# How The News Media Fail American Voters

POWER, CONFLICT, AND DEMOCRACY SERIES

*Robert Y. Shapiro, Editor*

Power, Conflict, and Democracy:
American Politics Into the Twenty-first Century
*Robert Y. Shapiro, Editor*

This series focuses on how the will of the people and the public interest are promoted, encouraged, or thwarted. It aims to question not only the direction American politics will take as it enters the twenty-first century but also the direction American politics has already taken.

The series addresses the role of interest groups and social and political movements; openness in American politics; important developments in institutions such as the executive, legislative, and judicial branches at all levels of government as well as the bureaucracies thus created; the changing behavior of politicians and political parties; the role of public opinion; and the functioning of mass media. Because problems drive politics, the series also examines important policy issues in both domestic and foreign affairs.

The series welcomes all theoretical perspectives, methodologies, and types of evidence that answer important questions about trends in American politics.

---

John G. Geer, *From Tea Leaves to Opinion Polls: A Theory of Democratic Leadership*

Kim Fridkin Kahn, *The Political Consequences of Being a Woman: How Stereotypes Influence the Conduct and Consequences of Political Campaigns*

Kelly D. Patterson, *Political Parties and the Maintenance of Liberal Democracy*

Dona Cooper Hamilton and Charles V. Hamilton, *The Dual Agenda: Race and Social Welfare Policies of Civil Rights Organizations*

Hanes Walton, Jr., *African-American Power and Politics: The Political Context Variable*

Amy Fried, *Muffled Echoes: Oliver North and the Politics of Public Opinion*

Russell D. Riley, *The Presidency and the Politics of Racial Inequality: Nation-Keeping from 1831 to 1965*

Robert W. Bailey, *Gay Politics, Urban Politics: Identity and Economics in the Urban Setting*

Ronald T. Libby, *ECO-WARS: Political Campaigns and Social Movements*

# How The News Media Fail American Voters

*Causes, Consequences, and Remedies*

Kenneth Dautrich and Thomas H. Hartley

Columbia University Press / *New York*

Columbia University Press
Publishers Since 1893
New York Chichester, West Sussex
Copyright © 1999 Columbia University Press
All rights reserved

Library of Congress Cataloging-in-Publication Data
Dautrich, Kenneth.
    How the news media fail American voters: causes, consequences,
and remedies / Kenneth Dautrich, Thomas H. Hartley.
        p.   cm.
    Includes bibliographical references and index.
    ISBN 0-231-11176-2. — ISBN 0-231-11177-0 (pbk.)
    1. Press and politics—United States.   2. Journalism—Political
aspects—United States.   3. Elections—United States.   I. Hartley,
Thomas H.   II. Title.
PN4888.P6D367   1999
071'.3—dc21                                                      98-33369
                                                                      CIP

Casebound editions of Columbia University Press books are printed on permanent and durable
acid-free paper.
Printed in the United States of America
c 10 9 8 7 6 5 4 3 2 1
p 10 9 8 7 6 5 4 3 2 1

# contents

# acknowledgments

Lately, the news media have become all to easy to criticize. The limitations of news organizations, and the people who staff them, and their product, have been explored at great length by scholars, critics, and the media's own pundits. This book shows that the American voters, too, perceive many of the same weaknesses in the news media. It also documents the great extent to which voters rely on news organizations for their information about electoral politics. Some voters report using a surprisingly wide variety of news shows and publications quite regularly. Others focus on a discriminating set of high-quality news sources. Most rely on mainstream news shows and report watching them with a regularity that is impressive.

It is this last point that is, ironically, at the root of a problem with the news media. The great strength of American news is that it is protected from government influence by the First Amendment; the concomitant weakness, however, is that news organizations must fund themselves. Responsiveness to the public, for the most part, must be achieved through the market and not through politics or government regulation. We suggest that the market mechanism does not lead news organizations to respond to the public's dissatisfaction. This is because of the willingness—or diligence—of viewers who continue watching, listening to, or reading news that dissatisfies them in many ways. News organizations that can maintain their ratings and circulation—and their revenues—by relying on an audience that continues to use the news independently of whether they are satisfied with it have little incentive to respond to the public.

The research that underlies this book was sponsored by the Media Studies Center in New York City, which is an operating program of the Freedom Forum. Without the center's generosity we would have been unable to explore these linkages between the news media and the public. In particular, we would like to thank Larry McGill, Bob Giles, and Charles Overby for their commitment to studying public attitudes toward the news and their confidence in us to carry out the primary research that supports this book.

The University of Connecticut and the Political Science Department provided us with a base from which to pursue this project, and we thank all our colleagues there for their support in carrying out this project.

The staff of the Center for Survey Research and Analysis at the University of Connecticut also provided invaluable assistance. The interviewers under the direction of Lilly Markons worked diligently on the data collection effort. Jennifer Dineen and Chris managed the project wonderfully, and Melanie Chebro provided superior administrative support in working with our manuscript.

Columbia University Press, its editorial staff, and anonymous reviewers provided valuable suggestions that greatly improved the manuscript.

We would like to thank the respondents—voters, journalists, and politicians. Without their cooperation this book would have been impossible.

Finally, we would like to thank our families for their love, support, and patience while we conducted these surveys and wrote this book.

# How The News Media Fail American Voters

# Campaigns Are Unthinkable,
# Save in Terms of the News Media

In this book we provide an evaluation of the institutional performance of the news media in its coverage of U.S. presidential elections. Using the 1996 election as a case study, the book scrutinizes how the U.S. electorate used the news media throughout the campaign, and how it evaluated the news media's performance. A large-scale, election-long panel study of American voters from January through November of 1996 served as the main source of data in our examination of Americans' use and opinion of election news coverage.

We explain how voters use and evaluate the news media, and discuss the impact of these evaluations on the electorate's continued use of the news. Our approach differs from most recent work in political communications, which focuses on questions such as how much information is needed (Popkin 1991), how citizens learn from the news media and election campaigns (Graber 1988; Neuman, Just, and Crigler 1992), what information is paid attention to and when (Krosnick 1988), what is remembered (Graber 1988), how political information mediates the impact of news (Zaller 1991), how news influences opinions (Iyengar 1991; Iyengar and Kinder 1987), and how voters use the media to construct a framework for the electoral environment (Just, et. al, 1996). Earlier research in this area recognized the potentials and limits of mass media's effectiveness as a provider of information, but it did not sufficiently explore the extent to which the voters themselves perceive that the quality of the news is high or low. Nor did earlier research explore the impact that perceptions of performance have on voters' future use of the news media.

Two important assumptions about U.S. politics provide justification for a thorough examination of voters' evaluations of the performance of the news media in covering presidential campaigns. First, the active and uninhibited transmission of political campaign information forms an important cornerstone of U.S. democracy, providing credible and useful information to voters (Converse 1964; Key 1966). But the importance of that information depends on how useful and how credible the voters perceive those sources of information—including the news—to be. Second, Americans rely heavily on the news media for information about candidates, campaigns, and elections. Alternative sources of information exist but are less frequently used, as we will show in this book, by the contemporary U.S. electorate. And reliance on the news media for election information has grown over the years. News organizations are not one among many sources of information. For most voters, they are increasingly their primary source of information. The increasingly important role of the news to voters places the news media in a lofty position in U.S. democracy, and makes voters' evaluation of the news a vital concern.

We argue that the news media should be evaluated by voters. But we also think that it should be evaluated as a political institution. One goal of the First Amendment to the U.S. Constitution, in guaranteeing of freedom of the press, is to ensure the independence of the press from government control and to allow the free flow of information so that the electorate might become a more informed and more capable citizenry. That the media are largely free of government control is especially evidenced when the U.S. news media are compared with those in other democracies such as Great Britain and France (Abel 1981).

> It is only a slight exaggeration to describe publishing as the only branch of American industry or commerce that is guaranteed by the Constitution a sturdy immunity from government interference. Although the First Amendment guarantee is less than explicit, the federal government has—with rare exceptions—taken a hands off attitude toward the industry, respecting above all its immunity against interference with the editorial process (Abel 1981:6).

Activities of the news media that are important for democracy include transmitting current information, educating the public, monitoring the activities of government, verifying the accuracy of public officials' statements, and encouraging the public to become interested and participate in politics. Others have made arguments for considering the news media to be a political institution. For example, Cook (1997) argues that the collection of disparate news organizations in the United States should be considered a political institution because they preside over a sphere of society, bearing primary responsibility for the transmission of information; because they display similar and enduring norms and operating procedures; and because these procedures have an effect on the content of the information transmitted. For us, the assumption that the transmission of information is vital, and the assumption (which we discuss later) that the organizations comprising the news industry are the primary actor that accomplishes this task, are the key characteristics that lead us to consider the news media to be a political institution.

The media's role is important because citizens' knowledge and participation in elections are necessary to the success of democratic government. The amount and quality of information that the media supply to voters during an election campaign influences what they know and whether they participate. The voters' evaluation of the news media provides an indication of whether news organizations are providing this information in a way that is appealing and useful to voters, and voters' assessment of the news media may impact the confidence in the news media and the likelihood that they will continue to use the news media as a source of information. That the goals of the news media extend beyond those of democratic government—news organizations also provide entertainment, and they earn money for their corporate owners—may change the constraints on these organizations, but it does not change the fact their political functions are of considerable consequence.

In focusing on the news media as a key political institution in the U.S. electoral system, we explore voters' orientations toward the news media across a variety of dimensions. These dimensions include usage of the news during the election campaign, overall evaluation of news content and news sources, perceptions of the presence and extent of different sources of political bias, the usefulness of news information in making voting decisions, evaluations of election news content, and evaluations of different news sources. In our research we found that the media are failing many voters on these dimensions.

Our evaluation of the institutional performance of the news media through the eyes, ears, and minds of the electorate is largely based on a national panel survey of the U.S. electorate conducted during the 1996 presidential campaign. The study was sponsored by the Freedom Forum Media Studies Center and conducted at the University of Connecticut. We interviewed an initial national voter sample of over 2,000 individuals in January and February 1996, before the New Hampshire primary. Of these, we re-interviewed 503 respondents at three additional points in time—immediately after the national party conventions in early September 1996, right after the last presidential debate in mid-October 1996, and immediately after election day in November 1996. The larger sample size of the initial panel (January-February) allowed us to identify patterns of media use among a variety of voter audiences (see chapter 2).

All four panel waves examined voter use of the news for election information and gauged voter opinion on various aspects of election coverage. Many questions were repeated across the waves of the panel, facilitating the measurement of change and stability in voter attitudes through the campaign. Also, unique sets of questions were administered at various time points to examine opinions of coverage of particular aspects of the campaign (e.g., coverage of conventions and debates).

The rest of this chapter does two things. First, it describes the importance of the news media in U.S. elections. Mass media is pervasive, and recent research has presented evidence suggesting that media influence on the attitudes and behavior of voters is greater than was once thought. Moreover, the decline in voter attachments to political parties may have led to an increase in ticket-splitting, as well as a tendency of partisan outcomes to switch from one election to the next, rather than remaining stable following a realignment. In such a context of declining partisanship and pervasive use of the news media, the power of the media becomes vitally important. If we view the American voter as an individual seeking information needed to make a voting choice in the classical democratic view, then elections are now unthinkable save in terms of the news media.

Second, the chapter discusses the way in which we examine the news media. We point to problems that other scholars have found when they examine the news media's role in presidential campaigns. The news media include more sound bites rather than lengthy quotes, and they focus more on strategy and negative coverage rather than on issues. In later chapters, we show that voters also perceive many, if not all, of these failings in the news media. We also justify the importance of describing voters' dissatisfaction with aspects of the news. Although the news media collectively serve as an important institution in electoral politics, little attention has been paid to whether the news media have an incentive to be responsive to the criticisms of voters. The news media lack a political mechanism for voters to influence the media's behavior. Assessing the responsiveness of the media to voters requires us to describe the criticisms of voters, not only those of scholars.

## The Importance of the News Media in Contemporary Elections

The mass media have had a profound impact on transformations in U.S. electoral politics. Candidate communications have changed dramatically with the decline of local party organizations and the rise of a reliance on television news and spot advertisements. The rise of national party organizations has not led candidates to rely on these organizations rather than pursuing their own individual fund-raising and advertising.

The way in which journalists and news organizations cover electoral politics has also changed a great deal, particularly since the 1950s. The contemporary mass media environment for U.S. elections is the product of several interrelated sets of factors: changes in the rules by which elections are conducted, most notably the rise in prominence and prevalence of primary elections, which enhanced the role of voters (Joslyn 1984; Keeter and Zukin 1983); changes in the U.S. electorate that include lower levels of partisanship and increased focus on candidates in presidential campaigns (Wattenberg 1996); and the continued, extensive coverage by journalists and media organizations of election news and advertisements (Patterson 1980; Jamieson 1992). Taken together, these trends have had the effect of increasing the role and influence of the news media in U.S. electoral campaigns, and particularly presidential campaigns. The contemporary American electorate depends on the news media for campaign information. In thereby increasing its institutional importance in U.S. electoral politics, the news media has, to an extent, replaced the role played earlier by political parties.

### The Influence and Pervasiveness of the News Media

The media have a pervasive presence in American life. By the age of 18, a typical American has spent more time watching television than attending school; and on average, about seven hours of every day is spent watching TV, reading a newspaper or magazine, or listening to the radio (Neuman 1991). From television sitcoms, to "shock" radio shows, to coverage of the O. J. Simpson trial, to the sports section in newspapers, the media offer a primary source of entertainment to many Americans (Neuman 1991). Similarly, from the evening network news, to Sunday morning political talk shows, to talk radio, to the front pages of newspapers, the media has become the principal source of information.

Americans' engagement with the mass media readily extends to electoral politics, particularly presidential campaigns. Voters in the 1996 election unequivocally reported the news media to be their dominant information source for learning about the campaign. When we asked where they got most of their information, as many as 79 percent of voters said "the news media," and only 7 percent said "conversations they had with others." On a daily basis, many voters reported that they used a variety of media to satisfy their need for information—72 percent used TV news daily, 60 percent used newspapers daily, and 51 percent used radio every day to learn about the campaign.[1]

With this significant presence of the mass media in the eyes, ears, and minds of voters, it is not surprising that contemporary U.S. presidential campaigns have become candidate-centered and media-driven—1996 was no exception.

E. E. Schattschneider's (1942) admonition that U.S. elections are "unthinkable save in terms of the parties" should, in the contemporary age of U.S. politics, be reconsidered. Now, U.S. elections are unthinkable save in terms of the news media. Modern campaigns occur within the context of a omnipresent mass media environment—an environment that has become a steadfast part of U.S. political culture. For better or worse, Americans experience campaigns mostly through the lens of the news camera, the pens of the journalist, the mouths of radio talk show hosts, and, increasingly, the information superhighway.

Whereas early voting behavior research questioned the impact of news media campaign coverage on voters' decision making (Lazarsfeld, Berelson, and Gaudet 1944; Campbell et al. 1960), changes in the news media environment and the way researchers conceptualize that environment have suggested that news does play an important role in voters' decisions.

Just et al. (1996), in their analysis of the media's role in the 1992 presidential election, found that campaigns are not merely exercises in political reinforcement but provide the context in which voters learn about and evaluate the candidates. Gelman and King (1993) further discuss the important role of the campaign to voters, and conclude that the political information environment of the campaign provides fundamental variables that influence voter behavior. Zaller (1991), Page and Shapiro (1992), and Lupia (1994) have found that the political information environment can have a great influence on political attitudes. Just et al. (1996:89) apply this finding to election campaigns and find that the news media are "a resource for citizens trying to make sense of the political world and reach electoral decisions."

This growing body of literature suggests that campaigns serve to prime voters, set agendas, reinforce attitudes, and hold candidates accountable to an agenda. As the news media are largely the vehicle through which voters experience the presidential campaign, the modern electorate's experience with a campaign is largely a media experience. The growing body of literature that suggests that campaigns matter, together with the pervasiveness and key role of the news media in campaigns, highlights the importance of understanding voter uses and attitudes of the news media. It also highlights the need to better understand and evaluate the performance of the news media as a democratic institution.

*Decline in Party Identification and Rise in Volatility*

The weakening of party ties has allowed the news media to assume a more prominent role in U.S. elections, although the causal connection between the rise of the news media and the decline of parties is difficult to establish (Patterson 1993). Nevertheless, one is hard-pressed to ignore two sets of long-term trends that have occurred over roughly the same period of time—the growth of the media and rise of candidate-centered campaigns on the one hand, and the significant changes in the U.S. electorate's political attitudes and behavior on the other. These trends include a decline in partisan attachments, a decline in party voting, and an increase in volatility in presidential election outcomes since 1944. There has been a clear pattern of decline in voter attachment to the parties. Table 1.1 shows the percentage of voters who consider themselves a Democrat or Republican in presidential election years since 1952, as measured in the National Election Studies (NES). In addition to this long-term decline in attachments to the political parties, the 40-year-trend seen in presidential election-year NES surveys demonstrates increasing neutrality toward both parties (Wattenberg 1996). In 1952, only 13 percent of Americans expressed neutral feelings, while in the 1992 presidential election, 32 percent were neutral toward the parties.

As a stable force in the U.S. electorate, partisanship is thought to play a useful role in the stability of the political system generally (Wattenberg 1996). In our two-party system, it gives party leaders an expected base of public support in elections (Converse 1966). Stability and persistence can also be seen in the transference of party identification from parent to child (Jennings and Niemi 1983) and the tendency for new political information to reinforce and add to one's pre-existing partisan identification (Fiorina 1981).

**TABLE 1.1** Percent Who Consider Themselves to be a Republican
or Democrat

| Election
Years | Percent
partisan |
| :---: | :---: |
| 1952 | 75 |
| 1956 | 73 |
| 1960 | 75 |
| 1964 | 77 |
| 1968 | 70 |
| 1972 | 64 |
| 1976 | 63 |
| 1980 | 64 |
| 1984 | 64 |
| 1988 | 63 |
| 1992 | 61 |

Source: National Election Studies.

The outcome of U.S. presidential elections may be characterized as
"volatile" since the rise in prominence of the news media and the move
toward candidate-centered campaigns. In the thirteen presidential contests
between 1944 and 1992, only two successive elections produced similar
voting outcomes: the 1952–1956 landslide Republican victories, and the
1980–1984 large Republican victories.

Aside from these similar successive outcomes, there have been massive
shifts in partisan outcomes from one election to the next. The Democratic
landslide in 1944 was followed by an unexpected and very slim Democratic victory in 1948, which was followed by a Republican landslide in 1952.
The 1956 Republican landslide was succeeded by a narrow Democratic
margin in 1960, followed by a Democratic landslide in 1964, only to be met
with a slim Republican victory in 1968. The 1972 large Republican victory was followed by a close Democratic win in 1976, which was followed
by a Republican landslide in 1980. The Reagan re-election was succeeded
by a slimmer Republican victory in 1988, and then a Democratic win in
1992 where Clinton achieved only 44 percent of the popular vote. The rise
of the mass media election has been met with a corresponding high degree
of voter volatility.

Another interesting trend in the U.S. electorate over the past four
decades is an increase in split-ticket voting. This trend complements the
decline in partisanship and the increase in volatility trends in that it further
suggests that the stable, persistent attitude of party identification is acting

as less of a guide to voters. In 1996, we asked voters whether they always voted for the same party for president or whether they voted for candidates of different parties across presidential elections. We found that 63 percent have voted for different parties in presidential elections while 37 percent say they always have voted for the same party. The level of splitting the party vote across presidential elections has changed dramatically since 1952. In 1952, the NES found that only 29 percent of voters had cast a vote for two different parties across presidential elections—a 34-percentage-point shift.

Our 1996 voter panels also indicate a significant level of ticket-splitting activity within elections. Fully 71 percent of registered voters say that when voting they typically split their ticket by voting for candidates from different parties. An increase in ticket-splitting is also confirmed by examining the individual vote intentions in presidential and house contests from 1952 through 1992. Split-ticket vote intentions accounted for 12 percent of voters in 1952, compared to 36 percent of voters in 1992.

During the decades when the news media rose in importance as a source of election information, there have been clear shifts in political attitudes (e.g., decline in partisanship) and political behaviors (e.g., split-ticket voting) of the U.S. electorate. Although it is difficult to prove that the emergent role of the news media is directly responsible for these shifts, it is not unreasonable to suggest that the role of the news media as a political institution deserves further study.

## Evaluating the News Media's Institutional Role: Scholarly Perspectives and Voters' Perspectives

In this book, we describe the ways in which voters use the news media, their evaluations of media, and how the two interact in presidential elections. The next two sections justify our focus on voter's evaluations by suggesting that scholars also have found limitations in the ways that news media cover elections. First, we discuss the existing literature in which scholars have scrutinized and criticized the form and content of the news over a range of elections. Second, we discuss long-term trends in the public's confidence in the news media, presenting aggregate evidence that suggests lower confidence in the news media in recent years. Later chapters show that in 1996 the voters gave the news media lukewarm overall evaluations; in addition, we show that voters agreed with some, if not all, of the scholarly criticisms. Taken together, the overall long-term decline in confidence in the news media, the criticisms of the news content asserted in scholarly studies, and the agreement of the public with many of these criticisms, suggests that the news media should take notice and become more responsive to the criticisms of the electorate.

### Criticizing Content

We are not the first to argue that the media are failing U.S. voters. Media critics have pointed to grave limitations in the ways that television and newspapers cover elections. For years, scholars and pundits have pointed to the need of news organizations to appeal to the audience and maintain ratings. This imperative has led to a variety of shortcomings. For example, news has become little more than sound bites and attractive images, geared mainly to keeping homes tuned to that station between dinner time and prime time (Adatto 1990; Hallin 1990; Gans 1980). Newspapers, too, have devoted smaller and smaller amounts of space to candidates' quotes and speeches (Stempel and Windhauser 1991).

A different change in the news is the increase in skepticism in news stories in the post-Watergate era (Taylor 1990). Moreover, the dictates of news as a profession and an industry lead reporters to use events schemas, covering events that are of ongoing concern, dramatic, and thus news-worthy (Jamieson 1992). This skepticism comes in part from journalists' view that politicians are strategic players seeking personal advantage (Weaver 1972). Timely and novel news stories have a strong impact on the audience (Graber 1993:116–20), and thus provide one way to retain a large audience, boost ratings, and increase profits. These, and other, limitations of the media are associated with lower levels of trust in the news media as an institution.

Because strategy and conflict make for eyecatching stories, election coverage tends to focus on strategy—"what did this candidate gain by taking this position"—rather than focusing on the pros and cons of that issue position. Increasingly, the contestants in presidential races have received such negative coverage (Robinson and Sheehan 1983; Patterson 1993). In the aggregate, controversies and strategy have come to occupy a far larger portion of coverage than policy issues (Clancy and Robinson 1985; Lichter, Amundson, and Noyes 1988). Coverage of strategy and the horse race, focusing on which candidate is ahead and why, was once dealt with in separate articles that seem few by comparison with today's coverage. Now, stories about strategy and the horse race dominate coverage, both because of the quantity of the stories and because strategy has become increasingly embedded in stories about the issues that candidates represent (Anderson and Thorson 1989).

Even a candidate who is trying to focus on a new and salient issue position is more likely to be covered by the news if the speech discussing the issue is accompanied by dramatic footage. The news of that event is more likely to report the speech and its impact on the horse race polls than to include expert commentaries on the possible consequences of the policies articulated in the speech. Scholars argue that the result is news that is less informing and useful for the voter than it could be.

What news there is focuses more on commentary and less on fact. And the facts that are covered are "objectivistic," meaning that it matters less that the focus of the story is on an important or interesting topic than that journalists can point to some type of concrete evidence, preferably quantitative, that they can use to defend their story as being impartial (Robinson and Sheehan 1983).

These findings have been of peripheral interest to political scientists, who have focused most of their energy on illustrating the weakness in political discourse between elected officials and the public. They have focused more on showing how news inform and influence the electorate (Iyengar and Kinder 1987; Iyengar 1991; Neuman, Just, and Crigler 1992), and less on studying the lack of credibility of news channels and how this might influence how people receive information. They have been more interested in showing that the public is able to work with incomplete information and use contextual knowledge to make decisions in the absence of specific facts (Popkin 1991) than in suggesting that people may not learn from the news because they do not trust the news.

The public agrees with some, but not all, of the scholarly criticisms. Failure to address voter dissatisfaction may result in lower levels of confidence in the news media. Restoring the authoritative voice of the media will certainly require media organizations to listen closely to the voters. If the news media fail to pay attention, then it is difficult to see how the media can remain a responsive political institution.

### The Importance of Evaluating Institutions

If the news media, taken together, do comprise a political institution, then it is as important to study the public's evaluation of the news media as it is to study the public's assessment of other political institutions. Yet scholars have put much more effort into studying and criticizing other institutions. A separate stream of research has emerged for example that ana-lyzes the public's criticism of Congress (Mann and Ornstein 1994; Hibbing and Theiss-Morse 1995). Little attention, on the other hand, has been paid to the responsiveness of the news media to the needs of American voters.

Scholarly criticisms of Congress have focused on a long list of poten-tial failings that are thought to be serious because they might contribute to a decline in responsiveness of Congress, as an institution, to the public. For example, incumbents are seen by some to have the ability to gain too many advantages, ranging from the perquisites of office to a greater capac-ity for raising the money necessary to run today's costly election campaigns. These advantages result in a high rate of incumbents being re-elected for reasons that are independent of voter satisfaction (Mayhew 1974). Both in-cumbents and challengers have incentives to emphasize only areas of broad consensus in their campaigns, denying voters information on areas where candidates differ (Page 1976; Shepsle 1972; Enelow and Hinich 1981). Scholars fear that these developments may allow incumbents to safeguard their ability to get re-elected, and thereby decrease their need to respond to the public.

These criticisms of Congress differ in two ways from scholarly criticisms of the news media. First, although some think that Congress may be unre-sponsive to the mass public, the news is thought to cater to a mass audience. It is this tendency to broadcast to the mean viewer that may result in exces-sive focus on strategy and scandal. Second, whereas members of Congress are thought to be more responsive to attentive publics, interest groups, and specific constituents' needs, we think that the mainstream news media appear to cater less to the smaller audiences who seek out more detailed and sub-stantive information. Despite the differences in the criticisms of Congress as a political institution and the news media as a political institution, the responsiveness of both should be a concern. Journalists have continued their frequently documented pattern of reporting information that dissatisfies a large part of the public. Despite the criticisms of scholars and voters, jour-nalists continue to focus more on the strategy and conflict and less on the policy positions voters need to make their decisions.

The news media's apparent lack of responsiveness raises questions because there is no political mechanism by which the public could exer-cise influence, should dissatisfaction mount to high levels. Few would doubt that an extremely dissatisfied public could use the electoral system to vote against incumbents, even if they outspent and out campaigned their oppo-nents. Moreover, remedies to the problems of incumbency are available, for example, campaign finance reform that could allow elections to restore the accountability of our representatives. Unlike Congress and the presidency, however, the mass media have no electoral feedback from the voters. The only direct feedback that acts upon the mass media is ratings that influence the revenues of news shows. And, as we suggest in the final chapter, ratings are a poor way to hold media accountable because viewing behavior can remain stable even as confidence in the media declines if the link between opinion and behavior is weak.[2]

In recent decades, as confidence in other institutions has waned, the public's trust in the media has declined. Examining the trends in confidence in the news media and other political institutions gives us a historical context into which to place this study.

Throughout the 1970s, with the exception of Jimmy Carter's election year, the National Opinion Research Center's (NORC's) measure of confidence in institutions showed that confidence in the news media was relatively high: in comparison to other political institutions, the public had more confidence in the press than in Congress or the president. Perhaps because of Watergate, 20 to 25 percent of the public reported that they had "a great deal" of confidence in the press, while the executive branch and Congress typically attracted the confidence of only about 15 percent of the public (figure 1.1). Compared to private institutions, the public had about the same amount of confidence in the press as it did in major companies, but banks and financial institutions enjoyed more confidence from the public (figure 1.2).

By the early 1980s, the proportion of the public with a great deal of confidence in the press fell to 15 to 20 percent, our confidence in Congress rose from about 10 to about 15 percentage points, and confidence in the executive branch rose to about 20 percentage points (figure 1.1). Over the same time period, confidence in business and financial institutions also rose to 25 to 20 percentage points (figure 1.2).

In the mid-1990s, confidence in Congress fell to 5 to 10 percent. Personal and political scandals, congressional-presidential gridlock, and the emergence of C-SPAN (which allowed the public to view of the slow, confusing deliberations of Congress) may have led to this decline in public trust (Asher and Barr 1994; Patterson and Magleby 1992; Mann and Ornstein 1994). Confidence in the news media has declined as well; only about 10 percent of the public reported having a great deal of confidence in the media (figure 1.1). At the same time, confidence in private-sector institutions such as business and financial institutions, which had declined during

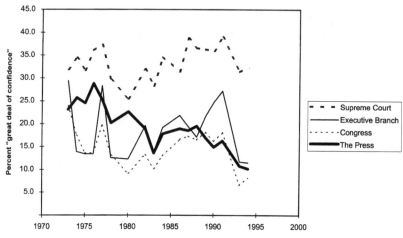

**FIGURE 1.1** Public confidence in political institutions
*(Source: National Opinion Research Center—NORC—various years).*

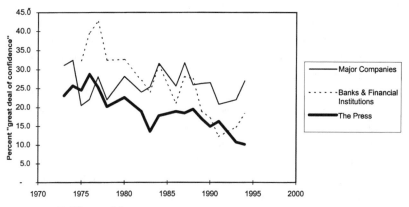

**FIGURE 1.2** Public confidence in nongovernment institutions
*(Source: NORC, various years).*

the recession of the early 1990s, rose somewhat (figure 1.2). By 1994, only about 10 percent of the public reported having a "great deal of confidence" in the press.

The American mass media is a political institution unlike any other, but it, too, experiences higher and lower levels of trust from the public. When trust in the media declines, negative implications for democracy may result. Lower levels of confidence in the media may deprive the public of some of the essentials of democracy: a source of current information and public education that it can trust and a watchdog for public officials in which it has confidence. Without a trustworthy source of information, the public is left without the ability to discern the important public issues of the day, the differences between candidates in elections, and whether what the candidates and advertisers are telling them is accurate. And a public that does not know which candidate stands for what may be less likely to vote and more likely to become cynical regarding elections.

Voters do, however, have resources that ameliorate these problems. Individuals may have the ability to detect bias in the news and control for it when they use information gleaned from media sources in their decision making. Individuals may be inundated with a barrage of stories about horse race and strategy, yet still be able to glean from the news a few facts about relevant candidate characteristics and policy alternatives (Graber 1988). Finally, if voters are dissatisfied with election coverage in the media they use the most, they may simply switch to another channel or another medium. Alternatively, they might choose to use the news less. Either option would give news organizations an incentive to respond to the dissatisfaction of voters. The final chapter of this book explores whether voters do, in fact, behave in this way.

It is in part because of the decline in the legitimacy of mass media that this book focuses on the problems voters see with the news. Solving the problem of declining trust requires addressing the criticisms of the electorate, not those of scholars. We are optimistic that the news can change to conform more to the expectations and needs of voters, but restoring the confidence of voters in the news media will likely take time. Just as legitimacy may remain for a time in the face of limited effectiveness, we expect that a lack of legitimacy will remain for a time even after reforms of the media have satisfied its critics in the public.

## Methodology

This book uses the findings from a national voter panel study conducted for the Media Studies Center by the University of Connecticut during the 1996 presidential campaign, from the pre-New Hampshire primary period through election day. The study contacted registered voters at four time-points in 1996:[3] in early February before the New Hampshire primary, in early September after the party conventions, in mid-October after the last presidential debate, and in early November immediately after the presidential election.

Each wave of interviewing focused on issues pertaining to media use and media performance in covering the presidential campaign. Many media use and media performance items were repeated over a number of panel waves, allowing us to track changes in voter evaluations of the news media through the campaign. The survey instruments used for all four waves of interviewing may be found on the web site at the University of Connecticut's Center for Survey Research and Analysis (www.CSRA.uconn.edu).

Interviewing for all four panel waves was conducted by telephone. The questionnaire for each panel wave averaged 18 to 22 minutes in length. A total of 503 voters were interviewed for all four panel waves.

The response rate for the initial wave of the panel study was 66 percent. This initial wave included interviews with a national sample of 2,007 voters. To obtain these interviews, we contacted 3,041 respondents, and 66 percent (our response rate) agreed to complete the survey. The sampling frame for wave 2 included a subsample of these 2,007 voters. The recontact rate (which is the response rate across waves) for the September panel wave was 77 percent; from September to October it was 83 percent; and from the October wave to the November wave it was 88 percent. Therefore, the response rate from the first panel wave to the final panel wave was 56 percent. A total of 503 voters were interviewed for all four panel waves.

The great advantage of the panel study is that it allowed us to compare individual-level change over time. We were able to determine which individuals changed their patterns of media use (chapter 2), whether individuals rated the news higher if they had just (since the last wave) obtained enough information to make up their minds on how to vote (chapter 4), and whether individuals who rated the news worse were less likely to continue using the news (chapter 7). The panel design meant taking the risk of sensitizing respondents, so that they may have responded differently to survey questions than they would have if they had only been interviewed once. Table 1.2 compares respondents in our September and November panels with independent cross sections that were interviews completed at the same time. With respect to vote intention, members of the panel showed no significant differences from the independent cross section in September on presidential and congressional vote choice questions. The same was true in November. No differences were found beyond what we would expect from fluctuations due to sampling error alone, although panel members were slightly more likely to report voting for Dole and for congressional

**TABLE 1.2** Comparing Panels and Independent Cross–Sections

| | N | Presidential Vote Choice | | | | Congressional Vote | | | Party Identification | | | |
|---|---|---|---|---|---|---|---|---|---|---|---|---|
| | | Clinton | Dole | Perot | | Democrat | Republican | | Democrat | Republican | Independent | |
| **September** | | | | | | | | | | | | |
| Panel (W2) | 512 | 48% | 36% | 7% | 9 | 35% | 36% | 29 | 35% | 36% | 25% | 4 |
| Cross–Section | 337 | 52% | 36% | 6% | 6 | 31% | 33% | 36 | 34% | 31% | 28% | 7 |
| **November** | | | | | | | | | | | | |
| Panel (W4) | 512 | 48% | 39% | 7% | 6 | 46% | 45% | 9 | 38% | 37% | 22% | 3 |
| Cross–Section | 489 | 44% | 32% | 7% | 17 | 42% | 38% | 20 | 35% | 30% | 28% | 7 |

Republicans. Comparing the party identification of respondents in the panel and independent cross sections, we found again that the difference between the two groups was within the range of what we would expect from sampling error, although again we find that respondents in the panel were slightly more likely to report identifying with the Republican party.

## Organization of the Book

Evaluating the news media's institutional performance in covering presidential elections involves understanding both how and why voters use the news to obtain election information, and how voters evaluate election coverage. Chapters 2 and 3 examine voters' use of the news during the 1996 election (chapter 2) and provide an explanation for news usage patterns (chapter 3).

Chapters 4 through 6 present our findings on how voters evaluated the media's coverage of the presidential election. Specifically, chapter 4 looks at overall evaluations of new media performance, how those evaluations changed over the course of the campaign, and differences in evaluations of the news product versus evaluations of the news-gathering process. Chapter 5 provides an evaluation of bias or balance in the news coverage of Campaign '96, and chapter 6 examines voter perceptions of news content and various news sources. Chapter 7 explores the consequences of performance: do voters' perceptions of news impact their use of the news for information about the campaign? Chapter 8 summarizes the conclusions of our research on voter uses and opinion of the news media's election coverage, and suggests how the news may become more responsive to the U.S. electorate.

**2**

—

# Media Use in the 1996 Campaign

This chapter and the next provide information about patterns of behavior that voters exhibit when they follow the election news. We discuss how closely people follow the election, and which sources of information they use to do so. This information is basic but important because one of the key assumptions of this book is that the news media is the most important provider of information to voters. This chapter provides evidence supporting that assumption. In addition, the information on media use will help us in later chapters when we make sense of which people—defined not only by demographic and attitudinal characteristics but also by their news gathering habits—are critical of different aspects of the programming content of the news. It will also prove helpful for showing that it is not only those who use the news least who criticize it the most. In chapter 7, we assess the *consequences* of voter dissatisfaction with the news. Are voters so dissatisfied they change their patterns of media use? Or do their habits of news use—outlined in this chapter and the next—lead them to continue using the news throughout the election campaign despite their dissatisfaction?

We begin by outlining some of the theories scholars have proposed for why people use the news. We then show that the news media, not personal conversations or advertisements, were voters' primary source of information about the 1996 election. We describe how closely voters followed the news over the course of the 1988, 1992, and 1996 presidential campaigns. Although the number of people following the 1996 election closely was smaller than in previous years, many voters did go to the effort needed to expose themselves to political information.

We then go on to describe the frequency with which voters use a variety of news sources that provide coverage ranging from fairly detailed and sophisticated to superficial. At one extreme are the elite media—several shows that feature political elites and experts and avoid summarizing the news in quick sound bites. Taken alone, each of these shows attracts a relatively small audience. Taken together, however, they capture a substantial part of the market. Talk radio has also attracted a substantial audience. The mainstream news sources—television (national and local broadcasts), newspapers, and radio—are each used with very high levels of frequency by many voters. At the other extreme we find tabloid television, which attracts a certain number of viewers.

Finally, we discuss the patterns of voters' media use, and show that voters differ not only on which particular sources they use, but how they combine them. Some voters—"news junkies"—use a wide variety of news, ranging from mainstream news to more sophisticated sources such as the *NewsHour* with Jim Lehrer, Sunday morning political talk shows, and commentary-filled political talk radio shows. These people are truly exposed to what Graber (1988) described as a flood of information, and the fact that some individuals are willing to go to such extremes of information gathering may have important implications for the future of the news (Neuman 1991). Another group of voters is more discriminating in its habits, restricting news gathering to a narrow range of sophisticated media. These viewers are more likely to watch other elite media shows and more likely to use mainstream news sources (e.g., network television, newspapers) more intensively.

## Why People Use the News

Scholars have proposed a variety of explanations for why people use the news. For the purposes of this book, the most revealing finding of this research is what it tells us about the political motivations of individual voters: either they follow the news to gain information about the election, or their energy is spent gathering the news for some other reason.

This distinction is important because after we discuss the criticisms that voters have of the news media—criticisms that some scholars share—we ask whether voters' dissatisfaction leads them to change their viewing behavior. If voters seek information about substance—issues, candidates' stands on the issues, the character of the contestants and how the election will affect them—then those voters who find the news lacking relevant stories might seek alternate sources of information. If voters prefer news that is not filled with stories about strategy and scandal, then those who share such criticisms might follow the news less frequently or change to a different media outlet. On the other hand, if voters are following the news for reasons that are tangential to the substance of electoral politics, then we might expect changes in their viewing habits to be independent of substantive criticisms.

Most theories of why Americans use the media suggest that the latter is the case. Uses and gratifications theories suggest that people spend time following the news if they find personally relevant and attractively presented messages.[1]

Bennett (1988) suggests three reasons that individuals may have for following the news. They may be engaging in surveillance, gathering news to make a voting decision. Alternatively, they may be seeking entertainment—using the news for fodder in their conversations with friends and family, or simply to pass the time. Finally, people may use the news for psychological adjustment, finding information in the news to support what they already believe or to make themselves feel more secure.

Of these three motives, only the goal of gathering information to make a vote choice may lead to politically relevant changes in viewing behavior. Only voters who follow the news in order to make an electoral choice change to a different medium if they think they are getting too little information or are having to wade through too much irrelevant material to get the information they need. Only individuals who are engaged in the practical enterprise of finding what they need to know to cast a vote might turn off the television or put down a newspaper. This behavior is politically relevant because it gives news organizations incentives to change their content to better inform the voters. But to the extent that these same voters are also entertained by the news, made to feel more secure, or gain satisfaction from the reinforcement of their beliefs, they may continue to use the news even if they are critical of it. In this manner they contribute to the ratings that news organizations require, despite their dissatisfaction.

Empirical studies of news use patterns also suggest that most people are seeking entertainment rather than pragmatically gathering information. Scholars tend to think that people are not inclined to expend much effort gaining knowledge of public affairs. This is why many people gravitate to television news—they perceive it to be easier to decode. Similarly, audiences tend not to choose shows that are informative or sophisticated (Neuman 1991:103–22).

Whatever each voter's motivation, we show in the remainder of this chapter that the electorate as a whole spent a great deal of effort seeking information across a surprisingly large variety of sources. We now turn to a description of how voters in the 1996 election used the news.

## News as a Primary Source of Information

A key assumption underlying this book is that voters use the news media as their primary source of information. To the extent that they do, the close study of the news media as a political institution becomes important. The vast majority of voters report that their information about the campaign comes primarily through the news, rather than conversations or advertisements. This pattern persists throughout the election year (table 2.1). In the preprimary panel held in February, 72 percent of our panel got most of their information from the news media. By the time the Republican and Democratic national conventions were over and the general election season had begun, approximately 80 percent of our panel were using the news media as their primary source of information. The data, like the findings of the Pew Research Center, suggest that the news media play a commanding role in informing voters.

At the individual level, voters tend to retain the same primary source of information. Table 2.2 shows that most voters in our survey who relied on the news media as their primary source of information maintained that reliance: 73 percent of individuals who said they got most of their information from news media in preprimary poll said the same in the postconvention survey. From August to September, 76 percent of individuals maintained their reliance on news. And from September to November, 75

**TABLE 2.1** Primary Source of Information about Presidential Campaign

|  | Preprimary | Postconvention | Postdebates | Postelection |
|---|---|---|---|---|
| From the news media | 72% | 80 | 80 | 77 |
| From paid political advertisements | 3 | 3 | 2 | 2 |
| From conversations you have with others | 6 | 5 | 7 | 9 |
| Other/combination | 18 | 12 | 11 | 11 |
| Don't know/Refused | 1 | ★ | ★ | 1 |

N = 494 registered voters; ★ = less than 1%.

TABLE 2.2 Change in Primary Source of Information about
Presidential Campaign (percent)

|  | February to Postconvention | Postconvention to Postdebate | Postdebates to Postelection |
|---|---|---|---|
| From news media to conversations/ads | 10 | 12 | 14 |
| Same | 73 | 76 | 75 |
| From conversations/ads to news media | 17 | 12 | 11 |

N = 494 registered voters; ★ = less than 1%.

percent maintained their reliance on news as their most important source
of information. Over these same time periods, much smaller percentages
of registered voters changed from relying primarily on the news to an alternate source of information such as conversations or political advertisements.
And voters who tended to gather information from advertisements or conversations were not likely to shift to a reliance on the news media. From
the first wave of the panel study to the second, only 17 percent of voters
shifted from other sources of information to the news media. From August
to September, and then from September to November, even smaller percentages of voters who had not relied primarily on the news shifted their
primary source to the news media.

Aggregate data suggest that information gathering is part of many
Americans' daily lives.[2] Among the various news sources, television news
was the primary source of information for the largest number of individuals in our panel, about 50 percent, throughout the campaign (table 2.3).
This finding is consistent with the impressive audiences that television news
usually garners.[3] Far fewer, approximately 20 percent, named newspapers
as their primary source of news, and only about 12 percent used radio as
their primary source of information. At the aggregate level, the primary
source of news remained stable throughout the election season for voters
(table 2.3).

It is interesting to compare the findings for media use with surveys
taken before the campaign in September 1995 and afterwards in January
1997. During the 104th Congress and public debate over the Contract with
America, a Media Studies Center/University of Connecticut survey found
that 64 percent of the general public got most of their information from
television, and 20 percent named newspapers as their primary source. Before

**TABLE 2.3** Primary News Source in Presidential Campaign

| Information from | September 1995 Congress | Preprimary | Postconvention | Postelection | January 1997 |
|---|---|---|---|---|---|
| | | Presidential election | | | |
| Television news | 64% | 51% | 53% | 54% | 50% |
| Newspapers | 20 | 20 | 19 | 22 | 24 |
| Radio | 8 | 12 | 14 | 11 | 14 |
| Magazines | 2 | 2 | 3 | 2 | 2 |
| Other/combination | 3 | 15 | 11 | 11 | 3 |
| Don't know/Refused | | ★ | ★ | ★ | |

N = 494 registered voters; ★ = less than 1%.

Question wording: September 1995, "From which news medium would you say you get most of your information about Congress—television news, newspapers, radio, magazines, or some other medium?" Election year: "From which news medium would you say you get most of your information about the presidential campaign—from television news, from newspapers, from radio, from magazines, or from some other medium?" January 1997: "Overall, where would you say you get most of your news from—from television, newspapers, radio, magazines, or some other medium?"

the election, television news maintained its role as the predominant source of news. After the election, a January 1997 survey found that 50 percent of the public relied on television news as their primary source of information, and 24 percent relied mostly on newspapers. In aggregate, then, most of the voters relied on television news, and a smaller fraction relied on newspapers, during and outside of the election season.

Individual-level data gathered over the course of the election season bolsters these findings that many voters rely primarily on the news for their information. Table 2.4 shows that about 70 percent of those who said they got most of their information from television news in February said the same in August; the same percentage reported maintaining their reliance

**TABLE 2.4** Change from TV to Newspaper, Radio, Other as Primary Source of Media Information

| | February to Postconvention | Postconvention to Postelection |
|---|---|---|
| Change from TV to other | 15 | 14 |
| Same | 69 | 70 |
| Change from other to TV | 16 | 15 |

N = 494 registered voters; ★ = less than 1%.

on television news from August to November. Much smaller percentages changed their reliance from television news to some other source, or vice versa. An election campaign that the U.S. voter perceives to be lackluster does not, for many voters, imply that they will use the news with less frequency.

## Following the News: 1988, 1992, and 1996

Now that we have reviewed evidence regarding the dominance of the news media as a source of information for U.S. voters, we outline the patterns of news use in 1996, comparing it to the 1988 and 1992 presidential election years. By many accounts, the electorate was less interested in the 1996 than the 1992 campaigns (Ceaser and Busch 1997; Nelson 1997). A July 1996 study by Princeton Survey Research Associates found that 73 percent of Americans thought the campaign was dull. Of these, 34 percent said they found the campaign boring because of the way candidates were campaigning, 27 percent said it was because of the quality of the candidates, and 22 percent found it dull because of the way the press was covering the campaign.

While Americans reported paying less attention to the campaign than in 1992, it is important to note that it may have been 1992, not 1996, that was the anomaly. Table 2.5 shows that the public paid about the same amount of attention to the campaign in 1996 as in 1988. CBS and CBS/New York Times polls that track the percent of the public (and, after August, the percent of registered or likely voters) paying a lot of attention to the campaign show that in all three years interest picked up in February and March. In 1988 and 1996, attention remained at a fairly low level (20 to 30 percent paying a lot of attention) until the conventions. After the main events begin, and after the polls switched to sampling registered voters rather than all adults, polls show that the number of voters paying close attention to the campaign rises by about 10 percentage points. Unlike the other years, 1992 surveys showed more interest in earlier months. Then began a dramatic increase in interest. Between September and November, the proportion of voters paying a lot of attention to the campaign rose from 51 to 70 percent.

Our voter panel showed changes similar to the trends found by CBS and New York Times (NYT) polls (table 2.6). In February, about 27 percent of voters reported following the campaign very closely. By the time the

**TABLE 2.5** Attention Paid to Presidential Campaigns, Percent Reporting "A Lot" of Attention

|      | Oct.-Dec. | 1/19-20 | 2/20-24 | 3/22-4/2 | 5/8-15 |
|------|-----------|---------|---------|----------|--------|
| 1988 | 15        | 13      | 23      | 29       | 26     |
| 1992 |           | 17      | 26      | 29       | 38     |
| 1996 | 17        | 18      | 27      | 23       | 14     |
|      | **8/14-18** | **9/18-24** | **10/3-8** | **10/10-17** | **10/30-11/2** |
| 1988 | 33        | 35      | 38      | 33       | 39     |
| 1992 | 45        | 51      | 54      | 61       | 70     |
| 1996 | 34        | 39      | 39      | 42       | 40     |

Source: CBS and CBS/NYT polls. Samples: National adult through May, registered voters from August. In 1988, the estimates for 9/23 through 10/10 were based on probable electorate, which is a sample in which responses were weighted for participation in previous elections and intention to vote in November.

Question wording: How much attention have you been able to pay to the 1988/1992/1996 presidential campaign-a lot, some, not much, or no attention so far?

**TABLE 2.6** Following the Presidential Election Campaign

|                     | Preprimary | Postconvention | Postdebates | Postelection |
|---------------------|------------|----------------|-------------|--------------|
|                     | Percent following the campaign | | | |
| Very closely        | 27         | 32             | 38          | 35           |
| Somewhat closely    | 53         | 50             | 49          | 43           |
| Not too closely     | 15         | 13             | 10          | 14           |
| Not closely at all  | 5          | 5              | 3           | 8            |
| Don't know/Refused  | ★          | ★              | 0           | 0            |

N = 494 registered voters; ★ = less than 1%.

debates were concluded, 38 percent of voters were following the campaign very closely. Voters maintained this level of engagement with the campaign until the close of the election.

Although people were less interested in the 1996 election than was the case in 1992, this does not imply that people used the news less regularly. Voters followed the 1996 election more closely as the election campaign progressed and spent a great deal of time watching, listening, and reading a wide variety of news media from beginning to end.

## Mainstream Sources of Political Information

In studying how voters used the news media in the 1996 election, we began by asking people how often they used different types of media news sources. Individuals typically relied on multiple sources of information, so asking voters how often they followed different types of news, one at a time, allowed us to assess the extent to which voters use overlapping sources of information. Many people opted for television when searching for information, in part because its visual component increases its credibility (Neuman 1991:99; Graber 1993:203). Fully 72 percent of voters in our preprimary survey reported watching television news daily, while fewer (55%) listened to news on the radio that frequently (table 2.7). Newspapers were perceived to be less enjoyable and more demanding than television. They were also more likely to be used for seeking information rather than entertainment (Robinson and Kohut 1988; Graziano and McGrath 1986; Neuman 1991: 102). Newspapers were read daily by 60 percent of voters. A smaller percentage (22%) read news magazines like *Time, Newsweek,* or *U.S. News and World Report* every week. Overall, table 2.7 shows that a large percentage of voters used a variety of media daily to get information about politics. Apparently, low levels of interest did not prevent voters from remaining active in their use of the news media.

Television's predominance as a source of news came from local news rather than from national-network news (table 2.7). While overall television news use was very high, with 72 percent of voters watching television news of some kind every day, only 48 percent of them watched network news, compared to 63 percent who watched local newscasts.

**TABLE 2.7** Type of Media Used, Preprimary Survey

| | Overall Television | Network newscasts | Local newscasts | News-paper | Use of Radio news |
|---|---|---|---|---|---|
| Every day | 72% | 48% | 63% | 60% | 55% |
| Several times per week | 19 | 27 | 20 | 17 | 12 |
| About once per week | 5 | 10 | 6 | 12 | 5 |
| Less than once/week | 2 | 7 | 4 | 5 | 10 |
| Never | 2 | 8 | 7 | 6 | 18 |
| Don't know/Not applicable/ Not available | ★ | 0 | 0 | ★ | ★ |

N = 1804 registered voters; ★ = less than 1%.

These relatively high levels of media use were maintained throughout the election cycle. Table 2.8 shows the percentage of voters who reported using various types of media every day, television news being used most frequently (by between 68 and 75 percent of those polled) throughout the election season. Use of television news did not rise significantly as the election season heated up. Indeed, the number of television news viewers dropped from 75 to 68 percent between August and September. Comparison with a September 1995 pre-election poll of national adults (which includes those not registered to vote) shows slightly lower use (62%) among the general public outside of the election season.[4]

Newspapers are used with the second highest frequency; about 60 percent of voters (and 50% of the general public in September 1995) read newspapers daily throughout the election year. Radio news use also remained constant throughout the election season, with about 50 percent of voters listening daily. Comparison with the September 1995 poll showed the same percentage of the general public listening daily before the election season began.

The bottom half of table 2.8 presents comparable results from our panel. The panel, which was interviewed four times throughout the election season, reports similar use of the news as the entire sample, although they appear to use slightly more television news, and to be a little more likely to read newspapers.

**TABLE 2.8** Types of Media Used Frequently Throughout the Presidential Campaign (percent watching every day)

| | September 1995 | Pre- primary | Post- convention | Post- debates | Post- election |
|---|---|---|---|---|---|
| **From all data** | | | | | |
| News on television | 62 | 72 | 75 | 68 | 72 |
| Read newspapers | 50 | 60 | 61 | 61 | 60 |
| News on radio | 49 | 55 | 52 | 49 | 52 |
| Talk radio (several times/wk) | 15 | 17 | 23 | 22 | 23 |
| Number (registered voters) = | (1,500) | (1804) | (938) | (580) | (1033) |
| **From panel only** | | | | | |
| News on television | | 78 | 80 | 69 | 74 |
| Read newspapers | | 67 | 65 | 61 | 64 |
| News on radio | | 57 | 54 | 51 | 53 |
| Talk radio (several times/week) | | 21 | 25 | 23 | 26 |
| N = | | (494) | (494) | (494) | (494) |

Table 2.9 explores changes in mainstream news media use at the individual level. We found that 77 percent of voters maintained the same level of use (daily, several times per week, once a week, less than once a week, or never) between February and August. A large majority maintained the same frequency of use between August and September as well, with more decreasing their news use than increasing it. Between September and November, more increased than decreased their viewing of the news, but again the vast majority maintained the same level of use. Newspaper use was equally stable throughout the election campaign. Radio news use was somewhat less stable. Still, majorities of voters maintained the same level of use throughout the panel study.

## Niche Providers of Broadcast News

We also explored the extent to which voters used a variety of other sources of news, such as morning news shows and cable television. By examining the frequency of use of these media, we were able to show that some voters took advantage of the wide variety of available information. We also found more evidence to support the common assumption that convenience—the extent to which a medium is widely distributed—is a strong determinant of audience.

**TABLE 2.9** Change in Frequency of News Use During Presidential Campaign

|  | February to Postconvention | Postconvention to Postdebate | Postdebates to Postelection |
|---|---|---|---|
| **Change in TV news use** | | | |
| Decrease in use | 11% | 16 | 7 |
| Same use | 77 | 76 | 80 |
| Increase in use | 12 | 8 | 13 |
| **Change in newspaper use** | | | |
| Decrease in use | 17 | 14 | 9 |
| Same use | 71 | 74 | 80 |
| Increase in use | 11 | 12 | 11 |
| **Change in radio news use** | | | |
| Decrease in use | 23 | 19 | 13 |
| Same use | 57 | 66 | 70 |
| Increase in use | 20 | 16 | 17 |

N = 494 registered voters.

Two alternative sources of political information—morning news shows and cable television news—claim audiences that are substantial in size, but still much smaller than mainstream evening news shows (table 2.10). Morning news was watched daily by a smaller percentage of our panel (20 percent) than the 72 percent who watched network news daily, probably because of its timing. Most people who worked away from home do not have access to morning television news programming.

A logistical constraint similarly limits the distribution of cable television news. Neuman (1991:36) reports that cable access has stabilized at about 60 percent of U.S. homes. We found that about 74 percent of our panel of voters said they had cable television. Despite a distribution network that is more limited than broadcast news, cable television has captured a significant market share. One of its offerings, *CNN News,* is able to attract more frequent use than morning news shows. Whereas 20 percent of our panel watched morning news shows daily, 26 percent reported that they also watched *CNN News,* which is only available on cable television, on a daily basis.

Voters can also access a variety of niche providers. Used by far smaller audiences, each of these shows vary from "elite news" shows such as the *NewsHour* on PBS and ABC's *Nightline,* which often include political news, direct interviews of political leaders, and more sophisticated commentary. Jamieson (1992) compared the length of sound bites in several different shows and found that the average length of a sound bite was 52 seconds in the *NewsHour,* 33 seconds in *Nightline,* and only 10 seconds in ABC, CBS, and NBC weekday evening news shows. Other shows, like *Larry King Live!,* feature interviews with prestigious guests but also spend a significant proportion of their programming time on nonpolitical shows like the O. J. Simpson trial. At the other end of the spectrum are news magazine shows like *Dateline, 20/20,* and tabloid television shows like *Inside Edition* and *Hardcopy* that provide little if any political information.

Compared to the mainstream sources of news, each niche provider caters to small audiences. Yet if we consider niche providers as a whole, we find that voters using some combination of them with frequency comprise a group big enough to be worth studying. For example, if we consider individuals who watch any of the elite media with frequency—either the *News-Hour,* Sunday morning political talk shows, *Inside Politics* on CNN, C-SPAN or news programs on National Public Radio—we find that 29 percent find their way into a group that uses some combination of these news sources with fairly high frequency. Examples of these individuals might be voters

**TABLE 2.10** Alternative Markets for Television News Shows

| | Elite or Credentialed | | | | | | | | Uncredentialed |
| --- | --- | --- | --- | --- | --- | --- | --- | --- | --- |
| | Overall Television News Use | Morning news shows | Cable TV: CNN News | News Hour/ Jim Lehrer | Inside Politics | Nightline | Larry King Live! | Dateline or 20/20 | Tabloid TV** |
| Every day | 72% | 20 | 26 | 3% | 2 | 4 | 2 | 4 | 7 |
| Several times a week | 19 | 13 | 22 | 8 | 5 | 11 | 8 | 28 | 13 |
| About once a week | 5 | 6 | 11 | 7 | 7 | 11 | 9 | 39 | 13 |
| Under once a week | 2 | 9 | 9 | 14 | 11 | 19 | 16 | 17 | 17 |
| Never | 2 | 52 | 7 | 67 | 49 | 54 | 40 | 11 | 50 |
| No access | – | – | 25 | – | 25 | – | 25 | – | – |
| Don't know/ Not applicable | ★ | 0 | ★ | 1 | 1 | 0 | 0 | 0 | 0 |

N = 1804 registered voters; ★ = less than 1%; ** = *Inside Edition, Hardcopy*.

who watch the *NewsHour* and listen to National Public Radio several times a week, and also watch Sunday Morning talk shows every week. Or they might be people who follow C-SPAN daily and two of the other "elite" media several times a week. No single elite media outlet commands enough market share to match the penetration of the three networks or CNN's *Headline News.* Yet together, the elite media have penetrated a proportion of the electorate big enough that it deserves attention. Moreover, the finding that nearly a third of our sample expended the energy required to discover and use these sources of news is important. Such effort is not typical, and most voters do not go to such great lengths to gather information, but a substantial proportion do report extending themselves beyond the mainstream media. We argued that convenience determined who watches morning and cable TV news shows. We will show later that tastes for different types of information (elite vs. tabloid TV), rather than convenience, helps determine the choice of these niche sources.

Similar patterns were found in radio usage. Fully 54 percent of our interviewees were daily listeners to radio news of some sort, which is widely available on various channels throughout the day (table 2.11). In contrast, only 7 percent listened every day to political talk radio shows, and only 12 percent tuned in to news shows on National Public Radio. Fourteen percent listened to all-news radio stations every day.

Voters use the radio to gather news partly because of convenience—they can listen to the radio in their cars while they commute or while they work at home (Neuman 1991:89). Personal tastes of respondents determine who listens to news shows and all-news radio, as we will show later.

**TABLE 2.11** Niche Markets for Radio News Shows

| | **News** | | | |
|---|---|---|---|---|
| | Radio news | All-news radio | News on NPR | Radio Talk Shows |
| Every day | 54% | 14% | 12% | 7% |
| Several times per week | 12 | 6 | 9 | 9 |
| About once per week | 6 | 4 | 8 | 6 |
| Less than once a week | 10 | 11 | 13 | 12 |
| Never | 18 | 63 | 57 | 65 |
| Don't know/Not applicable | 0 | 1 | 1 | 0 |

Irregularly Used Sources of Information

When we think of sources of information, traditional outlets such as television, radio, and newspapers, which are used with great frequency by voters, come to mind. But the public can get information from many other, less well studied sources. Fully 65 percent of voters on our panel read politically oriented newsletters at some point during the election campaign, and 23 percent read at least one book about politics in the year prior to the election (table 2.12). Books and newsletters differ from the news media sources already considered because they are not published on a daily basis. Individuals who read political newsletters or books may be actively seeking information, not merely watching what they are exposed to in the normal course of events. A smaller percentage (13%) had heard of MSNBC, the joint venture between Microsoft and NBC, and had actually watched it.

Another small, but potentially important, source of political information is the Internet. The percentage of voters on our panel using the Internet was small, and many may have used it only a few times over the course of the campaign. Nevertheless, this source may prove to be important in future elections. By 1996, 61 percent of those in our panel used a computer at home or at work, a considerable number, although still fewer than those with access to cable television (table 2.13). Unlike cable, computers did not come connected to a source of information: as of 1996, only 27 percent of our interviewees had computers *and* access to the Internet. Given the small number of people who have a channel of access to the Internet, it is not surprising that only 5 percent of our panel of voters visited a politically oriented home page in February 1996. The percent getting access to the Internet (27–29%) and to politically oriented home pages (5–8%)

---

**TABLE 2.12** Less Frequently Used Sources of News

|  | Yes | No/Never | Don't know/ Refused |
|---|---|---|---|
| Ever read any politically-oriented newsletters | 65% | 35 | 1 |
| Read books about politics in past year | 23 | 77 | ★ |
| Watched MSNBC on television | 13 | 87 |  |
| Use a computer at home or at work. | 61 | 39 | ★ |
| Use a computer and have access to Internet | 27 | 74 | ★ |
| Visited politically oriented homepages | 5 | 95 | ★ |

N = 1804 registered voters; ★ = less than 1%.

Note: MSNBC question was asked in August.

**TABLE 2.13** Internet Access

|  | February | August | November |
| --- | --- | --- | --- |
| Percent using a computer and have access to Internet | 27% | 28% | 29% |
| Have visited any politically oriented home pages | 5 | 6 | 8 |
| Have visited news organizations' Internet sites | N/A | N/A | 12 |

N = 494 registered voters from panel.

remained stable over the course of the 1996 election. In addition, a small percentage of voters visited news organizations' home pages (12%). For now, the Internet is a source of information for only a small proportion of the electorate. If, however, access to the Internet grows and the political usage rate continues, the Internet may become a significant supplementary source of news about politics.

To summarize our findings so far, we have shown that voters paid less attention to the 1996 election campaign compared to 1992, if not to 1988. Nevertheless, a significant proportion of voters reported following the election closely. And when asked about their media use, many reported high levels of use of a variety of news media. Because the amount of time spent following the news did not dramatically increase when the election season began, we can surmise that voters in our survey regularly followed the news, and that they were simply maintaining their habits. Other research suggests that although people may spend a great deal of time following the news, the amount of attention and intensity that they devote to this task can be low.[5] Overall, we found that voters in our survey had the opportunity to become exposed to a wide variety of media, which suggests that they were certainly capable of evaluating the news.

## Media Use Indexes

Because we are interested not only in tracking use of individual news media, but also in showing the multiple sources of information that voters use and in determining the impact of media use on satisfaction with the media, we developed several indexes of media use that are used throughout the book to separate voters based on their media use.

The first index groups together individuals who regularly used any of several "elite media" shows, chosen because they include more in-depth coverage, including more interviews with political elites and experts or opportunities for political elites and experts to directly air their views to voters. Elite news sources included the *NewsHour* with Jim Lehrer, Sunday Morning political talk shows, *Inside Politics,* National Public Radio, and C-SPAN. The index for elite media use is divided into three categories for subgroup analysis. Voters who fall into the top category used several of the elite media daily or at least several times per week.

Another index separates voters into three categories according to their use of talk radio: those who listened to talk radio at least several times per week, those who used it once a week or less than once a week, and those who report that they never listened to talk radio.

We also distinguished voters who were frequent users of mainstream television, either network television or CNN news shows such as CNN's *Headline News.* Those who reported watching both types of television news shows every day, or watched one show every day and the other several times per week, were placed in the highest category. Those using both shows between once and several times per week (frequent but not daily consumers of mainstream television news) were placed in the middle category. Finally, those who used network television less frequently, tuning in to one several times a week but never using the other television sources, or using both less than once a week, were placed in the lowest category.

Our final index separates voters according to how often they watched tabloid television shows such as *Inside Edition* and *Hard Copy.* Voters were separated into two groups: those who watched tabloid television at least several times a week versus those who watched it once a week or less.

Here we use these variables to determine whether those who tended to use one type of news media—elite media, talk radio, network news, or tabloid television—tended to use different sorts of media. We expected to find that those who were motivated to seek out the greater and more direct content of elite media would have sought out other in-depth sources of information. In contrast, we expected those whose personal tastes led them to watch tabloid television would have sought out other news shows with less substantial content. Network news viewers and talk radio listeners would fall somewhere in-between.

## Patterns of News Media Use

So far, we have shown the frequency with which voters used single sources of media. The findings suggest that convenience and habit played a large role in whether different types of media reached broader or narrower audiences. The sections that follow suggest that personal taste mattered as well. Different types of viewers were more likely to watch or listen to different combinations of news shows. We first focus on those who used the elite media. This group can be divided into discriminating elite viewers who limited their intake of non-elite news, and news junkies who used not only elite news media but also a wide variety of other news sources. We next focus on talk radio users, who may have had a special interest in politics. Because talk radio is frequently used by some of the elite-news group, we look at the viewing patterns of talk radio audiences after we control for the effects of elite media use. Finally, we look at the patterns of news usage of those who used network television, a mainstream source of news; and we explore what other shows tabloid TV viewers use.

### Elite Media

Supplementing the mainstream news provided by network news and print media with other sources can give voters access to substantive information that they would be rarely exposed to otherwise (Jamieson 1992). Substantive, in-depth information is available through elite or "credentialed" sources (*NewsHour* with Jim Lehrer, Sunday Morning political talk shows, *Inside Politics,* National Public Radio, and C-SPAN) that are more likely to include longer and more substantive interviews with elites and experts as opposed to the "sound-bite" summaries offered by mainstream media journalists (see Popkin 1991).

After dividing voters into three groups according to how often they use elite media, we further separated them according to the extent to which they used a wide variety of other news shows, and whether they used those sources more intensively. Those who used a smaller number of alternate sources of media, and used them less intensively, we refer to as discriminating viewers. We called those who used elite media, but also used many other types of news media with great frequency news junkies. Controlling for the overall frequency of news use, we found different patterns of media use for those who used elite media and little else compared with those who used elite media combined with a wide variety of news media.

There was great variation in the frequency with which different groups of voters use the news (table 2.14). Among the discriminating viewers (table 2.14, top three rows), those who used elite media more frequently distinguished themselves from those who use few elite-media sources by being much more likely to turn to newspapers (58 vs. 46%), CNN (70 vs. 37%),

**TABLE 2.14** Mainstream Media Use among Elite News Viewers (percent using the other media sources daily/weekly or several times a week/month)

| | TV news (daily) | CNN News | Radio news | All-news radio | Newspapers (daily) | News magazines | N |
|---|---|---|---|---|---|---|---|
| Discriminating viewers | | | | | | | |
| High elite media use | 73 | 70 | 66 | 15 | 58 | 39 | 624 |
| Medium | 63 | 52 | 60 | 15 | 56 | 41 | 366 |
| Low elite media use | 59 | 37 | 53 | 9 | 46 | 31 | 213 |
| News Junkies | | | | | | | |
| High elite media use | 92 | 92 | 87 | 43 | 79 | 69 | 105 |
| Medium | 93 | 85 | 81 | 37 | 75 | 70 | 177 |
| Low elite media use | 86 | 77 | 85 | 34 | 78 | 64 | 319 |

television news (73 vs. 59%), and radio news (66 vs. 53%) for their other sources of news. The discriminating elites were not much more likely than their non-elite media counterparts to listen to all-news radio (15 vs. 9%) or read news magazines (39 vs. 31%) (tables 2.14 and 2.15).

We found different results when we focused on the news junkies, and compare elite and non-elite news viewers (table 2.14, bottom three rows). Regardless of whether they used elite media, the news junkies tended to read newspapers and news magazines with great frequency, watch television news, and listen to radio news. Among news junkies, elite media use had only one discernible affect on media use: CNN Headline news was watched with greater frequency (92 vs. 77%).

When it came to niche markets for news, we again found differences between the discriminating viewers and news junkies (table 2.15). Elite news users among both groups were somewhat more likely to have read political books. But among discriminating viewers the elite-news users were not much more or less likely to seek sources of information outside the high-information content mainstream news. We found that discriminating news viewers tended to have little time for shows with less news content, such as tabloid television, television news magazines, and talk shows, with the possible exception of talk radio (13 vs. 6%). Only about 24 percent of discriminating viewers watched television news magazines at least several times a week, and only 12 to 18 percent used tabloid television.

Among the news junkies, however, elite news users were more likely to use some shows that have at least occasional political content, such as political talk radio (37 vs. 28%), and watch shows that feature interviews

TABLE 2.15 Other Types of Media Use among Elite News Viewers (percent using the other media sources daily/weekly or several times a week/month)

| | NIGHTLINE | LARRY KING LIVE! | Talk Radio* | Read Political Books | Morning News | TV News Magazines** | Tabloid TV*** | Late Night |
|---|---|---|---|---|---|---|---|---|
| **Discriminating Viewers** | | | | | | | | |
| High elite media use | 10 | 9 | 13 | 30 | 20 | 24 | 12 | 16 |
| Medium | 8 | 8 | 9 | 22 | 24 | 26 | 18 | 19 |
| Low elite media use | 8 | 4 | 6 | 11 | 22 | 24 | 16 | 17 |
| **News Junkies** | | | | | | | | |
| High elite media use | 33 | 36 | 37 | 36 | 56 | 45 | 26 | 24 |
| Medium | 28 | 21 | 28 | 31 | 49 | 46 | 27 | 23 |
| Low elite media use | 24 | 15 | 28 | 21 | 56 | 55 | 27 | 27 |

* = e.g., Rush Limbaugh, Jim Hightower; ** = e.g., Dateline, 60 Minutes, 20/20; *** = e.g., Inside Edition, Hard Copy.

such as *Larry King Live!* (36 vs. 15%) and *Nightline* (33 vs. 24%). These shows apparently provided content (or entertainment) to the liking of elite news viewers—at least those who budgeted more time for the news. This search for news and entertainment, however, did not extend to television news magazines: among news junkies, elite users were less likely (45 vs. 55%) than non-elite media users to watch television news magazine shows such as *20/20*. They were, however, not any less likely to use tabloid television. Apparently, while those with a taste for elite news media were drawn to use other outlets with high information content (such as television news, CNN *Headline News,* newspapers, and books), they were moderately repelled by TV news magazines.

To summarize, the group of voters we called the discriminating elites turned to few sources other than the elite media. When they branched out, they were most likely to use relatively high-information, unsensational mainstream sources such as newspapers, television news, CNN news, radio, and books. In contrast, the group we called news junkies used the same sources as the discriminating elites, but added talk shows with occasional political content (and perhaps more entertainment value) like *Nightline, Larry King Live!,* and talk radio to their viewing list.

*Talk Radio Use*

Talk radio listeners are another group of interest in contemporary elections. Although earlier research portrayed them as socially isolated, alienated, and discontent, more recent research has suggested that talk radio audiences are more politically involved than the general public, more interested in politics, that they pay more attention to politics in the mass media, and are more participatory (Hofstetter et al. 1994; *Times Mirror* 1993). Not surprisingly given the origins of political talk radio, listeners are also more likely to be Republican and conservative, rather than Democratic and liberal (Bolce et al. 1996).

Considered as a whole, we found that talk radio listeners were more likely to use a wide variety of news media. Analyzing talk radio listeners in this way is misleading, however, because some talk radio listeners also used elite media while others did not. In order to control for the effect of elite media use, we broke down talk radio listeners into two groups: those who used elite media and those who did not.

Among those who used elite news media, voters who listened more to talk radio were no more attracted to television news (81 vs. 79%) or newspapers (63 vs. 67%) than those who did not listen to talk radio. Among those who did not use elite media, talk radio listeners were a little less likely (59 vs. 67%) to watch television news, and less likely to read newspapers (49 vs. 55%). This evidence suggests that talk radio listeners may be less likely to use some types of mainstream news media, although this tendency would have been masked if we had not controlled for elite media use. Besides spending less time using the mainstream news media, talk radio listeners who did not also use elite news media were slightly more likely to watch television news magazines (36 vs. 29%)—broadcasts that discriminating viewers eschewed and elite news junkies were unlikely to watch.

Other patterns of media use, however, were consistent for talk radio listeners who used and did not use elite news. Talk radio listeners apparently preferred news in easily accessible and entertaining formats. For both the elite and non-elite groups, talk radio listeners were a little more likely to watch CNN *Headline News* (81 vs. 74% for the elite group, 57 vs. 49% for the non-elite group), and were more likely to read news magazines (60 vs. 51% for the elite group, 39 vs. 31% for the non-elite group). Talk radio listeners were much more likely to use the radio in general: they were much more likely to listen to radio news and all-radio news. For talk radio listeners, as for all radio listeners, there was a "radio effect." Apparently, factors such as commuting to work made individuals more likely to listen to talk radio, and also made them likely to listen to radio news shows and all-news radio (tables 2.16 and 2.17).

Beyond the tendency of all talk radio listeners to prefer news in an easily accessible format, the differences that we found between elite and

**TABLE 2.16** Mainstream Media Use Among Talk Radio Listeners (percent using the other media sources daily/weekly or several times a week/month)

| | TV news (daily) | CNN HEADLINE NEWS | Radio news | All-news radio | Newspapers (daily) | News magazines |
|---|---|---|---|---|---|---|
| **Elite Media Users** | | | | | | |
| High talk radio use | 81 | 81 | 88 | 45 | 63 | 60 |
| Medium | 75 | 76 | 73 | 22 | 68 | 57 |
| Low talk radio use | 79 | 74 | 67 | 22 | 67 | 51 |
| **Non-Elite Media Users** | | | | | | |
| High talk radio use | 59 | 57 | 80 | 36 | 49 | 39 |
| Medium | 65 | 49 | 64 | 19 | 52 | 41 |
| Low talk radio use | 67 | 49 | 56 | 14 | 55 | 31 |

**TABLE 2.17** Other Types of Media Use Among Talk Radio Listeners (percent using the other media sources daily/weekly or several times a week/month)

| | NIGHTLINE | LARRY KING LIVE! | Talk Radio* | Read Political Books | Morning News | TV News Mags.** | Tabloid TV*** | Late Night |
|---|---|---|---|---|---|---|---|---|
| **Elite Media Users** | | | | | | | | |
| High talk radio use | 12 | 26 | N/A | 37 | 36 | 31 | 21 | 23 |
| Medium | 12 | 18 | N/A | 35 | 35 | 36 | 18 | 20 |
| Low talk radio use | 11 | 19 | N/A | 24 | 38 | 35 | 21 | 20 |
| **Non-Elite Media Users** | | | | | | | | |
| High talk radio use | 21 | 7 | N/A | 27 | 28 | 36 | 17 | 22 |
| Medium | 21 | 7 | N/A | 20 | 26 | 28 | 17 | 22 |
| Low talk radio use | 19 | 8 | N/A | 10 | 29 | 29 | 20 | 20 |

N/A = not applicable; * = e.g., Rush Limbaugh, Jim Hightower; ** = e.g., Dateline, 60 Minutes, 20/20; *** = e.g., Inside Edition, Hard Copy.

non-elite talk radio listeners suggest that talk radio listeners should not be considered as a monolithic group. In the previous section, we showed that some voters listened to talk radio as part of their general tendency to use a wide variety of media, including elite media and mainstream sources. In this section we showed that those voters who used both talk radio and elite media displayed a tendency to gather more information; those who used talk radio, but did not use elite media tended to gather less information and use the more entertainment-oriented television news magazines.

### Network News Watchers

So far, we have explored the media viewing habits of two special groups of media users: elite media users and talk radio users. In order to contrast the viewing habits of the elite and talk radio groups with a more main-stream group, we also examined the viewing habits of network news watchers (those who regularly watch ABC, CBS, NBC, or CNN news).

In contrast to the elite and talk radio listeners, network news watchers were more likely to watch almost everything. Table 2.18 shows that people who watched network news shows frequently were more likely to watch Sunday morning political talk shows such as *Meet the Press* and *Face the Nation* than were low network news users (53 vs. 35%). Network news viewers were also more likely to watch *Inside Politics* (18 vs. 0%), C-SPAN (31 vs. 5%), and somewhat more likely to watch the NewsHour with Jim Lehrer (15 vs. 8%). People who watched more network news were also much more likely than their counterparts to read newspapers (75 vs. 45% read daily) and news magazines (55 vs. 34%).

Network news watchers were more likely to use media that has a more popular format (table 2.19) and, like non-elite talk radio listeners, network

---

**TABLE 2.18** Elite Media Use Among Network News Users (percent using the other media sources daily/weekly or several times a week/month)

| | Lehrer NEWS HOUR | Sunday AM Political Talk Shows* | Inside Politics | National Public Radio | CSPAN |
|---|---|---|---|---|---|
| High network news use | 15 | 53 | 18 | 22 | 31 |
| Medium | 11 | 34 | 5 | 19 | 10 |
| Low network news use | 8 | 35 | 0 | 23 | 5 |

★ = e.g., *Meet the Press, Face the Nation, This Week with David Brinkley.*

**TABLE 2.19** Other Types of Media Use Among Network News Users (percent using the other media sources daily/weekly or several times a week/month)

| | NIGHTLINE | LARRY KING LIVE! | Talk Radio* | Read Political Books |
|---|---|---|---|---|
| High network news use | 22 | 26 | 21 | 28 |
| Medium | 16 | 8 | 14 | 20 |
| Low network news use | 6 | 2 | 13 | 21 |
| | Morning News | TV News Magazines** | Tabloid TV*** | Late Night |
| High network news use | 39 | 40 | 25 | 23 |
| Medium | 33 | 34 | 19 | 20 |
| Low network news use | 19 | 19 | 13 | 16 |

★ = e.g., Rush Limbaugh, Jim Hightower; ★★ = e.g., *Dateline, 60 Minutes, 20/20*; ★★★ = e.g., *Inside Edition, Hard Copy.*

news watchers were more likely to watch television news magazines (40 vs. 19%). They were also more likely to watch *Nightline* (22 vs. 6%) and *Larry King Live!* (26 vs. 2%). Those who regularly watched network news were also more likely to watch tabloid television (25 vs. 13%), morning news shows (39 vs. 10%), and late night talk shows like the *Tonight Show* (23 vs. 16%).

Those who watched a great deal of network news were not discriminating viewers. Even more than the news junkies, or the non-elite talk radio listeners, voters who watched a lot of network news tended to use a wide variety of news media, including media with little issue content.

*Tabloid Television Watchers*

Finally, we turn to those who frequently viewed tabloid television. Tabloid television viewers were more likely to watch network or local television news (85 vs. 69%), and CNN Headline News (73 vs. 62%), somewhat more likely than non-tabloid television viewers to watch the Sunday morning talk shows (45 vs. 36%), and somewhat more likely to watch C-SPAN (24 vs. 17%), but they were no more likely to use any of the other elite media sources, including the *News Hour* with Jim Lehrer, *Inside Politics,* or *National Public Radio* (table 2.20 and 2.21).

Nor were they more likely to read newspapers or news magazines. And they were no more likely than nontabloid television viewers to listen to radio news, all-news radio, or talk radio (tables 2.21 and 2.22).

**TABLE 2.20** Elite Media Use Among Tabloid Television Viewers (percent using the other media sources daily, weekly, or several times a week or month)

|  | Lehrer News Hour | Sunday AM Political Talk Shows* | Inside Politics | National Public Radio | CSPAN |
|---|---|---|---|---|---|
| High tabloid TV use | 13 | 45 | 11 | 17 | 24 |
| Low tabloid TV use | 11 | 36 | 9 | 21 | 17 |

★ = e.g., *Meet the Press, Face the Nation, This Week with David Brinkley.*

**TABLE 2.21** Mainstream Media Use Among Tabloid Television Viewers (percent using the other media sources daily or weekly or several times a week or month)

|  | TV news (daily) | CNN Headline News | Radio news | All-news radio | Newspapers (daily) | News magazines |
|---|---|---|---|---|---|---|
| High tabloid TV use | 85 | 73 | 64 | 24 | 62 | 47 |
| Low tabloid TV use | 69 | 62 | 67 | 24 | 59 | 45 |

**TABLE 2.22** Other Types of Media Use Among Tabloid Television Viewers (percent using the other media sources daily or weekly or several times a week or month)

|  | Nightline | Larry King Live! | Talk Radio* | Read Political Books |
|---|---|---|---|---|
| High tabloid TV use | 26 | 21 | 17 | 18 |
| Low tabloid TV use | 13 | 13 | 16 | 24 |

|  | Morning News | TV News Magazines** | Tabloid TV*** | Late Night |
|---|---|---|---|---|
| High tabloid TV use | 43 | 53 | N/A | 31 |
| Low tabloid TV use | 30 | 27 | N/A | 17 |

N/A = not applicble; ★ = e.g., Rush Limbaugh, Jim Hightower; ★★ = e.g., *Dateline, 60 Minutes, 20/20*; ★★★ = e.g., *Inside Edition, Hard Copy.*

In contrast, table 2.22 shows that tabloid television viewers were much more likely to watch television news magazines (53 vs. 27%), late night talk shows (31 vs. 17%), and morning news shows (43 vs. 30%). They were also more likely to watch *Nightline* (26 vs. 13%) and *Larry King Live* (21 vs. 13%). Tabloid television viewers were less likely to read political books (18 vs. 24%). Even more than those voters who watched a great deal of network news, those who viewed tabloid television were very likely to gravitate toward shows with high entertainment and low information content.

## Conclusion

In this chapter, we demonstrated that voters depended mostly on the news media for their election information throughout the course of the campaign. We described the tendency of many voters to use mainstream sources of news, and we also described how voters used a great many niche sources of news including elite news media, political talk radio, and tabloid news shows. The finding that in the 1996 election Americans used the news as their primary source of campaign information, the impressive frequency with which voters used various media for campaign information, and the wide variety of specific sources utilized all provide evidence that voters do indeed depend on the news media for election news and that it is therefore important to evaluate the news as a political institution. In addition, the finding that many Americans use a variety of sources of information—especially elite media news—is good news for democracy.

We also demonstrated that some voters—news junkies—used a wide variety of media, ranging from mainstream sources of information such as television, radio, and newspapers, to niche market sources such as the PBS *NewsHour*, National Public Radio, talk radio shows, and tabloid television. Finally, we discussed the patterns of media use among different groups: elite versus non-elite viewers, talk radio versus nontalk radio listeners, network news users and tabloid television users. Our results imply that personal tastes seem to determine not only whether people use the news, but also the packages of information sources that they put together for themselves.

We suggest that theories of why people use the news do not necessarily imply that the wide variety of outlets for information will lead to higher information content on the part of the news. News organizations follow the cues of their audiences, and most theory emphasizes that public motivations for following the news are tangential to the desire to gather political information. If the public is dissatisfied with the political information being provided by the news, and yet the public does not change its viewing behavior, then we would not expect news organizations to provide more content, even if other sources proliferate. Our findings in this chapter suggest that media use is driven to a large extent by habit and taste—things that are tangential to politics. Because it appears that the factors driving media use are what we would expect, we should (and did) find that criticisms the public has of the news media (covered in chapters 4-6) will not have a large impact on the public's continued use of the news. Before exploring voter assessment of news quality and usefulness, we examine factors more closely related to political engagement, and those that might be expected to change over time and in response to the electoral campaigns.

**3**
—

# Explaining Media Use

As we suggested in the first chapter, the news media have several responsibilities that have an impact on the electoral system. The news media are responsible for providing current information, educating the public, and monitoring the veracity of public officials. In addition, they often play a role in turning voters' attention toward certain topics—in this case, elections. In this chapter, we explore the relationship between the public's interest, knowledge, and news media use. News organizations can play a role in educating potential voters and interesting them in elections.

We found that people who are more interested in the elections are more likely to use the news. But the percentage of the public interested in the 1996 elections did not grow over the course of the campaign, suggesting that news organizations did not do a very good job of mobilizing voter interest. We also found that people with higher levels of political knowledge are more likely to use the news. These factors affect the costs and benefits of news use. That is, people with more interest in an election outcome—especially those who think they have something at stake—have an interest in participating in that election, but the costs of gathering the basic knowledge needed to participate may prevent them from doing so.[1]

Before discussing the effects of voters' interest on media use, we define what factors might lead voters to gather more or less information. We also look at the impact of voters' party identification on media use, assessing whether voters use party identification as a shortcut (implying that those who have strong party identification use the news less) or whether partisans are more likely to use the news because they are more engaged in the electoral process.

## Gathering Information

Scholars attempting to explain why individuals engage in electoral and other types of behavior have developed theories that differ somewhat from explanations based on habit or personal preferences. We draw on these theories to develop an explanation for why some voters spend more time using the news. In doing so, we focus on several factors, including how important voters perceived the outcome of the 1996 election to be, whether they participated in past elections, and their level of political knowledge as the election year began. The explanation developed here is intended to be a starting point for more elaborate explanations of media use.

The explanations presented here will help to bolster our discovery that dissatisfaction with news media campaign coverage does not arise from some narrow portion of the electorate. If those with higher levels of political knowledge and those who regularly participate in elections are more likely to use the news—and if these groups are equally likely to be critical of the news—then we can conclude that criticism of the news media is likely to be spread across groups that are more and less likely to use the news. It is not confined to a narrow group of sophisticates who expect more from the news media than do most Americans; nor is it confined to those who spend little time on the news and are least qualified to evaluate it.

These variables also help us assess the consequences of dissatisfaction (see chapter 7). If the variables discussed here are more important in determining who uses the news than are the satisfaction variables discussed later (see chapters 4 through 6), then the feedback from public to media is weak. If voter dissatisfaction does not lead to less use of the media, then the electorate will not have an impact on media organizations' bottom lines, and it becomes much more difficult to see what holds the media accountable.

In developing a theory for why voters use the news media, we begin by focusing on the costs and benefits of using the news, as well as on the resources that voters bring to bear when using the news. Those explaining the costs of political participation assume that voters often have little incentive to expend a great deal of effort gathering information and voting. Scholars focusing on the costs of political participation suggest that voters may need to use a variety of strategies to negotiate the voting process in the presence of limited information (Downs 1954; Popkin 1991). Voters are thought to be more likely to gather information if they think they have more to gain or lose from the outcome of the election. We show that individuals who care a lot about who wins are much more likely to follow the news very closely and to use a variety of media over the course of the election.[2]

In addition to being more likely to gather information if the perceived benefits are greater, we argue that voters use the news more if the costs to them are less. In particular, we argue that the cost of using the news may be very little if the voter has a great fund of experience and political information on which to draw. In contrast, the news offers less to those who have never voted, and those who have low levels of political information. For example, those who have voted before may be familiar with some of the candidates. They may have already assessed their character, and know something about their policy positions, making information obtained from the news media easier (and more rewarding) to assimilate. Those who do not know any of the characters or who are still becoming familiar with the patterns of electoral campaigns and the jargon of journalists and experts may gain less from the same news shows or articles.

Each potential voter enters the campaign with an initial level of experience and knowledge about the campaign that may have been gleaned from previous experience in elections or from prior exposure to the media. Already having this information reduces the costs of using the news for that voter. This information may be basic, such as the knowledge of when and how to register, how to sift news stories for information, and where to vote. These experiences are thought to be the reason why people who have voted frequently in previous elections are more likely to vote again (Wolfinger and Rosenstone 1980:chapter 3; Rosenstone and Hansen 1993: 136–41). Because following the news, like voting, is a task that is easy compared to other forms of political participation, we might expect that even the relatively modest gains in ability that arise from having voted before would be associated with higher levels of media use over the course of the election cycle.

Some knowledge—encapsulated in our variable for experience—can be carried from one election to another. Other types of knowledge must be gained continually if voters are to keep abreast of events. For this reason, we sought a measure of current electoral knowledge. At the beginning of the election season (late January to early February), we asked our panel of voters to name as many candidates as they could in the Republican primary. Those with higher initial levels of information about the candidates— information gleaned from following the news in the year preceding the campaign or from participation in previous election campaigns—might be expected to gain more information (and more satisfaction) from the news stories to which they are exposed. We expected those with higher initial levels of information to use the news more, and found that that, indeed, was the case.

If voters are more likely to gather information about politics when they are interested in the outcome of the election, it is also thought that they try to conserve their efforts. Voters are expected, for example, to use party identification as an information shortcut. Thus, we might expect voters with higher levels of partisanship to collect less information.[3] Other scholars have found, however, that those who have strong feelings of partisan identification are more likely to be cognitively involved in politics (Campbell et al. 1960). We also found evidence for the latter assumption. It seems that voters who are more partisan use a wider variety of news sources more frequently than voters who have a weak or nonexistent political party identification.

Our explanation of media use, then, focuses on what voters have to gain from spending time on the news. It also considers the costs of using the news and the resources that voters bring to bear. Other plausible factors come to mind,[4] but they will not be explored here.

## Perceived Salience of the Election

In the last chapter, we mentioned that interest in the 1996 election was lower than in 1992, but about the same as in 1988. In our survey, we asked two questions intended to measure directly the salience of the current (1996) election. The first question asked about the short term, whether respondents cared a lot, some, just a little, or not at all about who wins the election. The second question focused voters on the long term: we asked whether they thought the election would have a major impact on the direction of the country for decades to come, or whether things in the country would not be much different regardless of who won.[5] Table 3.1 shows the relationship between these two variables. Those who thought the election would have a major impact were much more likely to care "a lot" about the election (69 vs. 49%). Those who thought that things would not be much different were more likely to care some, a little, or not at all. The relationship between these two variables is statistically significant,[6] although a number of individuals still cared about the outcome of the election, despite thinking that things would be much the same no matter who won.

**TABLE 3.1** Comparing Measures of Salience

|  | Results of election will have a major impact | Things will not be much different |
|---|---|---|
| A lot | 69% | 49 |
| Some | 16 | 27 |
| Just a little | 5 | 9 |
| Not at all | 9 | 16 |
| (N) | (258) | (192) |

Question asked was, "How much you personally care about which party wins the 1996 presidential election?"

After the Republican victory in both houses of Congress in the 1994 midterm election, a victory that the Republican leadership attributed in part to specific policies intended to roll back the growth in government and entitlements (Rosenstiel 1997), it seemed important to test whether perceptions of the immediate salience of the 1996 election led voters to gather more information, but also to assess whether voters who thought the 1996 election might be a watershed event spent still more time using the news. In general, we found that the perceived long-term importance of the election had no impact on viewing. Voters had the same patterns of viewing regardless of whether or not they thought the election would have a major impact on the country for decades to come. Those who thought the 1996 election would have a major long-term impact were more likely to report following the news closely throughout the campaign, but were no more likely to increase the frequency with which they watched different types of news media.

However, those who reported caring about the 1996 election outcome did have significantly different viewing habits. Respondents were much more likely (46 vs. 17%) to report that they were following the election very closely if they stated in February that they cared a lot about the outcome of the election (table 3.2). This resulted in a 25- to 30-percentage point gap that maintained itself through most of the election, falling to a 20-percentage point gap only in the final weeks. Those who cared a lot about the election outcome were 10 to 15 percentage points more likely to watch television news daily and 15 percentage points more likely to listen to talk radio. They were also about 10 percentage points more likely to read newspapers daily when the election season heated up, and more likely to listen to radio news in the few weeks immediately prior to the election.

**TABLE 3.2** Use of News Media and Salience of Election (percent responding that they follow news closely and use news media)

| | Preprimary | Postconvention | Postdebates | Postelection |
|---|---|---|---|---|
| **Follow news about the election very closely** | | | | |
| Care a lot about election | 46 | 44 | 52 | 44 |
| Care some, little, or none | 17 | 20 | 24 | 25 |
| **Use television news daily** | | | | |
| Care a lot about election | 83 | 85 | 74 | 80 |
| Care some, little, or none | 71 | 69 | 63 | 65 |
| **Read newspapers daily** | | | | |
| Care a lot about election | 66 | 68 | 64 | 66 |
| Care some, little, or none | 67 | 58 | 56 | 60 |
| **Use political talk radio** | | | | |
| Care a lot about election | 27 | 31 | 29 | 34 |
| Care some, little, or none | 13 | 17 | 15 | 17 |
| **Use radio news** | | | | |
| Care a lot about election | 68 | 68 | 68 | 57 |
| Care some, little, or none | 66 | 64 | 64 | 46 |

N = 494 registered voters

We found similar results when we looked at the impact of self-reported interest in the election. This question was asked in the first, second, and third wave of the panel study. Table 3.3 shows that voters who said they were "extremely interested" in the election were much more likely to follow the news closely (50%) than those who were "very interested" (26%) or only somewhat interested (9%). This difference in time spent using the news between those more interested and those less interested in the campaign maintained itself throughout the election year. Throughout the course of the campaign, those extremely or very interested in the election were more likely to watch television news daily. In February and September, the first two waves of the panel, those who were "extremely interested" in the election were more likely to watch television news every day (84–90%) compared to those who were "very interested" (75%) and those who were somewhat interested or less (58 to 66%). By the third wave of the panel, in October, fewer of those who were "extremely interested" (76%), and fewer who were "very interested" (68%) watched television news daily. Similarly, fewer of those who were only somewhat interested in the election watched television news daily as the election progressed, maintaining the

**TABLE 3.3** Use of News Media and Interest in the Election (percent responding that they follow news closely and use news media)

|  | Preprimary | Postconvention | Postdebates |
|---|---|---|---|
| Follow news about the election very closely | | | |
| Extremely interested | 50 | 51 | 64 |
| Very interested | 26 | 27 | 35 |
| Somewhat interested | 9 | 10 | 11 |
| Use television news daily | | | |
| Extremely interested | 84 | 90 | 76 |
| Very interested | 75 | 75 | 68 |
| Somewhat interested | 66 | 58 | 58 |
| Read newspapers daily | | | |
| Extremely interested | 69 | 72 | 65 |
| Very interested | 63 | 61 | 61 |
| Somewhat interested | 65 | 54 | 56 |
| Use political talk radio | | | |
| Extremely interested | 26 | 32 | 34 |
| Very interested | 22 | 24 | 18 |
| Somewhat interested | 9 | 13 | 13 |
| Use radio news | | | |
| Extremely interested | 59 | 57 | 56 |
| Very interested | 56 | 56 | 49 |
| Somewhat interested | 56 | 44 | 47 |

N = 494 registered voters

gap between those who were interested in the election and those who were not. In addition, those interested in the campaign were more likely to read newspapers daily, much more likely to listen to political talk radio, and more likely to use radio news.

Perceived importance of election outcome also had an impact on the use of different news media. Those who cared a lot about the outcome of this election were more likely to use mainstream television news, most elite media resources, and were more likely to listen to talk radio. Table 3.4 shows that those who cared a lot about the outcome of the election were more likely to watch the *NewsHour* with Jim Lehrer, were much more likely to watch Sunday morning talk shows (46 vs. 30%), and somewhat more likely to watch *Inside Politics* and C-SPAN and listen to National Public Radio. Those who cared a lot about which party won were also significantly more likely to watch television news daily (77 vs. 65%) and more likely to watch

CNN *Headline News* (69 vs. 57 percent). They were not more likely to listen to radio news or use the print media. On the other hand, they were more likely to listen to talk radio. Salience of the election to the voters had no impact on the probability that individuals would use tabloid television, TV news magazine programs, or morning news shows. Nor did caring a lot about the election make people more likely to watch *Nightline* or *Larry King Live* (tables 3.5 and 3.6).

These results suggest that voters who thought they received a greater benefit from the news—information about an election in which they were interested—were more likely to use the news. Because overall levels of interest in the election did not rise over the course of the campaign (see chapter 4), it appears unlikely that the news media was able to spark enthusiasm. They did, however, take advantage of what enthusiasm there was.

### Electoral Engagement

In this section we explore the impact of past electoral participation on use of the news. If past participation is an indication that respondents were interested (and may remain interested) in politics, then we would expect

**TABLE 3.4** Elite Media Use and Salience (percent using the other media sources daily/weekly or several times a week/month)

| | Lehrer News Hour | Sunday AM Political Talk Shows* | Inside Politics | National Public Radio | CSPAN |
|---|---|---|---|---|---|
| Care a lot about election | 14 | 46 | 12 | 23 | 22 |
| Care some, little, or none | 7 | 30 | 6 | 17 | 12 |

* = e.g., *Meet the Press, Face the Nation, This Week with David Brinkley.*

**TABLE 3.5** Mainstream Media Use and Salience (percent using the other media sources daily/weekly or several times a week/month)

| | TV news (daily) | CNN News | Radio news | All-news radio | Newspapers (daily) | News magazines |
|---|---|---|---|---|---|---|
| Care a lot about election | 77 | 69 | 68 | 23 | 60 | 49 |
| Care some, little, or none | 65 | 57 | 64 | 17 | 57 | 45 |

**TABLE 3.6** Other Types of Media Use and Salience (percent using the other media sources daily/weekly or several times a week/month)

| | NIGHTLINE | LARRY KING LIVE! | Talk Radio* | Read Political Books |
|---|---|---|---|---|
| Care a lot | 18 | 17 | 21 | 27 |
| Care some, little, or none about election | 13 | 10 | 11 | 17 |
| | Morning News | TV News Magazines** | Tabloid TV*** | Late Night |
| Care a lot | 34 | 35 | 21 | 21 |
| Care some, little, or none about election | 30 | 29 | 19 | 21 |

★ = e.g., Rush Limbaugh, Jim Hightower; ★★ = e.g., *Dateline, 60 Minutes, 20/20*, ★★★ = e.g., *Inside Edition, Hard Copy*.

those who have voted frequently in past elections to use more news. In other words, those who benefit more from the news use it more. It is also possible that those who have voted before have gained basic knowledge about elections and voting that reduces the costs to them of voting. For this reason, we also suggest that those who start with more information, either basic knowledge gained from voting before or campaign-specific knowledge measured with factual questions, are also more likely to use the news more frequently.

Past electoral engagement could have an impact on media use for several reasons. First, people voted because they felt a sense of civic responsibility. That sense of responsibility might be expected to persist over time. Second, people who have voted in previous elections have gone through the cycle of trying to obtain enough information to decide for whom to vote. They may have discovered new sources of media information and developed an interest that carried over to non-election years. In addition, they may have voted in past elections because they were interested in the candidates or the policies at stake. Individuals who were interested in past elections may be more likely to be interested in the candidates and issues of the current election, some of which overlap with those of past elections. We found that voting in one or two out of the past three elections did not have a significant impact on media use. Only those who voted three out of the past three elections were more likely to use media news.

Table 3.7 shows the patterns of media use across the course of the election cycle for our panel of registered voters. Entries in the table are the percent of voters that followed the election "very closely" or used each type of media with great frequency. Because so many people reported that they watch television news and read a newspaper, we reported the percent of daily use; for radio news and political talk radio, we reported the percent who used those media daily or several times per week.

We find that individuals who voted in all three of the most recent federal elections (two presidential elections and one congressional midterm), are much more likely to report that they followed news about the election very closely at the outset of the election (43 vs. 19%, a gap of 24 percentage points). By the end of the election cycle, this gap had narrowed to 15 percentage points.

Past electoral engagement also led to more use of specific types of media. Those who had voted in every election were somewhat more likely to use radio news (70 vs. 61%) and more likely to listen to talk radio (26

**TABLE 3.7** Use of News Media by History of Electoral Engagement

|  | Preprimary | Postconvention | Postdebates | Postelection |
|---|---|---|---|---|
| Follow news about the election very closely |  |  |  |  |
| Very engaged | 43 | 42 | 47 | 42 |
| Not very engaged | 19 | 22 | 29 | 27 |
| Use television news daily |  |  |  |  |
| Very engaged | 80 | 84 | 72 | 78 |
| Not very engaged | 74 | 70 | 64 | 67 |
| Read newspapers daily |  |  |  |  |
| Very engaged | 71 | 69 | 66 | 69 |
| Not very engaged | 60 | 54 | 54 | 56 |
| Use political talk radio |  |  |  |  |
| Very engaged | 26 | 30 | 29 | 32 |
| Not very engaged | 14 | 17 | 14 | 17 |
| Use radio news |  |  |  |  |
| Very engaged | 70 | 72 | 70 | 72 |
| Not very engaged | 61 | 58 | 60 | 61 |

Note: Percent responding that they follow news about the election very closely, that they use television news or read newspapers daily, or that they listen to radio news or talk radio daily or several times per week.

"Very engaged" voters voted in previous two presidential elections and the 1994 mid-term. N = 494 registered voters vs. 14%). They were also more likely to read newspapers daily (71 vs. 60%). The impact of electoral engagement on these types of media use remained consistent over the course of the election. In contrast, the impact of voting history on television news viewing was sporadic. Only after the Democratic and Republican party conventions, and after the final weeks of the election, were those who had voted in all of the past three elections more likely to watch television news.

## Knowledge at the Beginning of the Campaign

Besides basic information gained by voting in past elections, voters may also begin the election campaign with a larger cache of information specific to the candidates in the race. We might expect those with more information to be better able to make sense of the news, and to gain more from watching it, with less effort (Zaller 1992).[7]

We measured political knowledge in the preprimary baseline survey by asking individuals how many candidates running for the presidency they could name. For a substantial portion of the electorate, initial levels of factual knowledge were quite low: 37 percent of voters could name no more than two candidates (usually President Clinton and one other). An additional 44 percent could name three or four candidates (usually Clinton, Dole, and one or two third-party candidates such as Perot or Forbes). The remaining 19 percent could name additional candidates. This division mirrors similar divisions of the electorate by political knowledge that others have found (e.g., Zaller 1992).

Those with higher levels of baseline political knowledge were much more likely to use elite media, including the *NewsHour* (18 vs. 7%), Sunday

---

**TABLE 3.8** Elite Media Use and Political Knowledge (percent using the other media sources daily/weekly or several times a week/month)

| | Lehrer NEWS HOUR | Sunday AM Political Talk Shows* | INSIDE POLITICS | National Public Radio | CSPAN |
|---|---|---|---|---|---|
| High political knowledge | 18 | 51 | 13 | 25 | 24 |
| Medium knowledge | 9 | 35 | 8 | 21 | 19 |
| Low knowledge | 7 | 29 | 8 | 16 | 10 |

* = e.g., *Meet the Press, Fact the Nation, This Week with David Brinkley.*

morning political talk shows (51 vs. 29%), *Inside Politics* (13 vs. 8%), National Public Radio (25 vs. 16%) and C-SPAN (24 vs. 10%) (see table 3.8).

In addition, those with higher initial levels of political knowledge were more likely to use all mainstream sources of news. While 78 percent of those with high levels of political information watched television news daily, only 64 percent of those with low levels of knowledge did so (table 3.9). Those with higher initial levels of factual information were much more likely to watch CNN *Headline News* (74 vs. 51%). Those with more initial factual knowledge were much more likely to read newspapers daily (72 vs. 47%) and read news magazines each week (57 vs. 36%). In addition, they listen with greater frequency to radio news (72 vs. 59%), and all-news radio (26 vs. 16%).

If those with higher levels of political knowledge were more likely to use elite and mainstream news media, they were not more likely to take advantage of many other types of media (table 3.10). Those with higher levels of political knowledge were no more likely than those with lower levels to watch shows that have some political content and appealed to the elite-media viewers. Specifically, they are not much more likely to watch *Nightline* (17 vs. 15%) or *Larry King Live!* (17 vs. 12%). They were no more likely to watch shows with even less political content, such as morning news shows (32 vs. 33%), TV news magazines (35 vs. 30%), or late-night television (19 vs. 20%). The two exceptions to this finding were talk radio and political books. The more knowledgeable voters were more likely to listen to talk radio (24 vs. 10%), and were more likely to have read books on politics (33 vs. 13%). We also found, interestingly, that those with higher initial levels of political information were *less* likely to watch tabloid television. Although only 13% of those with high levels of political knowledge watched tabloid television frequently, 27 percent of those with the lowest amount of factual knowledge did so.

---

**TABLE 3.9** Mainstream Media Use and Political Knowledge (percent using the other media sources daily/weekly or several times a week/month)

| | TV news (daily) | CNN News | Radio news | All-news radio | Newspapers (daily) | News magazines |
|---|---|---|---|---|---|---|
| High political knowledge | 78 | 74 | 72 | 26 | 72 | 57 |
| Medium knowledge | 73 | 65 | 68 | 21 | 60 | 46 |
| Low knowledge | 64 | 51 | 59 | 16 | 47 | 36 |

**TABLE 3.10** Other Types of Media Use and Political Knowledge (percent using the other media sources daily/weekly or several times a week/month)

| | NIGHTLINE | LARRY KING LIVE! | Talk Radio* | Read Political Books |
|---|---|---|---|---|
| High political knowledge | 17 | 17 | 24 | 33 |
| Medium knowledge | 15 | 15 | 15 | 31 |
| Low knowledge | 15 | 12 | 10 | 13 |

| | Morning News | TV News Magazines** | Tabloid TV*** | Late Night |
|---|---|---|---|---|
| High political knowledge | 32 | 35 | 13 | 19 |
| Medium knowledge | 32 | 31 | 19 | 21 |
| Low knowledge | 33 | 30 | 27 | 20 |

\* = e.g., Rush Limbaugh, Jim Hightower; \*\* = e.g., *Dateline, 60 Minutes, 20/20*; \*\*\* = e.g., *Inside Edition, Hard Copy.*

Table 3.11 shows how those with higher levels of initial political knowledge differed from others over the course of the campaign. Initially, those with high levels of political knowledge were much more likely to report following the election very closely (44 vs. 19%). As the campaign progressed, however, the proportion of those with lower initial levels of political knowledge who followed the election very closely increased. By the end of the campaign, the difference in how closely the two groups were following the election had narrowed considerably (41 vs. 30%).

When we look at voters' media viewing behavior, we see differences that were more durable across the course of the campaign. In February, those with higher levels of political knowledge were more likely to watch television news daily (82 vs. 72%), and were much more likely to read newspapers daily (72 vs. 59%). These differences were maintained until the end of the campaign: 78 versus 68 percent for daily television news viewing, and 68 versus 57 percent for daily newspaper reading. Those with more factual knowledge were more likely to listen to talk radio frequently (27 vs. 14%). This difference, too, was maintained throughout the election, with 31 percent of the high initial-knowledge group reporting frequent talk radio use, and only 20 percent of those with less initial political knowledge reporting that they frequently listened to talk radio in the final weeks of the election campaign.

Overall, we found that those with higher initial levels of political

**TABLE 3.11** Use of News Media and Exogenous Factual Knowledge (percent responding that they use news media frequently)

|  | Preprimary | Postconvention | Postdebates | Postelection |
|---|---|---|---|---|
| Follow news about the election very closely |  |  |  |  |
| High political knowledge | 44 | 42 | 47 | 41 |
| Medium-low political knowledge | 19 | 23 | 30 | 30 |
| Use television news daily |  |  |  |  |
| High political knowledge | 82 | 83 | 72 | 78 |
| Medium-low political knowledge | 72 | 71 | 64 | 68 |
| Read newspapers daily |  |  |  |  |
| High political knowledge | 72 | 69 | 67 | 68 |
| Medium-low political knowledge | 59 | 58 | 54 | 57 |
| Use political talk radio |  |  |  |  |
| High political knowledge | 27 | 29 | 29 | 31 |
| Medium-low political knowledge | 14 | 19 | 15 | 20 |
| Use radio news |  |  |  |  |
| High political knowledge | 69 | 73 | 71 | 71 |
| Medium-low political knowledge | 65 | 58 | 61 | 63 |

N = 494 registered voters

knowledge were much more likely to use a variety of elite and mainstream news media. They were also more likely to listen to talk radio, and less likely to watch tabloid television. Those with high initial levels of factual knowledge used more media than their low-knowledge counterparts, although over the course of the campaign more of the low-information group reported following the campaign closely.

## Party Identification as a Shortcut

The amount of information that must be managed by voters is so enormous that perhaps the greatest task they face—once they choose to become exposed to media—is managing information (Graber 1988). Many argue that partisanship is one information shortcut used by voters.[8] Instead of bearing the costs of gathering information regarding the policy positions of candidates in each election, voters can use their evaluations of the parties in past elections, which have been tallied and incorporated into their constantly revised assessment of the political parties, as a shortcut to help them make their voting decision. Such a view implies a tendency of voters to use as little effort as possible in their decision as to how they will vote (Downs 1954; Fiorina 1981). From another perspective, an individual who exhibits stronger partisanship—a stronger affective orientation towards a political party—is thought to be more involved in politics. We might expect such individuals to spend more time perusing the news (Campbell et al. 1960).

We found much evidence that supports neither perspective. For most news sources, the extent of partisanship has little effect on whether individuals use the different news sources more or less frequently. When we found partisan differences, they supported the assertions of Campbell et al. that partisanship is an indicator of engagement in the political process. Strong partisans are interested in elections and tend to use more news. They do not appear to be conserving their energy.

If partisanship is used as a shortcut (perhaps by organizing and filtering information), it does not appear to be used as a substitute for gathering news. Table 3.12 shows the impact of partisanship, controlling for how much the voters cared about the outcome of the election. If salience is not controlled for, then strong partisans are more likely to watch elite news shows. If we control for the importance of the election to the voter, however, we find that differences between partisans and nonpartisans were small, with one exception. Strong partisans were more likely than nonpartisans to watch Sunday morning talk shows (50 vs. 38% among those who cared about the election, 33 vs. 23% among those who did not care).

Without controlling for salience, we also found that partisans were more likely to use many of the mainstream news media. Controlling for salience, we found that strong partisans are more likely to read newspapers daily (63 vs. 54% for those who cared about the election, 65 vs. 50% for those who cared little). Among those who cared little about the election, strong partisans were more likely to watch CNN *Headline News*. But among the high salience group, partisans were less likely to listen frequently to radio news (table 3.13).

Strong partisans also were more likely to use some of the alternative sources of information (table 3.14). Among those who care a lot about the election, more strong partisans than nonpartisans watched *Larry King Live!* frequently (20 vs. 8%), and more of them listened to talk radio (27 vs. 8%).

**TABLE 3.12** Elite Media Use by Strength of Partisanship and Salience of Election (percent using the other media sources daily/weekly or several times a week/month)

| | Lehrer NEWS HOUR | Sunday AM Political Talk Shows* | Inside Politics | National Public Radio | CSPAN |
|---|---|---|---|---|---|
| **High Salience** | | | | | |
| Strong Republican or Democrat | 15 | 50 | 14 | 24 | 24 |
| Weak Republican or Democrat | 14 | 39 | 6 | 21 | 19 |
| Leaning Republican or Democrat | 13 | 44 | 12 | 26 | 24 |
| No partisanship | 11 | 38 | 11 | 23 | 17 |
| **Low Salience** | | | | | |
| Strong Republican or Democrat | 13 | 33 | 9 | 22 | 12 |
| Weak Republican or Democrat | 7 | 17 | 4 | 16 | 11 |
| Leaning Republican or Democrat | 7 | 35 | 7 | 17 | 14 |
| No partisanship | 5 | 23 | 7 | 16 | 11 |

* = e.g., *Meet the Press, Face the Nation, This Week with David Brinkley.*

**TABLE 3.13** Mainstream Media Use and Strength of Partisanship (percent using the other media sources daily/weekly or several times a week/month)

| | TV news (daily) | CNN News | Radio news | All-news radio | Newspapers (daily) | News magazines | N |
|---|---|---|---|---|---|---|---|
| **High Salience** | | | | | | | |
| Strong Republican or Democrat | 80 | 70 | 66 | 25 | 63 | 47 | 589 |
| Weak Republican or Democrat | 73 | 66 | 69 | 20 | 58 | 50 | 283 |
| Leaning Republican or Democrat | 70 | 68 | 69 | 27 | 57 | 58 | 149 |
| No partisanship | 79 | 67 | 77 | 17 | 54 | 48 | 48 |
| **Low Salience** | | | | | | | |
| Strong Republican or Democrat | 72 | 67 | 64 | 19 | 65 | 47 | 129 |
| Weak Republican or Democrat | 65 | 57 | 65 | 18 | 59 | 48 | 335 |
| Leaning Republican or Democrat | 63 | 57 | 64 | 15 | 56 | 46 | 240 |
| No partisanship | 67 | 49 | 62 | 18 | 50 | 41 | 147 |

**TABLE 3.14** Other Types of Media Use and Strength of Partisanship (percent using the other media sources daily/weekly or several times a week/month)

| | NIGHTLINE | LARRY KING LIVE! | Talk Radio* | Read Political Books | Morning News | TV News Magazines** | Tabloid TV*** | Late Night |
|---|---|---|---|---|---|---|---|---|
| **High Salience** | | | | | | | | |
| Strong Republican or Democrat | 20 | 20 | 27 | 29 | 38 | 36 | 22 | 20 |
| Weak Republican or Democrat | 16 | 15 | 14 | 25 | 29 | 31 | 22 | 24 |
| Leaning Republican or Democrat | 16 | 10 | 16 | 26 | 32 | 38 | 22 | 22 |
| No partisanship | 17 | 8 | 8 | 25 | 33 | 27 | 19 | 15 |
| **Low Salience** | | | | | | | | |
| Strong Republican or Democrat | 14 | 17 | 13 | 20 | 31 | 30 | 19 | 19 |
| Weak Republican or Democrat | 11 | 8 | 9 | 14 | 29 | 28 | 18 | 19 |
| Leaning Republican or Democrat | 14 | 10 | 9 | 22 | 30 | 30 | 19 | 26 |
| No partisanship | 18 | 11 | 14 | 16 | 30 | 29 | 20 | 19 |

* = e.g., Rush Limbaugh, Jim Hightower; ** = e.g., Dateline, 60 Minutes, 20/20; *** = e.g., Inside Edition, Hard Copy.

In addition, strong partisans were more likely to watch television news magazines among the high salience group (36 vs. 27%).

Data from our panel survey showed again that, throughout the course of the election, if partisanship had an effect on media use, it tended to increase the frequency of use of the news media (table 3.15). Among those who cared about the outcome of the election, strong partisans were more likely to report following the election very closely. In February, 56 percent of strong partisans reported following the election very closely, compared with 33 percent of others. Throughout the election, more of the strong partisans reported following the news very closely. In contrast, among those who did not care about the outcome of the election, we find *fewer* strong partisans following the election very closely in February. For the rest of the election season, however, strong partisans in the low salience group also were more likely to follow the news closely.[9] Therefore, conclusions drawn from the low salience group should be interpreted cautiously.

Table 3.15 also shows that strong partisans are more likely to watch television news daily. In February, more strong partisans watched television news daily than those who are not strong partisans (86% for strong positions vs. 78% for others). By August, this difference had dipped to below levels of statistical significance. After the debates, however, strong partisans were again more likely to watch television news more frequently (81 vs. 64% and 85 vs. 73%). As for newspapers, among the high salience group strong partisans were more likely to read newspapers, but only in the latter phases of the campaign. Strong partisans may have been somewhat more likely to read newspapers daily in February and August, but the difference emerged more strongly in September (72 vs. 55%) and November (71 vs. 60%). We found a consistent pattern of strong partisans listening more frequently to talk radio. In February, strong partisans in this group were much more likely to listen to talk radio frequently (at least several times each week). The greater tendency of strong partisans to listen to talk radio was maintained throughout the election: 34 vs. 28 percent in August, 34 vs. 22 percent in September, and 37 vs. 28 percent in November.

To summarize, we found no evidence that partisan identifiers were less likely to spend time using the news. On some measures, in fact, partisan identifiers were more likely to spend more time watching, listening, and reading various news sources. In many cases, however, how much an individual voter cared about the outcome of the election mattered more than partisan identification in determining whether voters spent more time on their viewing habits.

**TABLE 3.15** Use of News Media by Strength of Partisanship and Salience of Election (percent responding that they use news media frequently)

| | Preprimary | Postconvention | Postdebates | Postelection |
|---|---|---|---|---|
| **Follow news about the election very closely** | | | | |
| High salience | | | | |
| Strong partisans | 56 | 51 | 60 | 51 |
| Not strong partisans | 33 | 36 | 41 | 36 |
| Low salience | | | | |
| Strong partisans | 10 | 37 | 33 | 43 |
| Not strong partisans | 19 | 18 | 23 | 22 |
| **Use television news daily** | | | | |
| High salience | | | | |
| Strong partisans | 86 | 87 | 81 | 85 |
| Not strong partisans | 78 | 82 | 64 | 73 |
| Low salience | | | | |
| Strong partisans | 77 | 80 | 63 | 80 |
| Not strong partisans | 71 | 68 | 63 | 63 |
| **Read newspapers daily** | | | | |
| High salience | | | | |
| Strong partisans | 70 | 71 | 72 | 71 |
| Not strong partisans | 63 | 64 | 55 | 60 |
| Low salience | | | | |
| Strong partisans | 67 | 53 | 57 | 57 |
| Not strong partisans | 68 | 60 | 57 | 61 |
| **Use political talk radio** | | | | |
| High salience | | | | |
| Strong partisans | 33 | 34 | 34 | 37 |
| Not strong partisans | 20 | 28 | 22 | 28 |
| Low salience | | | | |
| Strong partisans | 17 | 23 | 27 | 30 |
| Not strong partisans | 13 | 16 | 13 | 15 |
| **Use radio news** | | | | |
| High salience | | | | |
| Strong partisans | 65 | 70 | 66 | 67 |
| Not strong partisans | 73 | 66 | 71 | 73 |
| Low salience | | | | |
| Strong partisans | 57 | 57 | 47 | 50 |
| Not strong partisans | 68 | 67 | 68 | 68 |

N = 494 registered voters

## Conclusion

In exploring the correlates of media use, our evidence suggests that voters behave, in their news-gathering habits, in ways that support the cost-benefit assumptions of authors such as Downs (1954), Popkin (1991), and Rosenstone and Hansen (1993). Those who think that the election outcome is more important to them are more likely to use the news more frequently. In addition, those who have capabilities that may make following the news less difficult—those who have gained basic knowledge about the electoral process by participating in past elections and those who have higher levels of initial political knowledge—are more likely to use the news media more often.

The only theory for which we found limited and somewhat contradictory evidence was that of partisanship. We found limited support for the assumptions that voters with higher levels of partisanship were more engaged in the election. For some channels of information, voters were more likely to report more frequent use, but when we controlled for the salience of the election to the voter we found that in many cases those with higher levels of partisanship did not exhibit higher levels of media use than those with lower levels of partisanship. Until we can disentangle partisanship from perceived importance of the election, it will be difficult to determine which factor has the greater impact on media use.

These findings of the impact of perceived importance of outcome, knowledge, and past voting on media use support a view of the press as serving the information needs of the interested public—those who are moved to action, those who see a need or hold an interest in voting and do so. In this vein, Lippman (1925:61–62) suggested that the press serves the function of helping interested citizens by providing "guides to reasonable action" through reporting the news. Our data indicate that in terms of news use, the more informed, concerned, and interested voter is indeed more likely to seek out campaign news. We do not find evidence that the news media has increased the interest that voters have in elections.

To this point in the book, we have outlined basic information about how voters use the news. We have shown that some voters use a great variety of news sources. Others use very few. We have shown that voters with particular needs—for example, for more in-depth and direct news— are more likely to gravitate toward certain news sources than others. Finally, we have explored some aspects of voters' political backgrounds and some political characteristics of voters and found that some of them can have an impact on news use.

Bearing in mind what we have learned, and especially that a substantial number of voters used a wide variety of news sources with great frequency, we move on to the next three chapters, in which we examine voters' evaluations of the news in the 1996 election, beginning with voters' overall evaluations of the news media in the 1996 presidential campaign.

**4**

—

# Scratching the Surface:
# Overall Ratings of Election Coverage

In this chapter we describe voters' overall satisfaction with the news media in the 1996 presidential election (chapters 5 and 6 discuss more detailed evaluations of the performance of the news media, from the voters' perspective). The evaluation presented is from the perspective of the U.S. electorate. As we discussed in the first chapter, other scholars have examined the content of news reporting as well as the effects of news information on voter learning and opinion formation, and assessed their findings in the context of media performance in covering elections. These next three chapters use survey data on voters' opinions to evaluate the performance of the media. We do not mean to imply that voter evaluations are the primary source for evaluating the institutional performance of the news media. Indeed, relying on the voters' perspective complements the findings of other approaches, such as content analysis, media effects, and information processing research, by suggesting that voters (sometimes) also have the same criticisms as scholars. In addition, measuring the subjective assessments of voters allows us to later assess the implications of dissatisfaction on continued news media use. Despite criticism of the news sources, it is clear that voters make extensive use of various news media, as we have demonstrated in the previous chapters.

In addition to voter use, democratic theory also advances the role of the news media in the politics of U.S. democracy. Lippmann (1922), in Public Opinion, noted that the world of politics is "out of reach, out of mind, and out of sight" for the typical citizen in the United States. The news media provide the pictures to the masses that become their reality of the political world. Democracy, at least from the classicist viewpoint, is based in large part on the supposition that citizens are capable of making informed decisions about candidates. Such a supposition requires citizens to become informed about the candidates and issues in a campaign. The news media bring the political world of democratic campaigns to voters so they are within their reach and sight. The data we presented in chapter 2 confirm that the electorate is, in fact, highly dependent on the news media for their election information.

In American democratic theory as well as in practice, then, the news media play a very important role in the U.S. democratic political system. Theoretically, the media is an independent (nongovernmental) source of information, providing objective information upon which voters may rely to make decisions on who will lead and run the nation. And, as we have pointed out, voters do depend mostly on the news media to obtain information about presidential campaigns. Such dependence highlights the prominent role of the news media as an institution in American society.

It is in this spirit that we provide voters' overall views of how good or bad a job the news media did in covering the 1996 campaign. Like overall presidential performance ratings and overall ratings of the economic performance of the nation, we use several general performance ratings of the news media as dependent variables in assessing overall performance. Chapters 5 and 6 provide more specific criteria, such as assessments of the existence and extent of political bias in news coverage, attitudes about the content of news reporting on elections (e.g., horse race coverage, issue coverage, coverage of third-party candidates), and feelings about the value of different media and different news formats for learning about the campaign.

Here we specifically address the following questions: How interested are voters in election news compared to other kinds of news and how do they evaluate election news compared to other kinds of news? What are voters' overall evaluations of news media performance in campaign 1996, and how did overall opinions of coverage change from the presidential primary phase of the campaign up through election day? Why did their evaluations change over time? Here, we look at the impact of voters' interest in the campaign, their need for information at different times during the campaign, and their overall evaluation of the news media. In addition, we examine whether voters rate the media more positively after they think they have received enough information about the election.

We then explore ratings of different news sources, finding that voters rate television coverage the best, and that voters are more likely to rate best the medium that they use the most. Finally, we ask whether voters distinguish between evaluations of the news product and evaluations of the process the media use in gathering election news. Do voters think that news coverage of the campaign is improving or deteriorating?

## Election News Compared to Other News

Despite the important theoretical role the news media play in presidential campaigns, and despite the widespread voter reliance on the news media for information about presidential elections, it is important to put in perspective the importance of news about elections for the American voter. Overall, Americans express a relatively low level of interest in news coverage of political campaigns compared to other kinds of news. The public is also less likely to offer positive ratings to the news media's coverage of political campaigns, relative to other kinds of news.

A 1997 survey of the American public conducted for the Freedom Forum shows that among eleven different categories of news, voters express less interest in news about political campaigns than any other category of news asked about (Dautrich, 1996).[1] That is, only 20 percent of Americans say they are either extremely or very interested in news about political campaigns, compared to 69 percent who are at least very interested in local news, 68 percent who express high interest in news about crime, and 59 percent who express that level of interest in news about the environment. Figure 4.1 also shows that more Americans are interested in international news, news about money and business, sports news, and news about the arts than they are in news about political campaigns. The public's appetite for news information about political campaigns is not very strong.

The same survey also shows that Americans are relatively less likely to think that the news media do a good job in covering political campaigns than they do in covering other topical areas. The lower ratings for campaign coverage may, in fact, be lowering the public's appetite for campaign news. Figure 4.1 shows that half (50%) of Americans give a positive rating of "excellent" or "good" in how the news covers political campaigns. At the same time 72 percent offer a similar positive evaluation of coverage of sports in the news, and two-thirds give a positive rating to coverage of local news and coverage of news about crime.

Despite the great theoretical importance as well as the large practical influence of the news media in U.S. political campaigns, Americans express a very low level of interest in coverage of political campaigns, and they offer

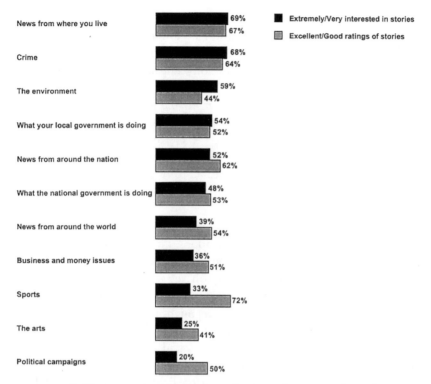

**FIGURE 4.1** Public interest in news stories and rating of coverage. These data are based on a national telephone survey of 1,500 conducted for the Newseum in January 1997. The survey was conducted by the University of Connecticut's Center for Survey Research and Analysis.

relatively low ratings of the news media's coverage of campaigns. It is within this context that we turn to an assessment of voters' overall evaluations of the news media's performance in covering the presidential campaign of 1996.

## Overall Evaluations of Media Coverage

The panel data allow us to trace overall assessments of news media coverage of the 1996 presidential campaign by observing responses to an item administered in our voter panel at each of the four waves: "Overall, how would you rate the job that the media are doing in covering the presidential campaign—excellent, good, only fair, or poor?"

Figure 4.2 shows panel responses to this question for each wave of interviewing. The figure shows a clear trend toward improved overall evaluations of news media coverage from the early primary period in February through the heart of the general election campaign. It also shows that the source of the increase in ratings is not from a decline in "don't know" responses. Rather, as the campaign wore on, the percentage of voters offering a negative rating of "only fair" or "poor" declined and those offering positive ratings of "excellent" or "good" increased. Forty percent of voters offered a positive rating of news media coverage at the outset of the primary season. This percentage increased to over half (52%) by the post-convention period, and again to nearly three in five (59%) by the end of the presidential debates.

What could have caused the change in viewers' overall ratings of the news media? We explore four explanations. First, voter ratings may have improved because they became more interested in the campaign. Voters more interested in the campaign might have rated the news better simply because they wanted information more, and so became more satisfied with the information available. Second, voters might have rated the news media higher at times during the campaign when they needed more information. If this is the case, then we should have found that more Republicans in 1996 rated the news media positively during the primaries when their need for information was greater (due to the large field of Republican candidates vying for the GOP nomination). Democrats, in contrast, with their largely uncontested primaries, should not have demonstrated a greater need for the news during the primary season. Third, voters may have rated the news

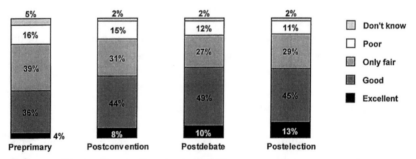

**FIGURE 4.2** Change in overall ratings of media coverage of campaign: February through November 1996. The question responded to was, "Overall, how would you rate the job the media are doing in covering the presidential campaign—excellent, good, only fair, or poor?"

media more highly after they have received enough information to make an electoral choice. After all, if viewers used the news for the pragmatic purpose of gathering information in order to cast their vote, then news that did not give them the information they needed might be rated more poorly while news that gave them the information they needed might be rated better. Fourth, it is possible that voters might have improved their overall rating if they saw an improvement in the problems that they saw in the news (this aspect is discussed in more detail in chapter 6). We begin by analyzing the impact interest in the campaign has on voter evaluation of the news.

*Interest in the Campaign*

One possible explanation for the increased ratings in media coverage might be that it was not media performance per se that improved, but that voter interest in the presidential campaign may have increased. It is possible that, as voters became more interested in the campaign, and wanted more information, they also became more favorable toward the channels of communication providing the campaign information. That is, as voter interest in the campaign increased, voters may have turned toward the media to satisfy their own information needs, possibly resulting in improved assessments of campaign coverage.

Although this "information demand" hypothesis sounds plausible, data from the panel study suggest that increased demand and reliance on news media for information did not contribute to the increased ratings. That is, from February 1996 through October 1996, voter interest in the campaign did not, in fact, increase. Interest remained fairly stable throughout this time, as shown in table 4.1. Four out of ten voters remained "extremely" interested in the campaign from the early primary season through the election, and about three-quarters of voters were at least "very" interested in the campaign from early in 1996 to election day. In fact, interest in the presidential election was remarkably stable throughout the election year. Also, if the demand for news about the campaign increased, we might expect to see an increase in use of the news media as the election drew closer. As we demonstrated in chapter 2, however, no such change in either frequency or nature of news media consumption habits occurred throughout 1996.

*Satisfaction After Receiving Enough Information to Vote*

Rather than simply an increase in demand for election news, it may be the case that the increase in positive evaluations resulted from voters managing to get the information they needed from news coverage. In other

**TABLE 4.1** Voter Interest in the 1996 Presidential Campaign

|  | Preprimary | Postconvention | Postdebate |
|---|---|---|---|
| Extremely | 40% | 41% | 39% |
| Very | 32% | 32% | 36% |
| Somewhat | 23% | 21% | 20% |
| Not too | 4% | 4% | 4% |
| Not at all | 1% | 1% | 2% |
| (Number) | (503) | (503) | (503) |

The question asked was, "How interested would you say that you are in the 1996 presidential election—extremely interested, very interested, somewhat interested, not too interested, or not at all interested?"

words, although there were aspects of media coverage that the public did not like—news presented in a confusing format, attention paid to subjects that are peripheral to their interests, or perceptions of bias in news stories (see discussion in chapters 5 and 6)—the public may have been able to gain the information it needed to make a voting decision (Zaller 1992; Robinson and Sheehan 1983; Patterson 1980). After obtaining this information, their ratings may have risen.

The results of our panel study show that in 1996, as the ratings of the media increased over the course of the election, the percentage of the public who reported receiving enough information to make a vote choice also increased significantly between February and September, and again between September (after the conventions) and October (after the debates). For example, in February, when only 31 percent said they received enough information to make a vote decision, only 40 percent of panel respondents offered a positive rating of news coverage, (see figure 4.3). By September, when 69 percent of voters thought they knew enough to cast a vote choice, 52 percent gave a positive rating to media coverage. And by mid-October, when fully 85 percent of voters said they knew enough to cast a vote, news media ratings hit the six-in-ten mark. As voters came to decide on a candidate, it is possible that they tended to credit the news media for providing the information necessary to cast their vote.

Panel data provide more evidence supporting this explanation. Table 4.2 shows the percentage of voters offering positive news media coverage ratings among three groups: (1) those said they had enough information to make a vote choice, and had said so before, (2) those who had just begun saying (in the current wave of the panel study) they had enough information, and (3) and those saying they did not have enough information. The

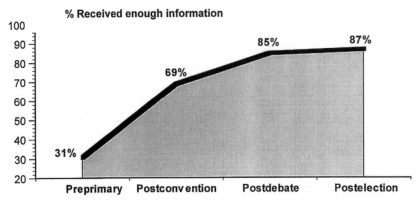

**FIGURE 4.3** Percent of voters who received enough information to make vote choice. The question responded to was, "At this point in the campaign, do you feel you have received enough information to make a vote decision, or do you need more information?"

table shows that toward the end of the campaign, those who had enough information to make an informed vote choice were more likely to give higher ratings than voters who did not have enough information. Moreover, in waves 3 and 4, when voters were re-interviewed at one-month intervals, we found that those who had just recently received enough information (within the past month) were the most likely of all to rate the news media positively.

By election day, 62 percent of those who thought they had enough information gave a positive media rating, and fully 68 percent of those who had just received enough information rated the news media positively.

**TABLE 4.2** Positive Ratings of Election News Coverage by Feelings that One Has Enough Information to Make Vote Choice (percent offering a positive rating)

| | Preprimary | Postconvention | Postdebate | Postelection |
|---|---|---|---|---|
| Have enough information to make a vote choice | 45% | 54% | 62% | 62% |
| Just received enough information to make a vote choice | | 52% | 68% | 67% |
| Do not have enough information | 38% | 55% | 56% | 37% |

The ratings for these groups were much higher than the rating (only 37% rated the news positively) given the news by those voters who thought they did not have the necessary amount of information to make their electoral decision. As more voters arrived at the feeling that they had enough information to make a vote choice, overall ratings of news media coverage increased. The fact that information about the campaign was made available to voters to help them in the vote decision process appears to have, at least in part, contributed to the trend toward higher ratings through the course of the campaign.

It is worth noting that waves 2, 3 and 4 of our panel study followed significant events in the election year (the party conventions, the debates, and the election outcome, respectively). As we shall see in chapter 6, the "direct exposure" events—the conventions and particularly the debates—are the kinds of news media information that voters value most highly. The jumps in the ratings from wave 1 to wave 2, and then again from wave 2 to wave 3, may be the result of the timing of key direct exposure events (conventions and debates) that voters find most useful. The media acting as a conduit of this direct exposure may have led to the higher overall ratings of the news at these time points.

It would appear, in general, that 1996 was a good year for the news media's ability to impart information to the voters. Pew Center polls conducted in November 1988, 1992, and 1996 showed that the proportion of the public that learned enough about candidates rose from 59 percent in 1988 to 77 percent in 1992. Compared to 1988, a much larger percentage of the public in 1992 and 1996 reported that it was able to learn enough about the candidates (see figure 4.4).

*Political Information Environment*

A third possible explanation lies in the nature of the political information environment (Page and Shapiro 1992) at the time of the panel interviews. The nature of the information passed through the news media to voters may have been more useful to different kinds of voters—most notably different partisan groups—at the time panel waves 2, 3, and 4 were conducted. At the time of wave 1, the focus was on the Republican primaries, as the Democratic incumbent President Clinton was not being challenged. The news focus was on the Republican primary, where Pat Buchanan was waging a significant challenge to frontrunner Bob Dole. One might expect that Democrats were less engaged and thus less enthusiastic about the news coverage of the campaign.

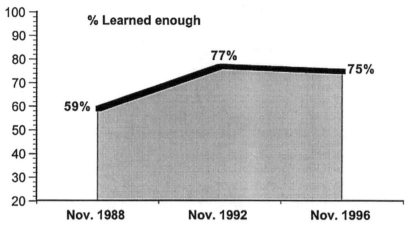

**FIGURE 4.4** Percentage of voters who learned enough about candidates *(Source: Pew Center surveys).*

Table 4.3 shows that although Republicans were less likely to offer high ratings at all waves of the panel, compared to other voters they were, in fact, even less likely to offer improved ratings as the campaign progressed from Republican-dominated news on the primaries to bipartisan news about the general election campaign (waves 2, 3 and 4). The partisan breakdown data show that through the campaign Republican voter positive ratings improved only modestly from February to October, and then dipped slightly by election day.[2]

Overall evaluations of news coverage by Democratic voters and to a lesser but significant extent by independent voters jumped sharply from February through October and provided the bulk of the overall increase in news ratings. These data suggest that at least part of the increase in ratings of media coverage (at least from wave 1 to wave 2) are based on a shift in focus from the Republican primaries to a broader focus on the general election campaign.

**TABLE 4.3** Percent Giving Positive Ratings of News Media Coverage by Partisanship

|  | Preprimary | Postconvention | Postdebate | Postelection |
|---|---|---|---|---|
| Republicans | 35% | 40% | 47% | 44% |
| Democrats | 44% | 64% | 78% | 76% |
| Independents | 39% | 56% | 55% | 62% |

*Quality of News Coverage and Overall Ratings*

A fourth possible reason for the increase in positive ratings of the media over the course of the election is that media coverage changed. In chapter 6 we show that, as the campaign progressed, the public's perception of the media's emphasis on different types of stories changed somewhat. Between February and November, a somewhat smaller proportion of the public felt that the media was paying too much attention to the personal lives of candidates. Between February and September, and then again between September and November, we found that fewer voters thought the media paid too little attention to issue positions and the effect of the election on themselves. Greater media focus on the kinds of campaign information that voters were more interested in may also have contributed to the trend toward higher ratings as the campaign progressed.

The national voter panel study appears to support several explanations for why voters' overall evaluations of media coverage of the 1996 election improved from February through election day. One is that the ability of voters to obtain from the news media at least the minimum information they need to cast their vote may have led voters to provide better evaluations of coverage as election day drew near, regardless of whether they liked the format in which the information was presented or whether the news was interspersed with less useful information. Second, voters may have rated the news media more highly when they demanded more information— during primaries for Republicans and for all voters as the election drew near. A third hypothesis, that overall ratings improved because from the voters' perspective the quality of news coverage of the campaign improved, was also supported (see chapter 6). One hypothesis, that voters improved their ratings of the news media as their interest in the campaign increased, was not supported. We now turn to an analysis of how the type of media voters used for political information may have influenced evaluations of overall news media performance.

## Satisfaction with Information Provided

In the last section, we suggested that voters who had received enough information to decide how to vote were more likely to rate the news media higher. Now, we ask which voters are more likely to think that they were well informed. Most American voters report that the news media is their dominant source of information about presidential campaigns. At all four waves of our voter panel study, at least 7 in 10 voters said they depended primarily on the news media to get campaign information. In the two panels conducted immediately prior to election day (the September and October waves), when voters were more apt to be seeking information about the candidates, about 8 in 10 voters said the news media was their dominant source of information.

Is one's sense of satisfaction that one has enough information to make a vote choice based, at least in part, on the type of news media used for campaign information? Previously, we demonstrated that one's sense of informed satisfaction varied positively with evaluations of media coverage. Here, we trace changes in the percent of voters who think they have received enough information over the course of the campaign, and examine whether use of certain kinds of news media has an effect on thoughts and decisions that one has enough information to make a vote choice.

Table 4.4 shows that the percentage of voters saying they had enough information to make a vote choice increased consistently through the campaign. It increased dramatically from 31 percent in February to 72 percent after the Republican and Democratic party conventions. After that, more modest increases occurred, to 87 percent after the presidential debates, and to 91 percent after the election. At the end of the election cycle, only 9 percent said they had not received enough information to make a vote choice. At the beginning of a series of primary races in February, only 31 percent of Republicans said they had enough information to make a decision. At that time, just before the New Hampshire primary, their party's field included five contenders. In contrast, because Clinton's bid for renomination was uncontested, the Democratic candidate was already chosen; in February many more Democrats (51%) said that they had enough information to cast their vote. By September, Democratic and Republican voters tended to exhibit similar levels of satisfaction with having enough information to decide on a candidate. Independents were less likely than

**TABLE 4.4** Percentage of Voters Saying They had Enough Information to Make a Vote Choice by Party Identification

|  |  | Preprimary | Postconvention | Postdebate | Postelection |
|---|---|---|---|---|---|
| All Voters | (512) | 31% | 72% | 87% | 91% |
| Republicans | (179) | 31% | 75% | 86% | 95% |
| Democrats | (186) | 51% | 75% | 90% | 93% |
| Independents | (109) | 23% | 68% | 81% | 89% |

partisans to think they had enough information, perhaps because they lacked the perceptual screen of a party identification to help influence their decision, or perhaps because independents tend to be less engaged in the electoral process.

Interestingly and with few exceptions, by late in the election season, use of particular forms of the news media—local and national TV, talk and news radio, print sources, books, and elite news media—did not appear to influence voters' sense that they have enough information to make a vote choice. As shown in table 4.5, light to heavy users of television and radio news were about as likely to say they have enough information for deciding on a candidate for the September, October, and November waves of interviewing. Heavier users of political talk radio, print news sources, and the elite news media tended to be slightly more likely to think they have enough information to cast a vote.

This finding did not hold early in the election season. During the early campaign period just prior to the New Hampshire primary, heavier users of certain media sources were much more likely to say they have information to make a vote choice. In February, heavier users of national television news were 20 points more likely than light users (48% to 28%, respectively) to feel they have enough information to vote. Similarly, heavier users of print and elite media sources were more likely to report having received enough information to make an electoral choice. Those who had read books on politics were also more likely to have already gathered the information they need.

After the election gets under way, then, it appears that voters' sense of having enough information to vote increases through the campaign regardless of which type of news medium voters use to get campaign information. By election day, the vast majority of voters said they have enough information to make a choice regardless of the media they use to gather information. The closer to election day, the more likely it is that use of any news source largely satisfies voters information needs. For example, by the November wave, nine in ten or more voters who either moderately or heavily used any of the ten news formats said they had enough information to make a vote choice. Accessing and using any source of campaign information appears to satisfy the informational demands of most American voters. Put another way, voter use of a news source for information about the campaign does not affect the satisfaction one has in thinking they have enough information to make a vote decision.

**TABLE 4.5** Voters Who Thought They Had Enough Information to Make a Vote Choice by Media Sources Used (figures are percentages)

| | All TV News | | | Local TV News | | | Tabloid News | | National TV News | | | Talk Radio News | | |
|---|---|---|---|---|---|---|---|---|---|---|---|---|---|---|
| | L | M | H | L | M | H | Y | N | L | M | H | L | M | H |
| Preprimary | 30 | 35 | 44 | 38 | 33 | 39 | 36 | 43 | 28 | 33 | 48 | 38 | 38 | 34 |
| Postconvention | 73 | 63 | 77 | 72 | 67 | 73 | 66 | 73 | 74 | 67 | 77 | 71 | 68 | 78 |
| Postdebate | 88 | 82 | 89 | 81 | 89 | 88 | 83 | 88 | 89 | 83 | 90 | 86 | 87 | 89 |
| Postelection | 90 | 93 | 92 | 89 | 89 | 93 | 86 | 93 | 90 | 91 | 93 | 89 | 94 | 96 |
| (N) | (152) | (147) | (203) | (80) | (101) | (321) | (105) | (397) | (108) | (216) | (178) | (297) | (100) | (105) |

| | Radio News | | | Print Media News | | | Political Books | | Elite Media News | | | ALL |
|---|---|---|---|---|---|---|---|---|---|---|---|---|
| | L | M | H | L | M | H | N | Y | L | M | H | |
| Preprimary | 42 | 31 | 38 | 29 | 35 | 44 | 35 | 44 | 30 | 30 | 49 | 37 |
| Postconvention | 71 | 71 | 74 | 71 | 73 | 72 | 71 | 75 | 69 | 70 | 76 | 72 |
| Postdebate | 86 | 87 | 88 | 84 | 87 | 87 | 86 | 88 | 85 | 87 | 89 | 87 |
| Postelection | 91 | 90 | 94 | 88 | 92 | 94 | 92 | 91 | 91 | 89 | 94 | 91 |
| (N) | (170) | (163) | (169) | (104) | (205) | (193) | (365) | (137) | (165) | (149) | (188) | (503) |

Key: L = Low; M = Medium; H = High.

### Ratings of Types of News Media Outlets

Our data indicate that voters in 1996 rate the performance of various media outlets differently. In the first panel wave (February), we asked the public to rate several different types of media outlets. Figure 4.5 shows that the public rates television news programs the highest, with 44 percent giving a rating of excellent or good. Newspapers are rated about the same, with 42 percent giving an excellent or good rating. In contrast, radio news programs are rated much lower, with only 33 percent rating radio news programs excellent or good.

These differences, however, appear to have more to do with actual usage of the three sources for campaign information. If we remove those who have no opinion on each medium rating item and re-percentage based only on those who used the medium, the gap between television, newspapers, and radio news shrinks considerably.

What appears to have happened is that people found a source of news that was more useful or convenient for their needs. Once they found a source, the ratings given to that source were consistent. That is, the evaluations that

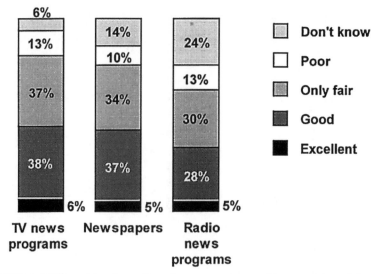

**FIGURE 4.5** Differential ratings of media coverage by specific news source. The question responded to was, "Overall, how would you rate the job that (rotate) are doing in covering the presidential campaign—excellent, good, only fair, or poor?" It was asked in February 1996.

users of TV news gave to that medium were very similar to the ratings that radio and newspaper users gave to those media in their coverage of the presidential campaign.

## Overall Evaluations of Media Coverage by Media Use

The preceding discussion demonstrated that voters' overall evaluations of media coverage of the 1996 campaign started at a low level in February (about 40% positive) and improved over the campaign to about 60 percent of voters saying that coverage was either "excellent" or "good." We looked at several explanations for the change and how different media were rated. In this section, we look at the possible impact of the use of particular news media on overall thoughts about campaign coverage. Does the use of certain kinds of news media have an effect on overall perceptions of news media coverage of presidential campaigns?

Many have speculated that the quality of the medium influences information gleaned by users of various media. Patterson (1980), for example, argued that those using print media were exposed to more information and had at their disposal more news about campaigns to process and use. Those relying on print media, having more information at their disposal, might offer higher ratings of the media's performance. The data presented in table 4.6 show that heavy print media users did tend to offer higher positive ratings of the media in 1996 than less frequent users of print media both early on in the campaign (the February wave) and at the end of the campaign (the November wave).

In February, 44 percent of heavy print users offered a positive rating to the news media, compared to 37 percent of both low and moderate users. And although no discernible relationship existed in the early general election campaign waves, by election day, 50 percent of low print users gave a positive rating compared to 61 percent of moderate print users and 64 percent of heavy print users.

Use of the television for election news bears a curious relationship to overall ratings of campaign coverage—moderate users of TV tended to offer higher ratings at most waves than light and heavy users of TV. Those who sought out little to no information from television and those who relied a great deal on television tended to be less satisfied with news media coverage of the campaign than moderate TV users. For example, by election day two-thirds of moderate TV users (66%) gave a high positive rating to news

TABLE 4.6 Voters Offering a Positive Rating to Media Coverage by Media Sources Used (figures are percentages)

| | All TV News | | | Local TV News | | | Tabloid News | | National TV News | | | Talk Radio News | | |
|---|---|---|---|---|---|---|---|---|---|---|---|---|---|---|
| | L | M | H | L | M | H | Y | N | L | M | H | L | M | H |
| Preprimary | 35 | 45 | 41 | 41 | 32 | 43 | 47 | 38 | 36 | 40 | 42 | 41 | 43 | 35 |
| Postconvention | 52 | 54 | 54 | 52 | 60 | 52 | 51 | 54 | 52 | 56 | 52 | 59 | 52 | 39 |
| Postdebate | 55 | 65 | 63 | 56 | 50 | 65 | 65 | 60 | 56 | 65 | 60 | 70 | 58 | 39 |
| Postelection | 51 | 66 | 61 | 54 | 60 | 60 | 63 | 59 | 51 | 63 | 56 | 64 | 63 | 44 |
| (N) | (149) | (146) | (199) | (79) | (100) | (315) | (105) | (389) | (105) | (213) | (176) | (294) | (97) | (103) |

| | Radio News | | | Print Media News | | | Political Books | | Elite Media News | | | ALL |
|---|---|---|---|---|---|---|---|---|---|---|---|---|
| | L | M | H | L | M | H | N | Y | L | M | H | |
| Preprimary | 39 | 37 | 44 | 37 | 37 | 44 | 41 | 39 | 39 | 40 | 42 | 40 |
| Postconvention | 52 | 59 | 51 | 57 | 48 | 57 | 56 | 48 | 53 | 53 | 53 | 53 |
| Postdebate | 65 | 59 | 59 | 63 | 61 | 61 | 66 | 49 | 64 | 59 | 60 | 62 |
| Postelection | 60 | 54 | 65 | 50 | 61 | 64 | 60 | 61 | 61 | 55 | 62 | 60 |
| (N) | (167) | (159) | (168) | (102) | (198) | (194) | (358) | (136) | (163) | (143) | (188) | (503) |

Key: L = Low; M = Medium; H = High.

coverage compared to 61 percent of heavy TV users and 51 percent of light TV news users.

Beyond the traditional distinctions among types of media, the contemporary news media environment raises many questions about the possible effects of use of a particular medium on orientations toward campaign coverage. The recent rise in usage of political talk radio and the rather negative orientations of political talk radio commentators and call-in guests is a case in point(Hofstetter et. al 1994; Katz 1991; Hollander 1996). As we demonstrated in chapter 2, more than one in ten voters tuned in to political talk radio on a regular basis to get news about the presidential campaign in 1996—and about half of all voters used at least some political talk radio for information during the campaign. The growing talk radio audience, along with talk radio's often negative orientation, raises serious questions about the impact of this negativity on voter attitudes toward many political institutions, including the news media.

Table 4.6 does, in fact, show that users—particularly heavy users—of political talk radio tended to hold lower opinions of overall news media performance. The differences were most pronounced during the general election campaign. In September non-users of talk radio were 20 percentage points more likely to offer a positive rating of news media performance; in October they were 31 points more likely, 20 percentage points more likely again by election day. Clearly, the political talk radio audience is one that is more negatively oriented toward the performance of the news media, and these election-year voter data tend to confirm the hypotheses advanced by Hofstetter.

Interestingly, users of the elite media were not more likely to offer higher ratings to the performance of the news media in 1996. We might expect that individuals who used these sources to have rated the overall news higher, if they included elite media as part of their definition of the news. Alternatively, if respondents did not include shows such as the *NewsHour* in their definition of the news, we might expect them to have rated the news lower than other respondents. Instead, we found no effect at all. Nor were differences found for those who claimed to have read a book about politics within a year or who heavily used news on the radio, local TV news, or national TV news. In fact, except for the print media and political talk radio usage differences, high and low use of other media sources did not seem to make much difference in perceptions of news media coverage of the presidential campaign.

Another way to understand the effect of media source use on attitudes about media performance is to examine how voters with different *primary* news sources differ in overall assessments of election news. Table 4.7 shows this relationship at three times during the 1996 campaign. Interestingly, those who depended mainly on television as a source of election information tended to provide higher overall evaluations of the news media than those who were newspaper-dependent, and particularly higher than those who are mainly radio-dependent—and they did so consistently from the beginning of the campaign in February through election day.

## Grading Media Versus Press Coverage

Another way of letting the public rate the press in its coverage of campaign 1996 was to ask them to give it a grade. Since 1988, the Pew Center for the People and the Press has asked the public to grade the press's conduct in national elections. Table 4.8 shows that the press received relatively low ratings in 1988, with only 30 percent of those polled giving As (8%) or Bs (22%).

According to the Pew Center tracking data, the press's conduct improved somewhat in the 1992 election: 36 percent gave the press either an A or a

**TABLE 4.7** Percent Offering Positive Rating of News Media Coverage by Main Source of News

**Depends Mainly on . . .**

|  | Television | | Newspaper | | Radio | |
|---|---|---|---|---|---|---|
| Preprimary | 45% | (258) | 37% | (98) | 23% | (56) |
| Postconvention | 59% | (260) | 43% | (90) | 41% | (64) |
| Postelection | 64% | (272) | 60% | (108) | 50% | (54) |

**TABLE 4.8** Grading the Media Overall and the Conduct of the Press

|  | A | B | C | D | F | DK |
|---|---|---|---|---|---|---|
| November 1988—Press Conduct (PEW) | 8% | 22% | 33% | 19% | 16% | 2% |
| November 1992—Press Conduct (PEW) | 11% | 25% | 29% | 16% | 15% | 4% |
| November 1996—Press Conduct (PEW) | 6% | 22% | 33% | 19% | 18% | 2% |
| November 1996—Media Overall (MSC) | 14% | 40% | 28% | 9% | 6% | 3% |

Key: DK = Don't know; PEW = Pew Center for the People and the Press; MSC = Media Studies Center.

B. Public grading of press performance deteriorated in 1996. According to the Pew Center, the press received low markings again for its conduct, receiving only 28 percent As or Bs.

The Pew Center's finding contrasts with that of the final wave of our Media Studies Center voter panel. Rather than focusing specifically on the conduct of the press, our study asked the public to grade the media overall. When rated on the overall job that it did, the press did better than when rated on its conduct: we found that 54 percent of the public was willing to give the media an A (14%) or B (40%), considerably higher than the rating of the press on its conduct.[3]

The differences in the grades given are likely the result of differences in question wording between the Pew Center and our voter panel. The apparent ability of the public to distinguish between different aspects of media coverage reflects differing findings from disparate question wording. The Pew Center study asked voters to offer a grade to the "press" for "how it conducted itself" during the campaign. The Media Studies Center survey asked voters to simply grade the media for their "coverage for their campaign." The differences in the grades offered between media coverage more generally and the conduct of the press suggests that voters make an important distinction between the news they get (measured by the Media Studies survey) and the manner in which the press goes about doing its job (measured by the Pew Center study). Clearly, voters were more enthusiastic about the news product than they were with the conduct of the press. Indeed, many of the more specific criticisms of the news media that were measured in the four-wave panel relate more to voter unease with the news gathering process and less with negative perceptions of news content.

For example, figure 4.6 shows that many voters are quite critical of a variety of aspects associated with how election news is gathered and how the press interferes with the election process itself. More than four out of five voters agreed that "the media lead candidates to avoid issues and perform for news cameras instead," thus indicting the news media for negatively affecting the campaign through the news gathering process. Further disdain for the news gathering process is evidenced in the finding that 76 percent say the media gave undue advantage to front-runners, and 77 percent agreed that the media have too much control in defining issues in the campaign. A large majority, 68 percent, found that news media coverage of candidates was confusing and unclear. And only 40 percent agreed with the statement that they were more likely to believe what the media said about candidates than to believe what the candidates say about themselves.

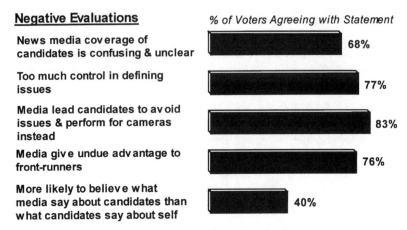

**FIGURE 4.6** Evaluations of different aspects of news media coverage (MSC/UConn).

Rather than behaving in a way that enhanced the electoral process, voters saw the media's news gathering practices and the conduct of the press as giving other actors incentives to behave in a manner that did not serve voter interests. Further, the specific criticisms that voters leveled at the news media related not as much to the news product provided, but to how the news media conducted themselves in gathering information and in influencing the electoral process. These findings corroborate the Pew Center findings of low grades given to the press for how they conducted themselves during the campaign, and further suggest that voter cynicism in the news gathering process characterizes public opinion of the news media.

## Conclusion

In this chapter we examined U.S. voters' overall evaluations of news media performance in covering the 1996 presidential election. We found that, compared to other types of news, Americans are much less interested in news about political campaigns. For example, Americans were three times more interested in local news and news about crime and the environment than they were in news about political campaigns. Although exposure to campaign information is high, and the electorate feeds primarily off of a diet of media coverage, its appetite for political campaign news is not particularly strong. Americans also rate coverage of other kinds of news higher than that of political campaigns. Although half of our panel rated coverage of political campaigns as excellent or good, about two-thirds rated other types of news as excellent or good.

With respect to coverage of the 1996 presidential campaign, voters' overall assessments of news coverage started below average (40% positive) during the early primary period, climbed to about average (50% positive) by the beginning of the general election campaign in September, and rose to a little better than average (60% positive) by mid-October and stayed at that level through election day. Analysis of the panel data suggest that U.S. voters' evaluation of election news substantively improved throughout the campaign, in part because perceptions of news quality improved, and in part because the news provided voters with the basic information they needed to make their voting choices. Their information needs apparently were satisfied. Increased subjective interest in the campaign did not provide an explanation for the improved ratings from February to election day.

Our data also suggest that use of particular media sources has an influence on ratings of coverage. Those who were heavier users of the print media were more positive about the job the media did in covering the campaign. Also, regular users of political talk radio during the campaign offered much lower evaluations of news media performance. Interestingly, use of the so-called elite media for gathering information on the campaign does not appear to have an influence on overall evaluations of the news media.

In this chapter, we also began to explore voter assessments of media coverage at a level deeper than the overall rating. We did this by comparing the results of an item asking respondents to offer a grade of A, B, C, D, or F to coverage of the campaign, with an item asking respondents to offer a grade to the press for how they conducted themselves during the campaign. Although more than half gave a grade of A or B to the more general question, fewer than three in ten gave a grade of A or B to the more specific question on press conduct. This finding suggests that voters are less favorable to the news gathering process than the news product (or the simple fact that the media provide information). When voters are asked to evaluate the media beyond an "overall" rating, they become less favorable. Although summary measures of performance are interesting, they mask much of the complexity in opinion about media performance. As we show in the next two chapters, voter opinions of news media coverage of elections becomes quite critical when scratching beneath the surface of the more general rating.

At a broad level, data in this chapter suggest that the news media functions satisfactorily as a political institution. The product of news on the campaign is viewed positively by about half of voters. Slightly more than half give a grade of A or B to media election coverage. From the voters' perspective, the overall institutional performance of the news media is neither an abysmal failure or a tremendous success. It is adequate.

# 5

# Tilting Left: Perceptions of
# Political Bias in Election Coverage

By providing information and education to the public, the news media occupy a prominent role in American society. This role—one that Jeffersonian democracy touts as critical to the functioning of U.S. politics—serves to promote an informed electorate. And, as watchdog of the government, the news media are critically important in the American democratic process.

U.S. journalism also tends to cover political campaigns as it does any other type of news event. Reflecting its role in the democratic process, the news media's characterizing principle of coverage is that of "objectivity," or as Weaver (1972) described it, acquainting a viewer or reader with the facts pertaining to a newsworthy event. The more recent emphasis of journalists on interpreting events and providing commentary in addition to straight reporting of the facts has led to more criticisms of the media, including assertions of political bias.

Perceptions of bias are an important aspect of evaluating the performance of the media. A perception of bias may limit the effectiveness of the news media's institutional role in providing information to voters. It is not enough for the news media to provide objective and balanced coverage. Voters' perceptions of the fair and unbiased institutional performance of the news media may serve as an important intervening factor likely to influence voter uses of media information and trust in that information. Just as Rosenthal (1996) has argued that perceptions of the ethical behavior of legislators is as important as the reality of ethical behavior, we make a similar argument that public perceptions of the fairness and unbiased performance of the news media are important in the evaluation of the American

Fourth Estate's role in promoting the democratic electoral process through objective reporting of the facts. The appearance and perception of political bias, or the lack thereof, is an important dimension to consider in an assessment of the performance of news media election coverage. Voter perceptions of fairness or bias in the news media may affect their uses of the media as well as their trust in the information provided. Those who perceive a bias in coverage may be less likely to rely on the information given.

Because (as we have shown) the public relies on the media for campaign information the news media needs to be a fair and unbiased source of political information for voters, in perception and reality. Because the news media provide an important filter (Patterson 1980) for what voters come to learn, know, and think about political candidates, the journalistic goals of balance and objectivity are paramount.

In this chapter, we evaluate elite and mass perceptions of partisan, ideological, and candidate bias in the news media throughout the 1996 presidential campaign. First, we review the origins of the norm of objectivity and the debate between other scholars regarding whether the content of election news coverage is biased ideologically and in partisan terms. Second, we examine the question of political bias from the perspective of journalists themselves, showing that journalists accept the possibility that bias might affect their work. Third, we look at this question through the eyes of members of Congress—a group that is the object of both election reporting and reporting of other political news. These political elites perceive bias in the media. Finally, we explore voter attitudes and perceptions of partisan and ideological bias to news reporting in the 1996 presidential campaign. We show that voters, too, perceive that ideology is a factor in the reporting of the news.

## Objectivity and Bias

The goal of objectivity is a relatively modern goal of American journalism. Joslyn (1984:101) notes that "In the early days of the Republic, the press was much more ideological and partisan than it is today. There was no separation between news and opinion or commentary, and papers unabashedly expressed partisan and philosophical viewpoints." Mainly born out of the economic need to appeal to wider audiences, the press gravitated toward less partisan and more fact-based reporting in the twentieth century. The credo of objectivity (see Schudson 1978) emerged as the dominant paradigm of media behavior in the first half of this century. This credo holds that news and commentary should be explicitly separate, and that the policy of news reporting should include fairness and balance, be fact-based and nonopinionated. The adoption of the norm of news objectivity, along with the development of the electronic media that appeals to large numbers of citizens, has established the U.S. news media as an important political institution in the American democratic system of government. In theory, the media have become the primary disseminator of facts, the chronicler of events, and the guardian of the truth. Despite this theoretical characterization of "objectivity," a recurring question in presidential campaigns involves the issue of whether or not political bias exists in the content of election news coverage.

Accusations of media bias are not new to U.S. political campaigns. In many campaigns, political actors have accused the media of bias. Careful scholarly research related to such accusations has sometimes found evidence of biased coverage, and sometimes found no evidence of bias at all. In 1952, for example, a study found that newspapers endorsing Eisenhower on the editorial page tended to give him more frequent and more positive coverage on their news pages (Sandman, Rubin, and Sachsman 1972:425). And in 1984, a study found that in one respect—the tone of coverage—the news favored the Democrats, but at the same time, the media consistently suggested the Republicans were more likely to win (Robinson 1985). In a content analysis of 1992 coverage, Lichter and Noyes (1996:212), in answering the question, "Is there a liberal bias?" concluded that, "The imbalance we found in the 1992 general election news coverage was pronounced, sustained, and overt."

The findings of bias are contradicted by more comprehensive studies, as well as by research focusing on other presidential campaigns, which suggest that coverage has not displayed a systematic ideological or partisan bias. Stempel (1965, 1969) found that fifteen metropolitan daily newspapers gave roughly equal coverage to Republicans and Democrats in the 1960, 1964, and 1968 presidential campaigns. Meadow (1973), in a content analysis of 1972 election coverage by the Philadelphia Inquirer, Philadelphia Evening Bulletin, and New York Times also found unbiased reporting. McClenegan (1978), in examining local coverage of eleven mayoral races in Texas found that newspapers actually gave more space to candidates they opposed on their editorial page. Robinson and Sheehan (1983) found that in the 1980 election contest, Republican and Democratic candidates received about the same share of good and bad press (with only a slightly more favorable tilt in favor of the Republican). In 1988, Lichter (1989) found little difference in the cumulative proportions of good and bad press for both parties. Graber (1993:263) asserts that "news people traditionally aim for rough parity in the number of stories about each candidate and rough parity in the balance of overtly favorable and unfavorable stories." Lichter and Noyes (1996:9) agree that "news organizations operate impartially" when it comes to frequency of coverage among candidates, and find that "[t]here is little evidence to support the contention that reporters intentionally and systematically provide favorable coverage to candidates with whom they agree on most issues, or manufacture criticism of candidates with whom they disagree" (16).

Explaining a systematic ideological bias in the content of the news by the ideological leanings of journalists would be difficult because bias is found in some years and not others, while the self-described liberal leanings of journalists is relatively constant over the years. A more probable explanation of bias that occasionally emerges is that the news media tend to focus on the horse race and insider issues such as the quality of campaign organizations and strategies. Early in the election year, the media tend to focus attention on the viability of candidates. Later in the race, they give a great deal of coverage to who will be the likely winner of the general election.

In more positive stories, winning is often attributed to effective campaign strategies in a series of more positive stories (although winners are also criticized). Falling behind is attributed to the problems of infighting and incompetence in campaign organizations, as well as lackluster strategic calculations. Gaffes by the frontrunners are noted by the press, but if particular problems do not change the status of the horse race, those issues focused on less than the failures of the campaign trailing in the polls. The tendency of the press to focus on strategy accounts, in part, for coverage that favors the Republicans in some years and the Democrats in others. Looking across many years it is not surprising that scholars have come to the conclusion that there is no systematic bias in press coverage of elections.

Scholars' findings of no systematic ideological bias in news coverage need not, however, imply that voters themselves see no bias in the media's coverage of elections. For example, if the media's strategic focus leads it in a single election to criticize the runner-up, who happens to be a Republican, some voters might see a bias. Moreover, voters might remember this perceived bias, rather than averaging across the decades as scholars do.

Voters might also detect bias in the form of particularly disturbing coverage, such as the media coverage of attack advertisements in the 1988 campaign (Jamieson 1992). Finally, voters might perceive partisan bias because of the public pronouncements of their leaders.

The 1996 presidential campaign was no exception. The campaign began in the context of a long series of criticisms by Congressional leaders that the media had a liberal bias. During the campaign, coverage was characterized by a great deal of focus on strategy (see discussion in chapter 6). Throughout the campaign, Senator Robert Dole frequently raised questions about a liberal-Democratic bias to news media coverage of the campaign. Republican congressional candidates made similar claims. Many of Dole's speeches focused on this perceived bias, with the result that many news segments covering the campaign, talk radio programs, television political talk shows, and newspaper editorials picked up Dole's cue and devoted air time and print space to the topic of political bias in the news. In the waning weeks of the campaign, the Dole camp specifically challenged the *New York Times'* coverage, claiming that their coverage of President Clinton exceeded—at least in magnitude—Dole coverage. The *New York Times* vigorously opposed Dole's charges. Scholarly analysis of bias in the 1996 election is still underway.

Regardless of whether the charges of bias are true, the voters in our survey perceived bias in news reporting of the 1996 campaign. This could have been either because of the rhetorical environment that many voters chose to believe, or because they actually found that there was a partisan bias to election news. We begin by presenting evidence regarding the ideology of journalists and their tendency to admit that bias might influence their coverage. We go on to show that many political elites also perceive partisan bias in the media. These findings serve to underscore our main findings that many voters in the 1996 election, like their leaders, perceived partisan bias in the media. Real or imagined, voter perceptions of partisan and ideological bias in the news are likely to affect evaluations of the role of the news media in covering campaigns.

## Political Orientations of Reporters and Editors

In this section, we explore assertions of partisan and ideological bias in media reporting by examining the political attitudes and opinions of reporters themselves. Evidence used to support contentions of political bias in election coverage are the political attitudes and voting behavior of the journalists themselves. Typical of such findings is a 1995 Media Studies Center-University of Connecticut survey of Washington, D.C.-based political journalists, which showed that 89 percent of journalists voted for Bill Clinton in the 1992 Presidential election (see table 5.1; Povich 1996).

In the highly publicized Media Studies Center survey, Washington, D.C.-based bureau chiefs and reporters (referred to in the rest of this chapter as reporters) claim to have voted for Clinton over Bush in 1992 by an overwhelming margin of thirteen to one (89% to 7%). Only 2 percent say they voted for Ross Perot. Keeping in mind that the actual vote outcome in 1992 was 44 percent for Clinton, 37 percent for Bush, and 19 percent for Perot, it is clear that reporters were much more inclined to vote for Clinton, and much less inclined to vote for either Bush or Perot than were other American voters. The survey findings refueled a common election-year debate on political bias in news coverage.[1] This finding is similar to Rosten's (1937) survey, which found that Washington correspondents were more likely to vote for Roosevelt than was the general public. Newspaper editors across the nation were also more likely than the electorate-at-large to vote for the Democratic ticket in 1992 (see table 5.2).

Ideologically (see table 5.2) there are also large differences between the electorate and the journalistic community. We found that six in ten reporters claimed to be either ideologically "liberal" or "liberal to moderate." This is similar to the 57 percent of Washington journalists who identified themselves as being liberal in 1961, and the 42 percent who said they were liberal in 1978 (Rivers 1962; Hess 1981). In addition, we found that three in ten newspaper editors claimed to be either ideologically "liberal"

**TABLE 5.1** Washington Reporter and Newspaper Editor Voting in the 1992 Presidential Race

|          | Washington Reporters | Newspaper Editors |
|----------|:--------------------:|:-----------------:|
| Clinton  | 89%                  | 60%               |
| Bush     | 7%                   | 22%               |
| Perot    | 2%                   | 4%                |
| Other    | 2%                   | 0%                |
| (N)      | (134)                | (100)             |

Note: Question asked was, "Did you vote for Bill Clinton, George Bush, Ross Perot, or some other candidate in 1992"?

The surveys of Washington reporters and newspaper editors were conducted in September and October 1995 by the Media Studies Center by the University of Connecticut.

**TABLE 5.2** The Politics of Journalists and the Public Compared

| | Washington-based Reports | Newspaper Editors (national) | New Journalists (1–10 years experience) | Public |
|---|---|---|---|---|
| Party Identification | | | | |
| Democrat | 50% | 31% | 40% | 34% |
| Republican | 4% | 14% | 14% | 28% |
| Independent | 37% | 39% | 34% | 25% |
| Other | 9% | 7% | 9% | 8% |
| Self-Described Ideology | | | | |
| Liberal (incl. lean) | 61% | 32% | N/A | 20% |
| Moderate | 30% | 35% | N/A | 34% |
| Conservative (incl. lean) | 9% | 25% | N/A | 27% |

N/A = not applicable

Note: Comparative data for the general public are from a Media Studies Center-University of Connecticut survey of 1,200 persons conducted in September 1995.

or "liberal to moderate." In contrast to these players in the media, only two in ten voters were liberal or leaned liberal in 1996.

A survey of 100 editors from the nation's approximately 1,400 daily newspapers showed a 60 to 22 percent margin for Clinton over Bush, with only 4 percent voting for Perot. Although not quite as exaggerated a slant as reporters, those making decisions about what news is fit to print were personally much more likely to support the Democratic candidate than either the Republican or the independent, when compared to the American public.

Such candidate preferences of newspaper editors and Washington reporters, especially when they are publicized, might be expected to raise important questions about *possible* sources of bias in news coverage. In addition to voting patterns in 1992, reporters and newspaper editors differed from the electorate in terms of their expressed partisan identification. The data in table 5.2, for example, show that reporters were sixteen points more likely than the rest of Americans to identify with the Democratic Party, and twenty-four points less likely to identify as a Republican. This table also shows that although newspaper editors were not more likely to be Democrats than the public, they were fourteen points less likely to be Republican.

A 1995 Freedom Forum-University of Connecticut national survey of "new journalists" (those who had been in the profession for no more than eleven years) also shows this nationally representative group of relatively newer journalists to strongly prefer the Democratic Party (40%) over the Republican Party (14%)(Medsger 1996).

The survey of reporters and newspaper editors also illustrated their feeling that they should be providing the more traditional "watchdog" and "objective" reporting roles (Johnstone, Slawski, and Bowman 1976; Weaver and Wilhoit 1986, 1996). In addition, they thought they should also be "suggesting potential solutions to social problems": 62 percent of reporters agreed with this as did fully 79 percent of newspaper editors (Patterson 1980; Graber 1993). This is indicated by the strong "civic journalism" inclination of reporters and editors to provide suggestions for solving social problems. Others have found that, in addition to reporting facts, many journalists have in recent decades adopted the role of interpreting the news. These attitudes, in and of themselves, do not seem problematic.

But considering that it is difficult if not impossible to suggest solutions to social problems outside the framework of partisan and ideological positions, and that journalists' personal ideological leanings are often liberal, it may not be surprising that news stories tend to favor the proposals of Democrats in government.

As we have demonstrated, survey data provide fairly strong evidence that at least three significant parts of the U.S. media establishment—Washington bureau chiefs and journalists, the nations' newspaper editors, and those journalists who are newer to the profession—differ dramatically from the electorate in their basic political orientations and in their voting behavior in 1992. In addition, a tendency for more journalists to vote Democratic and to lean to the Left are long-standing characteristics, dating as far back as 1937. All of these differences run consistently in the liberal and Democratic direction. And this information, relayed by party leaders in Congress and the media itself, might lead some in the public to say that they perceive bias in news content and coverage.

## The Link Between Opinions and Coverage

Actually, reporters may be the first to admit that their personal beliefs might influence their coverage of the news. "Are they biased? Of course, who isn't?" says Richard Reeves (1997:40) of other journalists. After all, self-recognition of an ideological perspective can be a journalist's first step in trying to take account of it and attempt to control it in his or her reporting. According to the their credo of "objectivity" (Patterson 1980; Joslyn 1984; Graber 1993), journalists are supposed to set their own predispositions aside when reporting the news. Those recognizing a tendency for journalists to prefer the liberal point of view and the Democratic Party in their personal lives tend to defend the objectivity of the profession on the grounds that it is possible to distinguish between personal preferences and objective reporting of the news.

Journalists themselves offer reasons for objectivity in reporting. First, most want to preserve their credibility with their audience, which includes readers of many persuasions. Second, most reporters need to be perceived as objective by their editors. And, they want to keep the respect of their peers (Reeves 1997:40//41). More pragmatically, other journalists assert that having been a reporter is a palliative for the ideologies that young reporters start their careers with. Lou Cannon (1997), for example, argues that early in their careers, many reporters lose their prejudices when they come into contact with people, ranging from political and business elites to the least privileged members of our society, who defy their expectations. And there is evidence that reporters do recognize the possible impact of their ideologies on their reporting.

The data from the survey of reporters suggest that many journalists agree that their personal beliefs can jeopardize the journalistic goal of objectivity. Washington reporters are willing to admit the possibility that their ideological leanings may influence their coverage of politics. When asked to provide a self-assessment of how often their own opinions affect their work, less than 1 percent say their opinions never affect their coverage. Fully 78 percent say that their own opinions affect their work at least "occasionally." Whether this happens consistently, and whether it is balanced by stories written from other perspectives, we cannot say.

In addition to efforts by journalists who try to mitigate the affects of personal (often liberal) ideologies, there is another reason that the news may not, in the end, be influenced by journalists' personal political orientations. Should journalists let bias creep into their stories, they are still confronted by the values and operating procedures of news organizations that are set by corporate management. These corporate values have a direct influence on which news makes it into print or is aired—an influence that declined through the mid-1980s but re-emerged to an extent in the 1990s (Rothman and Lichter 1986; Weaver and Wilhoit 1996). In addition, corporate values may have an indirect impact by socializing reporters in regard to which stories are newsworthy.[2]

Certainly, in some circumstances, the partisan leanings of journalists may appear to make their way into coverage. Survey data from Washington reporters on their coverage of the 1994 Republican Party's "Contract with America" provides a good example of a situation in which reporters themselves saw the possibility of bias caused, in this case, by an excessive focus on strategy.

The Contract with America became the centerpiece of the Republican Congressional campaign in 1994. In keeping with the tendency of the media to focus on strategy rather than substance (e.g., Patterson 1980; Jamieson 1992), there was significant discussion on the part of Democratic candidates and others that the Contract was a campaign gimmick. The Republicans, under the leadership of Newt Gingrich, adamantly defended the Contract as a serious proposal. Many credit Gingrich and the Republicans with successfully nationalizing the 1994 off-year election through the Contract with America.

In retrospect, fully 59 percent of reporters said they treated the Contract with America topic *only* as an election year campaign ploy, compared to 3 percent who treated it as a serious proposal. Only one-third of reporters say they covered the Contract story in both ways. That six in ten reporters did not report the Contract story as a policy proposal in covering the issue may suggest that in this case the media's tendency to focus on strategy biased actual coverage of the Contract with America in a direction that Democrats would have preferred. On the basis of this single case, where strategy and ideology overlap, we cannot say whether this bias was the result of a focus on strategy to the detriment of substance, which often happens in election campaigns, or whether the root cause was the journalists' ideology.

To summarize, we find evidence at the individual level that the ideology of journalists does not reflect that of the population as a whole. Whether their personal ideological predilections lead to a systematic ideological bias in news *content* is uncertain. In some circumstances it might, even though journalists' professional incentives may lead them back toward the center and the right. However, the much publicized personal orientations of journalists and the tendency of political leaders to assert that the news media are biased (much simpler notions to transmit to the public than that of gate keeping and professional norms), may lead the public to perceive bias, whatever the content of the news. Moreover, the tendency of journalists to focus on strategy may lead them to favor one side of a partisan debate over another, resulting in coverage that the public perceives as being ideologically biased.

In the remainder of this chapter, we document perceptions of bias, not only among the public but among those who lead them. We begin with a survey of members of Congress. We will see that, not only does the public think that their coverage may not be objective, members of Congress agree.

## The Perspective of Congress

In addition to examining perceptions of partisan and ideological bias from the vantage point of information suppliers(news media) and information receivers (voters), data from a 1995 survey of members of Congress provides a third and unique perspective on political bias in reporting.[3] Members have been candidates for office and have experienced, first hand, the performance of reporters. As legislators, they have also witnessed coverage of politically charged issues.

In addition, statements that representatives make characterizing the media, both directly to constituents and through the media, might help shape public opinion about the ideological makeup of the press corps. The unique perspective of members of Congress, from both sides of the political aisle, offers yet another answer to the question of whether there may be a political bias to media coverage.

When asked to assess the political orientation of the Washington-based national media, fully three-quarters of members characterized this group as either "liberal" (42%) or "liberal to moderate" (34%). Twenty percent said this group was best described as moderate; only 5 percent of the members of the 104th Congress described the Washington press corps as "moderate to conservative," and less than 1 percent thought the term "conservative" described the political views of the press.

Further, a majority (63%) of congressional members who described themselves as liberal thought that characterizing the national press as "liberal" or "liberal to moderate" was accurate. Similarly, 44 percent of Democratic members perceived this portion of the press to be "liberal" or "liberal to moderate." Conversely, not one of the conservative members described the Washington press corps as "moderate to conservative" or "conservative," and 94 percent of conservative members described the national press as "liberal" (57%) or "moderate to liberal" (37%).

Reporters covering Congress for regional and local news organizations were perceived by its members as being more moderate than their national press corps colleagues. Only 17 percent of members surveyed characterized regional and local reporters as liberal, compared with 42 percent who saw the national press as such, and 37 percent who used the phrase "liberal to moderate." And although only 5 percent of respondents characterized the national press as "moderate to conservative," 18 percent believed this to be true about the regional and local press.

Political elites at both ends of the ideological and partisan spectrum agreed that, politically, much of the press, especially the national press corps, could be described as liberal and Democratic. This congressional perspective, along with the data described here, reinforces the possible connection between the political orientations of the media and bias in coverage, and provides additional reasons why the public might perceive the press to have a liberal bias.

## The Perspective of Voters

We turn, finally, to voters' perceptions of bias in election coverage. Voters' perceptions of political bias in the media are significant for several reasons. First, the mass media are voters' primary source of campaign information (see chapter 3). To the extent that voters perceive that the information contained in the media is not fair and unbiased, they may turn from this source. Second, perceptions of bias might have an impact on the media's political legitimacy in our democratic system of governance. Given the news media's role in American democracy, such a decline in confidence might undermine one of the cornerstones of the legitimacy of government.

In addition to the media's role in conveying information, the U.S. public strongly endorses the media's watchdog function.[4] Given the media's broad and significant roles as a democratic institution, voter perceptions of media objectivity and fairness are important. Thus it is disconcerting that a wide variety of surveys conducted during the 1996 presidential campaign found that voters were quite skeptical of the news media's performance as a fair and unbiased source of election information. As figure 5.1 shows, the September wave of our panel study, for example, found that only one-third of voters agreed that "news media stories about the campaign provides unbiased accounts of what is happening in the campaign."

Further, perceptions of the news media as generally biased were much more pronounced among voters considering themselves to be Republicans or conservatives. Three-fourths of partisan Republicans and seven in ten politically conservative voters disagreed that the news media generally

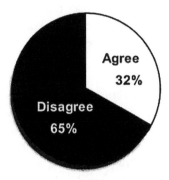

**FIGURE 5.1** Do the news media provide unbiased accounts of campaign? *(Source: MSC-UConn; preprimary survey wave N = 2,007.)*

provided unbiased accounts of the 1996 presidential campaign. Fewer, though still clear majorities, of Democrats, independents, moderates, and liberals sensed a general bias to coverage.

Other research conducted during the campaign similarly concluded that the public saw a general bias in news coverage. When asked if the media went to great lengths to make sure coverage is fair and balanced, only 32 percent answered "yes."[5] Another survey revealed a strong tendency for voters to think that television news coverage went beyond information provision and actually tried to influence voters into voting for a specific candidate.[6] The vast majority of voters not only perceived a general bias in election news coverage, but thought that news coverage overtly attempted to influence election outcomes. It would appear that reporters were unable to convince the public that they were practicing journalistic objectivity, at least in their campaign coverage.

Our voter panel data also provided insights on the perceived direction of bias in media coverage of the 1996 presidential campaign. The preprimary wave, postconventions wave, and postelection wave of the panel study each repeated the following two questions:

1. Overall, do you think news media coverage of the presidential campaign is biased toward the liberal point of view or conservative point of view, or do you think coverage is pretty evenly balanced?
2. And, overall, do you think news media coverage of the Presidential campaign favors the Democratic Party or the Republican Party, or do you think coverage is pretty evenly balanced?

Responses to these items allow us to trace perceptions of political bias (both partisan and ideological) through the campaign, and also to identify individual-level changes in these perceptions.

### Perceptions of Ideological Bias

When specifically asked about ideological biases in news reporting, about half (48%) of all respondents claimed coverage was about evenly balanced at the outset of the presidential primaries (see figure 5.2). The percentage of voters saying coverage was evenly balanced increased to 52 percent after the national party conventions, and then again to 59 percent in early November, immediately after the election.[7] Throughout the course of the campaign, then, about half to three-in-five voters were of the opinion that news reporting did not have an ideological bias.

Of those voters who did detect an ideological slant to coverage, many more perceived that slant to favor the liberal over the conservative point of view. This is perhaps not surprising given the tendency of Republican leaders to criticize the liberal bias of the media without response from Democratic leaders (see, e.g., Zaller 1991). Throughout the campaign, the percentage claiming a liberal bias remained relatively constant, at about three in ten voters. The decline in the overall percentage of voters detecting ideological bias came predominantly from those saying that there was a conservative bias to coverage. The percent that reported perceiving a conservative bias in the news dropped from 13 percent in the preprimary stage of the campaign to 4 percent by election day. That is to say, the increase in the percentage of those saying there was balance to coverage was drawn

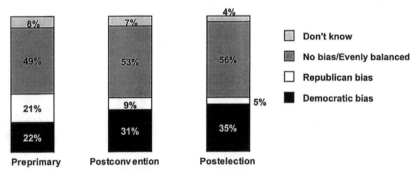

**FIGURE 5.2** Voter perceptions of ideological bias in coverage (MSC-UConn surveys).

from those who perceived a conservative bias early in the election cycle. As the campaign wore on, about 30 percent of the electorate continued to sense a liberal bias to news coverage.

If we look at self-professed liberal, conservative, and moderate voters separately, we see that many more conservative voters perceived an ideological bias to news reporting in 1996 (see table 5.3). By election day, only 37 percent of conservatives said coverage was balanced, compared to 68 percent of moderates and 73 percent of liberals. Not surprisingly, those conservatives who sensed a bias were much more likely to say there was a liberal bias (55%) rather than a conservative one (4%).

On the other hand, among the liberal voters who said there was a bias, about as many thought the bias was liberal (11%) as thought it was conservative (9%). Among the more neutral political moderates, 25 percent thought there was a liberal bias and 5 percent said there was a conservative bias in reporting on the campaign.

In addition to examining differences in perceptions of ideological bias by ideological reference groups, we also explore differences in perception of bias by media-dependence groups (shown in table 5.4). Television-dependent voters through the course of the campaign were least likely to sense that news coverage was characterized by a liberal bias. By election day, about three in ten TV-dependent voters said there was a liberal bias in election coverage, compared to 37 percent of newspaper-dependent voters and more than half of radio-dependent voters. With this lesser perception of a liberal bias, TV-dependent voters were most likely to say that news coverage was ideologically evenly balanced, with as many as 62 percent thinking this way by election day.

In terms of ideological bias, then, voters' perceptions of the news media's performance are mixed. On the one hand, more than half (mostly liberals and moderates) say that coverage is pretty much evenly balanced.

**TABLE 5.3** Perceptions of Ideological Bias by Ideological Reference Group

|  | Liberal | Moderate | Conservative |
| --- | --- | --- | --- |
| Liberal Bias | 11% | 25% | 55% |
| Conservative Bias | 9% | 5% | 4% |
| About Even Balance | 73% | 68% | 37% |
| (N) | (90) | (200) | (185) |

Source: Panel wave 4—November—of the voter panel study.

**TABLE 5.4** Perceptions of Ideological Bias by Type of Media Most
Dependent on for Election News

|  | Television | Newspaper | Radio |
|---|---|---|---|
| **Liberal Bias** | | | |
| Preprimary | 32% | 40% | 55% |
| Postconvention | 29% | 34% | 61% |
| Postelection | 29% | 37% | 54% |
| **Conservative Bias** | | | |
| Preprimary | 13% | 19% | 9% |
| Postconvention | 11% | 8% | 1% |
| Postelection | 5% | 7% | 2% |
| **Evenly Balanced** | | | |
| Preprimary | 51% | 36% | 29% |
| Postconvention | 56% | 45% | 32% |
| Postelection | 62% | 54% | 39% |

On the other hand, throughout the 1996 campaign, about one-third of
voters (many of them conservatives) steadfastly held the opinion that there
was a liberal bias to news.

*Perceptions of Partisan Bias*

A second component of political bias to reporting involves partisanship. The rhetoric of campaign 1996, and in particular the Republican cries
of a "liberal" media, that may have contributed to moderate and conservative voters' perceptions of a bias in news coverage, might also affect voters'
sense of a Democratic bias in news coverage. Figure 5.3 shows perceptions
of partisan bias in media coverage through campaign 1996. With respect to
the number of voters saying that coverage did not contain a partisan bias,
the same pattern emerges as with perceptions of ideological bias. In the
preprimary phase of the campaign, about half say there is no partisan bias
and by election day there is a modest increase in perceptions that the news
is balanced.

Two additional trends in perceptions of partisan bias are noteworthy:
an increase in opinions that media coverage favored the Democrats (from
22% in February to 35% on election day), and a decrease in perceptions of
a Republican bias over the same span (21% to 5%). By the campaign's end,
over one-third of voters thought news was slanted toward the Democrats.
As table 5.5 shows, Republican voters and, to a lesser extent, independent
voters perceived a slant to the news.[8] Among Republicans, fully 68 percent

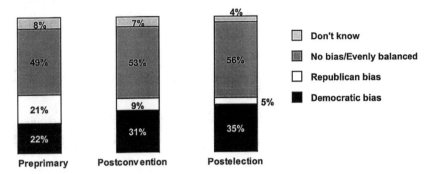

**FIGURE 5.3** Voter perceptions of partisan bias in coverage, 1996 (MSC-University of Connecticut).

said the news favored the Democratic Party. Democratic voters, however, were about as likely to think that the news favored the Republicans (7%) as the Democrats (11%).

It is possible that the nature of the medium might contribute to perceptions of partisan bias in coverage, so it is interesting to examine differences in perceptions of partisan bias across various media-dependence groups, namely, television, newspapers, and radio. Table 5.6 shows differences in perceptions of partisan bias over the course of the campaign.

The table shows large consistent differences in perceptions of a Democratic bias between radio-dependent voters on the one hand, and television and newspaper-dependent voters on the other hand. Early on in the campaign (February) radio-dependent voters were more than twice as likely to perceive a Democratic bias. However, through the course of the campaign, TV and newspaper-dependent voters became more likely to see a

**TABLE 5.5** Partisan Differences in Perceptions of Partisan Bias to the News

| | Partisan Identification | | |
|---|---|---|---|
| | Republican | Democrat | Independent |
| Democratic Bias | 68% | 10% | 26% |
| Republican Bias | 1% | 7% | 3% |
| About Even Balance | 28% | 78% | 68% |
| (N) | (181) | (189) | (109) |

These data are from wave 4 (November) of the voter panel study.

**TABLE 5.6** Perceptions of Partisan Bias by Type of Media Most
Dependent on for Election News

|  | Television | Newspaper | Radio |
|---|---|---|---|
| **Democratic Bias** | | | |
| Preprimary | 24% | 25% | 59% |
| Postsonvention | 30% | 36% | 52% |
| Postelection | 33% | 38% | 51% |
| **Republican Bias** | | | |
| Preprimary | 19% | 28% | 11% |
| Postconvention | 12% | 10% | 7% |
| Postelection | 5% | 6% | 2% |
| **Evenly Balanced** | | | |
| Preprimary | 53% | 42% | 25% |
| Postconvention | 54% | 44% | 39% |
| Postelection | 59% | 55% | 45% |

Democratic bias (24% to 33%, and 25% to 38%, respectively) while radio-
dependent voters became less likely to see a liberal bias (59% to 51%).
Despite these opposite trends among media-dependent groups through the
campaign, by election day radio-dependent voters were still more likely to
sense a Democratic bias in coverage.

To summarize, we found that many voters, especially conservatives and
Republicans, perceived ideological and partisan biases in media coverage.
The data further showed, quite convincingly, a strong tendency for voters,
especially conservatives and Republicans, to see a bias that runs in the
liberal and Democratic direction, with radio-dependent voters most likely
to think there was bias, and TV-dependent voters most likely to view coverage as being about evenly balanced.

*Perceptions of Bias in Candidate Coverage*
The most salient factor characterizing the contemporary era of U.S.
presidential campaigns is, perhaps, the rise of what Agranoff (1976) termed
the "candidate-centered campaign" (see also Salmore and Salmore 1989).
Candidates now often run campaigns that de-emphasize party ties. The
media have provided the means for candidates to bypass parties and appeal
directly to voters (see Fiorina 1990). Image-building strategies, particularly
for national elections, are often best achieved through electronic media
rather than through the parties.

In our consideration of political bias in coverage of the 1996 campaign, then, it is important to examine voter perceptions of how fair and unbiased coverage of the *candidates* was in 1996, apart from perceptions of ideological or pure partisan bias to coverage. Table 5.7 shows that, overall, strong majorities of voters thought that the major party candidates were treated either very fairly or somewhat fairly by the news media. Fully 89 percent of voters reported that President Clinton was given very fair or somewhat fair treatment, while slightly fewer (but still a strong majority) voters said Dole was treated at least somewhat fairly by the media.

It is clear from Pew Center and Media Studies Center surveys, however, that more voters (by 8 and 11 percentage points, respectively) thought that Bill Clinton was more fairly treated than was Bob Dole. Even more striking was the sense among voters that Ross Perot, the independent candidate, was not treated fairly. Fewer than half (46%) of Pew's respondents said that the press was fair in covering Perot, and only one-third of Media Studies Center respondents said media coverage of Perot was either very fair or somewhat fair. A Fox News survey found that voters were more likely to think that Clinton was given a free ride by the media than was Dole (40% to 28% respectively).

## Perception of Bias in Particular Media

In addition to measuring voter perceptions of the direction of political bias in election news, the February wave of the voter panel explored assessments of fairness and bias of particular news sources. Specifically, the voters were asked to give a "bias score" of between "1" and "7" (where 1 means not at all fair-biased and 7 means completely fair-unbiased) to fourteen

**TABLE 5.7** Fairness of Coverage of Presidential Candidates

|  | Fairness of Press in Covering: | | |
| --- | --- | --- | --- |
|  | Clinton | Dole | Perot |
| **Pew Center November 1996** | | | |
| Fair | 73% | 65% | 46% |
| Unfair | 24% | 32% | 44% |
| **MSC/UConn November 1996** | | | |
| Very/Somewhat Fair | 89% | 78% | 32% |
| Not too/ Not Fair | 8% | 19% | 45% |

specific types of media sources for campaign information. Table 5.8 shows (1) the mean bias scores offered by voters who were familiar with these different media to offer a rating (2) the percentage of voters giving a bias score of either "6" or "7," and (3) the percentage of all voters who were familiar enough to give a bias rating.[9]

Table 5.8 demonstrates some clear distinctions in voters' sense of fair and unbiased reporting across these different news media sources. The specific sources with the highest mean scores and favorable ratings of "6" or "7" were C-SPAN and the PBS *NewsHour* with Jim Lehrer. Column 3 shows that the somewhat smaller audiences for these sources (42% and 35%, respectively) provide the relatively higher fairness ratings. It is not the smaller audience size alone, however, that prompts the better fairness rating. Other sources with relatively less use (*Larry King Live!* and *The New York Times,* for example) have lesser familiarity among voters but receive lower fairness ratings. Sunday morning political TV shows, such as *Meet the Press* and *Face the Nation,* also obtain higher fairness scores.

Interestingly, CNN news tends to be viewed by voters as an election news source that is less biased than the network news or local TV news. As we discussed earlier in this chapter, some past research suggests that local TV news is more trusted than national sources. But as Just et al. (1996)

**TABLE 5.8** Voter Perceptions of Bias in Election Coverage across Different Media Sources

| Media Source | (1) Mean | (2) % 6 + 7 | (3) % Familiar |
|---|---|---|---|
| C-SPAN programming | 5.3 | 50% | 42% |
| Lehrer *Newshour* | 5.2 | 53% | 35% |
| Sunday Morning TV Shows (e.g., *Meet the Press*) | 5.2 | 46% | 48% |
| CNN news programs | 5.1 | 46% | 70% |
| Weekly news magazines | 4.8 | 33% | 57% |
| Local TV newscasts | 4.8 | 33% | 90% |
| Network newscasts | 4.7 | 33% | 92% |
| *New York Times* | 4.6 | 44% | 31% |
| All news radio | 4.4 | 39% | 45% |
| Internet | 4.3 | 28% | 14% |
| Local newspaper | 4.2 | 38% | 90% |
| *Larry King Live!* | 4.2 | 36% | 42% |
| Local call-in talk radio | 4.2 | 29% | 61% |
| Rush Limbaugh talk radio show | 3.1 | 20% | 55% |

point out, much has changed in the nature of the news information environment since the 1970s. They note that "there have been few attempts to chart the impact of these new developments on election coverage. In particular, many recent investigations lump the three major networks together or treat one network as a typical example. But the dominance of the three network news broadcasts in the 1970s has been succeeded by a more varied mix" (Just et al. 1996:91). Clearly, our data indicate that CNN does contribute variety to the mix—at least in terms of voter perceptions of the fairness of the election news.

## Conclusion

Our data, drawn from three unique perspectives—journalists, voters, and members of Congress—suggest four important findings. The first three relate to the news media. First, the political orientations of media professionals (such as Washington bureau chiefs and journalists, newspaper editors, and a national cross-section of newer journalists) do not reflect the distribution of political orientations of the American voter. The media professionals tend to be more liberal, more Democratic, and more likely to have voted for a Democratic candidate (at least in 1992). Second, reporters are willing to admit that their ideology may have an impact on their work. Third, we found that members of Congress from both sides of the aisle tend to see the Washington-based national media as either liberal or liberal-to-moderate. It is possible that these two characteristics of the media, and the tendency of political elites to assert that the content of the media is biased, may lead voters to see a bias in the news media.

Finally, our empirical evidence suggests that many voters do think the news media provide politically biased accounts of the campaign. From the perspective of voters, especially those who are conservatives and Republicans, there was a feeling during the 1996 campaign that news coverage tilted in favor of the liberal point of view, and in favor of the Democratic Party. Many voters on our panel sensed that Bill Clinton was treated more fairly in the press than Bob Dole, and that Ross Perot was treated far less fairly than the two major party candidates. Radio-dependent voters were most likely to sense bias, and TV-dependent voters were most likely to say that news coverage was about evenly balanced.

The news media play an integral role in the workings of U.S. democracy by setting the campaign agenda for voters and framing the coverage of the events (Iyengar and Kinder 1987). Our results raise serious questions in regard to balance and objectivity in coverage of the 1996 campaign. The perception of bias that characterized voter sentiment regarding media coverage of that presidential election may have implications for voter confidence in the news media, and for their tendency to continue to use the media over the long haul.

As a political institution, public perception that the press is providing unbiased and fair accounts of presidential campaigns is crucial. Because the news media are a voter's main source of information, those who think the news is less than objective have a hard time accepting campaign news at face value. Perceptions of political bias may diminish the value and credibility of the news product. And such perceptions may inhibit use of the news to make informed judgments. The acute sense among voters that news is characterized by political bias significantly compromises the institutional role of the press in U.S. elections.

# 6

# Evaluations of News Content
# and News Sources

In chapter 4 and 5, we noted several scholarly criticisms of the news media's coverage of presidential campaigns, based on content analyses and media effects research: a preoccupation with the horse race, an inclination to focus on personality stories, undue attention to campaign tactics and candidates strategies, lack of attention to nonmainstream major party candidates, a dearth of news information about issues and candidate positions, and lack of coverage that is meaningful to voters' decision making. Content analysis literature on media coverage and media effects literature tend to support these criticisms of election news performance, particularly with respect to television news coverage. Here we look at whether voters agree with these criticisms of the news.

The performance of the news media in the current era of U.S. campaigns is often characterized by criticisms that it focuses on trivialities and ignores substance. Bennett (1988:9), in describing what has come to be more or less the conventional wisdom about news media coverage, described the performance of the news media, and particularly television, as "superficial, narrow, stereotypical, propaganda-laden, of little explanatory value, and not geared for critical debate or citizen action." Patterson and McClure (1976:76) also point the finger at television news, finding that the nightly news produces little or nothing in the way of substance for viewers about the presidential campaign, and that its impact includes "a television audience obsessed with election nonsense."

Here we explore the voters' perspective on the content of election news coverage and the usefulness of different news sources in learning about the campaign. How do voters evaluate the content of news coverage? Do they perceive an excessive level of attention afforded to the horse race and personality stories? Are they interested in this type of information? Do they think there is a shortage of issue coverage, as the content analysis literature suggests? Do voters distinguish among different news sources and formats in terms of usefulness of the information?

We examine voter interest in a variety of types of election news coverage—news stories about which candidate is ahead in the race, about personal aspects of the candidates, about candidate issue positions, on how the election might affect Americans, about campaign strategy and tactics, and on third party candidates. In addition to measuring voter interest across these story types, we also measure opinion about whether the news media focus too much or too little attention on each type of story, and trace these opinions through the course of the campaign. From the perspective of voters, then, we provide a time-line evaluation of the news media's job in providing the kinds of information voters wanted about the campaign, and at what stages they wanted that information.

Also in this chapter, voter attitudes about the usefulness of a variety of news media sources and formats are explored. For example, do voters think they learn more about the campaign from particular news sources? Do they value journalistic analysis and commentary on election matters. And, what are voter impressions of the usefulness of such commentary?

## Election News Content in 1996

In assessing election coverage of the 1976 campaign, Thomas Patterson noted a strong tendency for the news media to prioritize coverage of voter opinion polls, particularly the polls that focus on the horse race (Patterson 1980). Brady and Johnston (1987) and Sigelman and Bullock (1991) provide similar findings and argue that news stories on the horse race displace more substantively important and useful information to voters, such as issue coverage, and that election coverage has increasingly focused more on where candidates stand in the race than where they stand on the issues (Johnson 1993; Robinson and Sheehan 1983). These researchers concluded that horse race coverage of the election tends to dominate news media information about presidential campaigns, as do personality assessments of the candidates.

Indeed, much research shows that the bulk of general election campaign coverage deals with the horse race. Stevenson et al. (1975) found that in the 1968 campaign, news coverage concentrated on who was winning, who was losing, and campaign staff and organization topics, with coverage of policy issues being almost nonexistent. In *The Unseeing Eye,* Patterson and McClure (1976) found that in the 1972 presidential campaign news coverage on television focused significantly more on campaign activity and the horse race than on policy positions and issues. They further claim that newspaper coverage focused on the horse race as well, although Graber (1993) found that print media were more prone to cover personality characteristics of presidential candidates.

In identifying the nature of news coverage of the 1992 presidential election, Just et al. (1996:99) segmented news stories based on the "main focus" of the story into four classification categories: (1) personal qualities, (2) chances of winning, (3) candidate's position on issues, and (4) campaign factors (e.g., campaign staff, organization, finances, and so on). They found that across network television, local television, and newspapers, "All three kinds of media put the greatest emphasis on candidate's personal qualities and their chances for election; issue positions come in third and campaign factors are last" (Just et al. 1996:100–101). These researchers also found that the three presidential candidates in 1992 were covered the same way across different media.

In a content analysis of news coverage of the 1996 election conducted by the Annenberg Public Policy Center, researchers found an under-reporting of issue coverage in the print media in 1996 compared to past presidential campaigns. They also found that issue coverage in the broadcast media in 1996 also dropped in comparison to such coverage in 1992. For example, based on an analysis of *New York Times, Washington Post,* and *Los Angeles Times* coverage, the percentage of front page stories on the campaign that focused on issues dropped from 39 percent to 26 percent from 1992 to 1996. For the weekday evening broadcasts at ABC, NBC, and CBS, the percentage of stories on issues was 34 percent in both 1992 and 1996.[1] For 1992 and 1996, then, only about one-third of nightly network coverage and coverage on the first page of three major daily newspapers focused on issues in the campaign.

The Annenberg Public Policy Center and the Center for Media and Public Affairs (CMPA) both reported an overall decline in the level of news media coverage of the 1996 campaign.[2] Comparing 1992 with 1996, the Annenberg Center found that the number of words devoted to broadcast campaign coverage was down 55 percent and the number of words in front-page newspaper campaign coverage was down 45 percent. The CMPA reported that during the general election campaign, the broadcast media devoted 45 percent less air time to campaign stories than in 1992, and 30 percent less than in 1988.

Of the broadcast coverage provided in 1996, CMPA found that nearly half (48%) of the stories focused on the horse race. Although high, it is interesting to note that the rate of horse race coverage actually declined in the broadcast media in 1996. Content analyses of 1992 and 1988 election coverage by CMPA found that in both previous election years, 58 percent of stories focused on the horse race. The 1996 analysis found that 37 percent of campaign stories dealt with policy stories, compared with 32 percent in 1992 and 39 percent in 1988. CMPA also reported that "the overall drop in campaign news [in 1996] meant that the total number of policy stories declined by 23 percent" (2). Available content analysis data, then, find that in 1996 about half of broadcast news coverage focused on the horse race, and about one-third on policy matters. Past literature and recent content analysis of election news content largely agree that the plurality, if not majority, of news stories focus on the horse race and campaign strategy, while substantially less news is about issues and candidate positions on issues.

The large focus on the horse race is not surprising given the amount of polling during the campaign. Since 1976, the number of polls available for news media consumption has proliferated, to put it mildly. In 1996, there were five national daily tracking polls, numerous other organizations conducting national polls on the horse race at various points during the campaign, and statewide voter polls being conducted in forty-eight of the fifty states. The amount of information on the horse race that was available to the news media was quite extensive in 1996.

Interestingly, though, an analysis of four of the five national daily tracking polls during the last month of the election found virtually no change in vote choices accounted for by the polls (Dautrich and Hartley 1997). Despite the lack of a story in the polls (except that there was no change in vote choice), the broadcast media still devoted half of its campaign coverage to horse race stories. Perhaps the overall decline in news coverage of the 1996 election that both Annenberg and CMPA documented suggests that if the race is not interesting (i.e., there are few changes), then there will be less coverage because other types of stories are less "newsworthy." That is, it appears that overall content of coverage may be a function of the volatility of the horse race.

The news media focus on the horse race and personal qualifications of candidates means "that citizens wanting to learn about the candidates' qualifications or issue positions during the campaign would have to be either extremely lucky or unusually perseverant to find any of this material" (Joslyn 1984: 144). How does the U.S. voter react to the supply of news information about the presidential campaign? Are voters simply more interested in the horse race, as many journalists and news executives suggest? Do they think that issue coverage is sufficient in helping them make vote decisions? Do voters make distinctions between the value of different news formats and news sources for election information?

We now turn to an investigation of what U.S. voters thought about the content of news coverage in 1996. In evaluating news media performance as an institution, content analysis of reporting provides only part of the answer. How the American voter perceives the amount and quality of information is a critical factor in evaluating the performance of the news. In short, any assessment of the new media's institutional performance in U.S. presidential elections must take into account voter attitudes of news content. We now turn to this assessment.

## Voter Evaluations of Election News Content

Our 1996 voter panel study measured voter opinion on six different categories of election news stories:

- which candidates were ahead and which were behind
- personal lives of the candidates
- campaign strategies and tactics
- candidate stances on issues
- how the election outcome might affect people like you
- third party and independent candidates

In the baseline survey, voters were asked to express their level of interest in each of these six types of news stories as either "very interested," "somewhat interested," "not too interested," or "not at all interested." Also, in three of the four waves of the panel (February, September, and November), voters were asked if the news media devoted "too much," "too little," or "about the right amount" of attention to each of these six types of news stories. These data allow us to measure voter interest in different types of election news content as well as perceptions of the imbalance in reporting of different types of news throughout the course of the campaign.

*What Is Given Too Much Coverage?*

Table 6.1 shows that through the 1996 campaign, voters consistently said "too much" news media attention was paid to stories about the horse race and to stories about the personal lives of the candidates. As the campaign wore on, voters became increasingly of the opinion that the news media was providing too much attention to which candidate was ahead and which were behind, with 46 percent saying there was too much focus on that issue in February, 50 percent saying that in September, and a clear majority— 57 percent—thinking that way by election day. Few voters said that the news provided too little focus on the horse race.

These findings indicate that, from the perspective of election news consumers, the news media provide disproportionate attention to candidates' chances of winning. It appears that voters' own assessments of news election coverage is consistent with the findings of much content analysis and media effects research, which shows that horse race stories are excessive (Patterson 1980; Brady and Johnston 1987; Sigelman and Bullock 1991; and Johnson 1993).

Similarly, voters expressed dissatisfaction with the media's focus on personality stories, particularly in the early stages of the primary campaign season when as many as 68 percent of voters said "too much" attention was given to stories about the personal lives of the candidates. Through September this number declined slightly to 63 percent, and by election day dissatisfaction was at 50 percent. Again, voters agreed with many media scholars and critics regarding the amount of focus the news places on personality stories of candidates.

Finally, more U.S. voters tend to be of the opinion that there is too much news media focus on stories about campaign strategies and tactics. About one-third of voters consistently said through campaign 1996 that strategic and tactical-oriented stories were excessive, and about one-fifth or fewer thought there was too little focus on these types of stories.

Other findings in the voter panel confirm these concerns about election news content. For example, fully 83 percent of U.S. voters agreed with the statement: "the media lead candidates to avoid issues and perform for the cameras instead."[3] This finding suggests that not only do voters feel too little news focuses on issues, but voters believe that the media actively contribute to less candidate discourse about the issues.

*What Is Given Too Little Coverage?*

At the same time voters thought too much attention was paid to the horse race and to personality stories, Table 6.1 shows that voters in our

**TABLE 6.1** What Voters Want and What They Get from Election News

| Voter Interest in Types of Stories: | % Very Interested January/February 1996 | % saying "Too Little" and "Too Much" Attention in Media | | | | | |
|---|---|---|---|---|---|---|---|
| | | January/February 1996 | | September 1996 | | November 1996 | |
| | | Too little | Too much | Too little | Too much | Too little | Too much |
| Who's ahead/who's behind | 22% | 8% | 46% | 7% | 50% | 2% | 57% |
| Personal lives of candidates | 14% | 10% | 68% | 12% | 63% | 11% | 50% |
| Candidate's issue positions | 77% | 51% | 8% | 46% | 8% | 45% | 7% |
| Campaign strategies | 26% | 21% | 33% | 18% | 34% | 15% | 34% |
| Effect of election on you | 72% | 51% | 11% | 43% | 13% | 38% | 12% |
| Third party candidates | 27% | 49% | 10% | 44% | 13% | 58% | 5% |

Questions asked: "Please tell me how interested you are in the following types of news stories about the presidential campaign—very, somewhat, not too or not at all interested"; and, "Do you think the news media devotes too much, too little, or about the right amount of attention to stories about . . .?"

panel consistently thought that "too little" media attention was being paid to candidate issue positions throughout the campaign. In February, half of voters said that "too little" media attention was being paid to issues, nearly half (46% and 45%) continued to think this way in September and November. In February, September, and November, fewer than one in ten voters said "too much" media focus was on the candidates' issue stands. So, although voters thought an overabundance of news information was made available on the horse race and the personality of the candidates, many also thought that not enough news was available on substantive issue-oriented coverage.

Voters were similarly critical of a shortage of media coverage of third party and independent presidential candidates. From February to September, 49 percent and 44 percent of voters said "too little" attention was given to third party candidates. By election day, nearly three in five (58%) voters thought that third party candidates were not getting their fair share of news coverage. By November, only one in twenty said that third party candidates were receiving too much coverage. The voter panel data further confirmed the finding that voters thought third party candidates were given short shrift in that 76 percent of voters responding in February agreed with the statement: "the media give undue advantage to front-running candidates."

The 1996 voter also perceived a shortage of news information regarding how the election outcome might affect them. Half (51%) said too little media attention focused on this in February, 43 percent thought that way in September, and 38 percent were under that impression by election day. Only about one in ten voters thought that "too much" news focused on how the election might affect voters at each of these three time points.

### Voter Interest in Different Kinds of Election Stories

Clearly, voters sensed an imbalance in the content of news coverage of campaign 1996—an imbalance toward coverage of the horse race and stories about the personal lives of the candidates and away from stories about candidate issue positions, news about third party candidates, and information on how the election outcome might affect them. Interestingly, table 6.1 also shows that the types of stories voters said were the subject of too much media focus were also the types of stories in which voters expressed less interest.

Only 22 percent said they were very interested in the horse race, and 14 percent were very interested in stories about the personal lives of the candidates. About one-quarter of voters were very interested in stories about campaign strategies and tactics. On the other hand, more than three-quarters (77%) of voters reported being very interested in candidate issue positions and in how the election outcome might affect them. The content bias that voters perceive in the news, then, runs in the opposite direction of what voters say news content provides.

Viewed as a news information supply and voter demand function, these data clearly suggest that the information supplied by the media in certain areas (namely information about candidate issue positions, third party candidates, and how the election outcome might affect Americans) is not sufficient. Likewise, voters are saying there is a clear oversupply of less important news about the campaign (the horse race, the personalities of the candidates, and strategy and tactics).

The lack of responsiveness of news content to voter information needs and desires raises serious questions about the performance of the media in the 1996 presidential campaign. The demand for particular types of campaign news—issue positions of the candidates and news about how the election outcome might affect voters—was not satisfied by the news media. The important institutional function of the news in the U.S. electoral process—to provide information needed by voters to cast an informed vote —apparently was unfulfilled.

*Evaluations of Election News Content by News Sources Used*

Earlier we reviewed some research that suggested that news provided across different forms of media varied in content. For example, Patterson and McClure (1976) found that television coverage was particularly prone to focusing on the horse race. Graber (1993) also found that print media were more likely than other forms of media to cover stories related to the personality characteristics of candidates. More recently, however, Just et al. (1996) found that the three presidential candidates in 1992 were given about the same level of horse race, personality characteristic, and issue coverage across different media.

The voter panel data allowed us to examine voter perceptions about the supply of various story categories broken down by media sources the voters actually used to get information. This allowed us to ask whether those who used certain kinds of media were more or less likely to think there was too much or too little focus on different types of election news. Such an analysis provides insights into voter assessments of the supply of election news based on the sources they use.

Table 6.2 shows perceptions of news focus across the six story categories, broken down by the particular type of media that voters were *most* dependent on for information about the presidential election. The table also shows changes in this relationship over the course of the campaign.

Those primarily dependent on radio for election news were consistently more likely than TV and newspaper-reliant voters to say there was too much focus on the horse race. In September and November 1996, for example, about seven in ten radio-dependent voters thought that too much attention was given to the horse race, whereas six in ten newspaper-dependent voters and about half of television-dependent voters expressed that sentiment in the same time period. Those using television as their most relied upon news source were least critical of the media's focus on the horse race. This finding is quite interesting, given the past finding of Patterson and McClure (1976) indicating that television is most likely to focus on the horse race. Although a possible explanation is that TV-reliant voters are more likely to want news about the horse race, our data suggest otherwise.[4]

Consistent with Graber's findings, our voter opinion data found that newspaper-reliant voters were more likely to say *that* too much attention was given to personality-oriented stories about the candidates. In September and November, those more dependent on newspapers were about 10 points more likely than TV-dependent voters to say that there was too much focus on the personality of the candidates.

Regarding the kinds of stories voters said they were most interested in—stories about the issue positions of the candidates—TV-reliant voters were less critical of the news media's lack of attention. Table 6.2 shows, for example, that by election day four in ten TV-reliant voters thought too little focus was given to candidate issue positions compared to 51 percent of newspaper-reliant voters and 56 percent of those who relied mostly on radio for their news about the election.[5]

Finally, table 6.2 shows the differences in media-reliance categories across voter perceptions about the amount of attention given to third party and independent candidates. From September to November 1996, the perception that there was too little focus on those candidates increased substantially (from 43% to 56% among TV-reliants and 41% to 67% among newspaper-reliants). By election day, however, only 44 percent of radio-dependent voters said there was too little focus on third party and independent candidates.

Cross-tabulation can provide another way to look at the relationship between media use and voter perceptions. Tables 6.3 through 6.8 provide

**TABLE 6.2** Perceptions of News Content Focus by Main Media Source Used

| How much focus on . . . | Television | | | Newspaper | | | Radio | | |
|---|---|---|---|---|---|---|---|---|---|
| | February | September | November | February | September | November | February | September | November |
| **A. Horse Race** | | | | | | | | | |
| Too much | 41% | 46% | 53% | 48% | 57% | 61% | 54% | 72% | 70% |
| Too little | 8% | 6% | 1% | 7% | 7% | 2% | 5% | 2% | 2% |
| About right | 48% | 41% | 43% | 42% | 34% | 36% | 39% | 23% | 20% |
| **B. Personality** | | | | | | | | | |
| Too much | 69% | 54% | 45% | 69% | 66% | 53% | 70% | 60% | 54% |
| Too little | 9% | 16% | 11% | 9% | 11% | 9% | 11% | 23% | 19% |
| About right | 18% | 25% | 41% | 19% | 20% | 36% | 14% | 14% | 24% |
| **C. Issue positions** | | | | | | | | | |
| Too much | 5% | 10% | 6% | 6% | 4% | 3% | 5% | 3% | 4% |
| Too little | 52% | 41% | 42% | 60% | 48% | 51% | 66% | 59% | 56% |
| About right | 39% | 43% | 49% | 32% | 45% | 45% | 29% | 35% | 39% |
| **D. Strategy & Tactics** | | | | | | | | | |
| Too much | 31% | 35% | 32% | 40% | 35% | 38% | 30% | 32% | 44% |
| Too little | 22% | 18% | 13% | 17% | 12% | 13% | 23% | 20% | 15% |
| About right | 42% | 39% | 50% | 39% | 46% | 45% | 43% | 35% | 33% |
| **E. Outcome effect** | | | | | | | | | |
| Too much | 8% | 13% | 10% | 14% | 11% | 12% | 16% | 23% | 22% |
| Too little | 49% | 42% | 40% | 55% | 46% | 44% | 55% | 46% | 28% |
| About right | 36% | 37% | 46% | 25% | 36% | 41% | 23% | 26% | 44% |
| **F. Third Party** | | | | | | | | | |
| Too much | 12% | 14% | 4% | 10% | 21% | 6% | 9% | 11% | 0% |
| Too little | 43% | 43% | 56% | 53% | 41% | 67% | 55% | 51% | 44% |
| About right | 39% | 36% | 35% | 32% | 29% | 26% | 30% | 32% | 52% |

Question asked was, "Where do you get most of your news about the campaign?"

cross-tabulations of the type of news story covered and the medium used in accordance with voter perceptions of levels of coverage.

An interesting relationship of media source to story coverage is shown in table 6.3. Talk radio listeners were much more likely to say there was too much horse race coverage, particularly during the general election campaign period. In contrast, table 6.4 shows that those who make greater use of talk radio were much less likely to think there was too much coverage of personality stories of the candidates.

**TABLE 6.3** Amount of Focus on Horse Race by Use of News Sources

|  | Television | | | Newspaper | | | Radio | | |
|---|---|---|---|---|---|---|---|---|---|
|  | Low | Medium | High | Low | Medium | High | Low | Medium | High |
| **February** | | | | | | | | | |
| Too much | 45% | 50% | 42% | 44% | 45% | 47% | 37% | 48% | 48% |
| Too little | 5% | 7% | 8% | 5% | 9% | 7% | 13% | 5% | 6% |
| About right | 47% | 40% | 46% | 47% | 42% | 44% | 46% | 45% | 43% |
| **September** | | | | | | | | | |
| Too much | 53% | 52% | 53% | 45% | 50% | 64% | 52% | 52% | 54% |
| Too little | 7% | 5% | 4% | 5% | 7% | 3%★ | 5% | 4% | 6% |
| About right | 35% | 36% | 39% | 41% | 37% | 32% | 37% | 36% | 38% |
| **November** | | | | | | | | | |
| Too much | 56% | 54% | 59% | 56% | 56% | 59% | 56% | 57% | 57% |
| Too little | 3% | 1% | 1%★ | 1% | 3% | 1% | 1% | 2% | 1% |
| About right | 36% | 42% | 39% | 41% | 37% | 38% | 39% | 38% | 40% |

|  | Tabloid TV | | Talk Radio | | | Elite | | |
|---|---|---|---|---|---|---|---|---|
|  | No | Yes | Low | Medium | High | Low | Medium | High |
| **February** | | | | | | | | |
| Too much | 47% | 39% | 46% | 39% | 51% | 44% | 44% | 47% |
| Too little | 7% | 9% | 6% | 9% | 7% | 3% | 11% | 7% |
| About right | 43% | 50% | 46% | 45% | 41% | 48% | 44% | 42% |
| **September** | | | | | | | | |
| Too much | 56% | 42% | 48% | 46% | 73% | 48% | 53% | 57% |
| Too little | 4% | 10%★ | 5% | 8% | 1%★ | 6% | 5% | 4% |
| About right | 35% | 44% | 40% | 41% | 22% | 39% | 35% | 36% |
| **November** | | | | | | | | |
| Too much | 60% | 46% | 54% | 52% | 68% | 56% | 55% | 59% |
| Too little | 2% | 1%★ | 1% | 1% | 2%★ | 1% | 2% | 1% |
| About right | 36% | 52% | 42% | 43% | 28% | 40% | 40% | 37% |

**TABLE 6.4** Amount of Focus on Personality Stories by Use of News Sources

| | Television | | | Newspaper | | | Radio | | |
|---|---|---|---|---|---|---|---|---|---|
| | Low | Medium | High | Low | Medium | High | Low | Medium | High |
| February | | | | | | | | | |
| Too much | 70% | 68% | 69% | 72% | 65% | 70% | 67% | 66% | 74% |
| Too little | 10% | 12% | 7% | 8% | 12% | 8% | 11% | 11% | 7% |
| About right | 15% | 16% | 21% | 17% | 18% | 19% | 15% | 19% | 18% |
| September | | | | | | | | | |
| Too much | 57% | 61% | 59% | 63% | 59% | 55% | 52% | 55% | 67% |
| Too little | 16% | 15% | 11% | 11% | 17% | 15%★ | 20% | 14% | 10%★ |
| About right | 24% | 20% | 24% | 21% | 18% | 29% | 23% | 24% | 21% |
| November | | | | | | | | | |
| Too much | 46% | 45% | 54% | 52% | 52% | 43% | 40% | 47% | 56% |
| Too little | 12% | 16% | 7% | 7% | 12% | 15% | 11% | 13% | 10%★ |
| About right | 38% | 36% | 37% | 38% | 33% | 39% | 45% | 37% | 33% |

| | Tabloid TV | | Talk Radio | | | Elite | | |
|---|---|---|---|---|---|---|---|---|
| | No | Yes | Low | Medium | High | Low | Medium | High |
| February | | | | | | | | |
| Too much | 70% | 66% | 75% | 63% | 59% | 73% | 67% | 67% |
| Too little | 9% | 11% | 7% | 11% | 14%★ | 9% | 9% | 10% |
| About right | 17% | 19% | 15% | 24% | 19% | 14% | 18% | 21% |
| September | | | | | | | | |
| Too much | 59% | 59% | 70% | 48% | 38% | 63% | 56% | 57% |
| Too little | 14% | 15%★ | 9% | 16% | 27%★ | 12% | 17% | 13% |
| About right | 24% | 17% | 17% | 32% | 29% | 19% | 22% | 27% |
| November | | | | | | | | |
| Too much | 49% | 47% | 58% | 39% | 32% | 51% | 51% | 46% |
| Too little | 11% | 11% | 6% | 14% | 24%★ | 10% | 10% | 13% |
| About right | 36% | 42% | 33% | 42% | 42% | 36% | 36% | 39% |

## Voters' Evaluations of Election News Sources

A wide variety of media outlets and information sources are available to voters, ranging from print and electronic stories and reports, to direct exposure events on television (such as the debates), to commentary provided on talk radio and Sunday morning TV talk shows, to paid political advertisements. The September wave of our election study sought to obtain feedback from voters as to the kinds of news media sources that were relatively more and less effective in helping them learn about the candidates and the campaign.

**TABLE 6.5** Amount of Focus on Candidate Issue Positions by Use of News Sources

| | Television | | | Newspaper | | | Radio | | |
|---|---|---|---|---|---|---|---|---|---|
| | Low | Medium | High | Low | Medium | High | Low | Medium | High |
| February | | | | | | | | | |
| Too much | 5% | 5% | 7% | 8% | 3% | 6% | 6% | 6% | 5% |
| Too little | 61% | 56% | 52% | 53% | 56% | 58% | 56% | 55% | 57% |
| About right | 31% | 37% | 38% | 37% | 36% | 35% | 36% | 36% | 35% |
| September | | | | | | | | | |
| Too much | 11% | 3% | 8% | 7% | 7% | 8% | 8% | 10% | 5% |
| Too little | 51% | 48% | 39%★ | 45% | 48% | 44% | 46% | 42% | 49%★ |
| About right | 36% | 42% | 48% | 43% | 40% | 44% | 39% | 42% | 45% |
| November | | | | | | | | | |
| Too much | 3% | 4% | 9% | 8% | 3% | 6% | 4% | 6% | 6% |
| Too little | 47% | 47% | 43%★ | 39% | 51% | 46% | 46% | 46% | 44% |
| About right | 45% | 49% | 47% | 49% | 44% | 47% | 47% | 46% | 48% |

| | Tabloid TV | | Talk Radio | | | Elite | | |
|---|---|---|---|---|---|---|---|---|
| | No | Yes | Low | Medium | High | Low | Medium | High |
| February | | | | | | | | |
| Too much | 5% | 10% | 5% | 6% | 7% | 3% | 6% | 7% |
| Too little | 58% | 48%★ | 56% | 53% | 59% | 54% | 56% | 57% |
| About right | 35% | 37% | 37% | 36% | 31% | 39% | 36% | 33% |
| September | | | | | | | | |
| Too much | 7% | 10% | 7% | 7% | 9% | 6% | 10% | 6% |
| Too little | 47% | 42% | 45% | 42% | 51% | 43% | 48% | 46% |
| About right | 43% | 42% | 44% | 46% | 34% | 46% | 38% | 43% |
| November | | | | | | | | |
| Too much | 5% | 8% | 6% | 4% | 6% | 8% | 5% | 4% |
| Too little | 46% | 43% | 43% | 44% | 52% | 40% | 47% | 49% |
| About right | 47% | 46% | 48% | 51% | 41% | 50% | 46% | 45% |

Existing research on media effects tends to show that use of newspapers for information and voter exposure and attention to salient campaign events—such as the nominating conventions and the presidential debates—has at least a marginal influence on voter knowledge and understanding of the campaign (Delli Carpini and Keeter 1996). Research also indicates that voter attentiveness to television news on the election contributes little, if anything, to voter learning (Patterson and McClure 1976; Patterson 1980).

In evaluating the institutional performance of the news media, the perceptual perspective of voters is critical. Media effects are only one way of

**TABLE 6.6** Amount of Focus on Strategy and Tactics by Use of News Sources

| | Television | | | Newspaper | | | Radio | | |
|---|---|---|---|---|---|---|---|---|---|
| | Low | Medium | High | Low | Medium | High | Low | Medium | High |
| **February** | | | | | | | | | |
| Too much | 34% | 34% | 30% | 38% | 32% | 27% | 36% | 31% | 33% |
| Too little | 21% | 20% | 22% | 17% | 21% | 25% | 17% | 20% | 24% |
| About right | 36% | 39% | 45% | 38% | 41% | 42% | 41% | 41% | 39% |
| **September** | | | | | | | | | |
| Too much | 35% | 31% | 36% | 35% | 34% | 34% | 34% | 31% | 38% |
| Too little | 20% | 20% | 14% | 14% | 21% | 18% | 22% | 15% | 18%* |
| About right | 37% | 38% | 41% | 42% | 33% | 41% | 35% | 40% | 40% |
| **November** | | | | | | | | | |
| Too much | 35% | 33% | 36% | 38% | 32% | 35% | 36% | 35% | 35% |
| Too little | 11% | 16% | 15% | 12% | 15% | 15% | 12% | 16% | 14%* |
| About right | 44% | 48% | 45% | 44% | 45% | 47% | 45% | 42% | 50% |

| | Tabloid TV | | Talk Radio | | | Elite | | |
|---|---|---|---|---|---|---|---|---|
| | No | Yes | Low | Medium | High | Low | Medium | High |
| **February** | | | | | | | | |
| Too much | 33% | 30% | 35% | 31% | 27% | 39% | 33% | 27% |
| Too little | 20% | 25% | 20% | 23% | 24% | 13% | 24% | 26%* |
| About right | 41% | 37% | 40% | 39% | 43% | 40% | 41% | 40% |
| **September** | | | | | | | | |
| Too much | 34% | 34% | 38% | 28% | 31% | 32% | 39% | 32% |
| Too little | 18% | 17% | 16% | 18% | 22% | 15% | 21% | 17% |
| About right | 40% | 36% | 38% | 45% | 34% | 41% | 33% | 42% |
| **November** | | | | | | | | |
| Too much | 35% | 36% | 36% | 35% | 31% | 34% | 34% | 37% |
| Too little | 15% | 10% | 13% | 15% | 17% | 13% | 15% | 14% |
| About right | 44% | 52% | 45% | 44% | 47% | 47% | 44% | 44% |

providing feedback on performance. The direct opinions and attitudes of the news consumer provide a critical dimension in assessing the job of the news media. To obtain this perspective, in the September wave of the panel study voters were asked to provide their own assessment of the relative value of news sources and news formats in helping them learn about the campaign and arrive at vote decisions. Respondents were presented with ten different news sources and formats and asked whether they learn "a lot," "some," "just a little," or "nothing at all" from these sources and formats.

**TABLE 6.7** Amount of Focus on How Election Outcome Might Affect You by Use of News Sources

| | Television | | | Newspaper | | | Radio | | |
|---|---|---|---|---|---|---|---|---|---|
| | Low | Medium | High | Low | Medium | High | Low | Medium | High |
| **February** | | | | | | | | | |
| Too much | 10% | 12% | 10% | 9% | 7% | 16% | 10% | 14% | 8% |
| Too little | 55% | 54% | 45% | 49% | 58% | 45%★ | 54% | 45% | 55% |
| About right | 28% | 27% | 39% | 33% | 29% | 34% | 30% | 34% | 31% |
| **September** | | | | | | | | | |
| Too much | 13% | 14% | 15% | 12% | 15% | 15% | 17% | 13% | 13% |
| Too little | 42% | 48% | 37% | 41% | 43% | 42% | 47% | 42% | 39% |
| About right | 40% | 29% | 38% | 38% | 34% | 36% | 31% | 35% | 40% |
| **November** | | | | | | | | | |
| Too much | 9% | 14% | 15% | 11% | 12% | 15% | 8% | 14% | 14% |
| Too little | 41% | 39% | 34% | 33% | 44% | 37% | 40% | 36% | 38% |
| About right | 41% | 43% | 48% | 49% | 42% | 42% | 45% | 44% | 44% |

| | Tabloid TV | | Talk Radio | | | Elite | | |
|---|---|---|---|---|---|---|---|---|
| | No | Yes | Low | Medium | High | Low | Medium | High |
| **February** | | | | | | | | |
| Too much | 10% | 11% | 9% | 11% | 13% | 7% | 13% | 12% |
| Too little | 52% | 47% | 53% | 44% | 51% | 59% | 49% | 46% |
| About right | 31% | 36% | 31% | 37% | 31% | 27% | 34% | 35% |
| **September** | | | | | | | | |
| Too much | 14% | 13% | 14% | 11% | 16% | 15% | 16% | 12% |
| Too little | 41% | 44%★ | 39% | 44% | 49% | 40% | 44% | 42% |
| About right | 38% | 29% | 38% | 37% | 29% | 38% | 34% | 37% |
| **November** | | | | | | | | |
| Too much | 13% | 11% | 11% | 12% | 18% | 10% | 14% | 14% |
| Too little | 38% | 38% | 35% | 38% | 45%★ | 40% | 32% | 40% |
| About right | 44% | 48% | 48% | 47% | 32% | 47% | 46% | 41% |

Table 6.9 shows that among the eleven types of media information asked about on the survey, voters in 1996 said the single most valuable type made available to them for campaign learning was "live coverage of the presidential debates." Fully 45 percent of voters said they learned "a lot" from live debate coverage. Viewing the debates live was clearly perceived as the best type of media-provided information for campaign learning. The second most desirable medium for campaign learning—where about 30 percent say that there is "a lot" to be learned—was consumption of TV or newspaper news stories.

**TABLE 6.8** Amount of Focus on Third Party Candidates by Use of News Sources

| | Television | | | Newspaper | | | Radio | | |
|---|---|---|---|---|---|---|---|---|---|
| | Low | Medium | High | Low | Medium | High | Low | Medium | High |
| **February** | | | | | | | | | |
| Too much | 8% | 16% | 10% | 14% | 10% | 10% | 9% | 13% | 11% |
| Too little | 49% | 46% | 45% | 47% | 50% | 44% | 56% | 46% | 41%* |
| About right | 38% | 33% | 38% | 31% | 37% | 42% | 29% | 37% | 42% |
| **September** | | | | | | | | | |
| Too much | 13% | 16% | 15% | 14% | 13% | 18% | 14% | 13% | 18% |
| Too little | 47% | 44% | 39% | 42% | 44% | 42% | 45% | 44% | 40%* |
| About right | 36% | 31% | 35% | 34% | 35% | 34% | 35% | 31% | 38% |
| **November** | | | | | | | | | |
| Too much | 3% | 5% | 5% | 2% | 4% | 7% | 1% | 6% | 4% |
| Too little | 56% | 63% | 55% | 60% | 55% | 57% | 66% | 48% | 62%* |
| About right | 36% | 27% | 35% | 32% | 35% | 32% | 28% | 38% | 31% |

| | Tabloid TV | | Talk Radio | | | Elite | | |
|---|---|---|---|---|---|---|---|---|
| | No | Yes | Low | Medium | High | Low | Medium | High |
| **February** | | | | | | | | |
| Too much | 11% | 13% | 11% | 7% | 17% | 12% | 11% | 12% |
| Too little | 46% | 48% | 48% | 49% | 40% | 50% | 49% | 41% |
| About right | 37% | 35% | 36% | 40% | 36% | 32% | 35% | 43% |
| **September** | | | | | | | | |
| Too much | 15% | 16% | 11% | 13% | 28% | 14% | 15% | 15% |
| Too little | 42% | 43% | 45% | 40% | 37%* | 39% | 46% | 43% |
| About right | 35% | 30% | 35% | 37% | 31% | 38% | 32% | 33% |
| **November** | | | | | | | | |
| Too much | 5% | 1% | 4% | 3% | 7% | 2% | 4% | 7% |
| Too little | 56% | 62% | 60% | 61% | 47%* | 62% | 57% | 53% |
| About right | 33% | 33% | 31% | 31% | 42% | 31% | 32% | 36% |

The next tier of preferred sources for campaign learning included magazine articles, TV journalistic analysis and commentary, and TV debate format programs—each of which were identified by about two in ten as a source where a lot of information is learned. Two-thirds or more of voters said they learned very little or nothing at all about the candidates and the campaign from these sources: talk radio, Sunday morning political talk shows, newspaper journalist analysis and commentary, and paid political advertisements.

It is interesting that live debate coverage ranks high above the remaining ten categories of media information in that it involves direct unmediated

**TABLE 6.9** Usefulness of Different Kinds of Campaign Information Provided by the News Media

|  | A lot | Some | Little | Not too | Not at all |
|---|---|---|---|---|---|
| Watching debates live | 45% | 27% | 13% | 5% | 9% |
| Reading newspaper stories | 32% | 36% | 19% | 4% | 9% |
| Watching TV news stories | 30% | 39% | 22% | 4% | 4% |
| Reading articles in magazines | 21% | 33% | 20% | 7% | 19% |
| TV journalist analysis and commentary | 18% | 27% | 25% | 16% | 13% |
| Watching TV debate programs | 18% | 19% | 14% | 10% | 38% |
| Talk radio | 15% | 17% | 17% | 11% | 39% |
| Sunday A.M. political talk shows | 15% | 16% | 12% | 12% | 44% |
| Newspaper journalist accounts of candidates performance | 14% | 30% | 25% | 14% | 16% |
| Paid political ads | 5% | 18% | 27% | 28% | 21% |

Question asked was, "Generally, how much do you learn about the candidates and the campaign from each of the following ...?" (September 1996)

exposure to candidates, whereas nine of the other ten items involve information mediated by a journalist or reporter. The single exception is paid political advertisements, which are viewed by only 5 percent of voters as providing "a lot" of information about the candidates and the campaign. Other survey data collected during the campaign suggest that although direct exposure to the debates was valuable, journalistic accounts and commentary on the debates were problematic. For example, in an October 1996 news poll, Fox News found voters thought that debate commentary was more likely to try to influence one's opinion about who won the debate than it was to put the debates into context for news consumers.

### Attitudes about Journalistic Commentary

Data from panel waves 2 and 3 offer insights into another criticism of the news media's campaign coverage—the extent to which journalists provide commentary on campaign events rather than on reporting on them. A content analysis of broadcast election news in 1996 by the Center for Media and Public Affairs found that nearly three-quarters of air time on news stories about the campaign was "consumed by network anchors and reporters discussing the campaign," while only 13 percent showed comments from the candidates themselves.[6] What do voters think about the commentary provided by journalists? Do they prefer news stories that include such commentary or not? How valuable is journalist commentary as a source of information for voters in helping to arrive at a vote decision?

In panel wave 2 (September) of our study, administered after the party conventions, we asked panel respondents if they would prefer watching the conventions with or without journalistic commentary. In panel wave 3 (October) of the study, administered after the presidential and vice presidential debates, we asked voters if they would prefer watching the debates with or without journalistic commentary. Figure 6.1 shows that in both instances, more voters opted for watching these events without journalistic commentary.

Regarding coverage of the party conventions, 52 percent preferred watching the events without the commentary of journalists and 43 percent wanted to hear journalists' commentary. The margin rejecting journalistic commentary increased for coverage of the debates—59 percent preferred not having the commentary and only 35 percent opted for having the commentary.

Likewise, the print media version of journalistic commentary—newspaper endorsements and editorials about a candidate—appeared to matter little to voters. Figure 6.2 shows that less than one-third were aware of a newspaper's endorsement of a candidate; 18 percent of voters said they actually took the time to read the editorial in which the endorsement was made; and only 3 percent said the endorsement had an influence on their own opinion about the candidates.

## Conclusion

This chapter provided an assessment of election news content from the perspective of voters. We also discussed opinions about the value of a variety

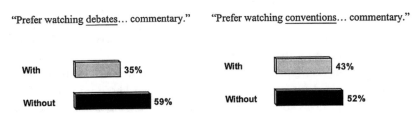

"Prefer watching <u>debates</u>... commentary."   "Prefer watching <u>conventions</u>... commentary."

With — 35%       With — 43%

Without — 59%       Without — 52%

**FIGURE 6.1** Attitudes about journalistic commentary on the presidential campaign.

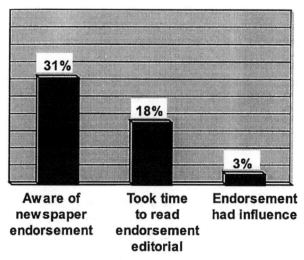

**FIGURE 6.2** Role of newspaper endorsements of candidates (MSC/RC).

of different campaign news sources for voter learning. In terms of news content, we found that voters themselves confirm what other research—such as media effects and content analysis of news—has shown. There is too much news about the horse race and stories relating to the personalities of the candidates; at the same time there is too little news about candidate issue positions, third party and independent candidates, and how the election outcome might affect voters. Further, the sense that the news media put too much focus on the horse race increased as election day drew closer. During the general election campaign season about half of voters in our panel thought that there was too little news on third party candidates and candidate issue positions.

We showed that voter interest is highest in the kinds of election news stories that are given too little attention—stories about how the election outcome might affect "voters like you," and stories about candidate issue positions. Fully three-quarters of our panel were "very" interested in this type of news. Very few respondents were interested in the kinds of news stories that are over reported in the news—about the personal lives of the candidates and about the horse race.

Those depending primarily on newspapers were more likely to think that news focused too much on personality stories. Those using radio as a prime election news source were most likely to express frustration about the overabundance of horse race coverage. And those depending mostly on

TV for news appeared to be least critical of the media's tendency to ignore issue coverage.

We also explored voter attitudes about how much they learned from various news sources and formats. By far the single best source of news in terms of learning about the candidates was live coverage of the debates. Nearly half of voters said they learned a lot from watching the debates. Voters told us that the next tier of sources for campaign learning included newspaper stories and television news stories. Talk radio, Sunday morning political talk shows, and journalists' accounts of candidate performance provided little in the way of voter learning; and voters said that newspaper endorsements had little to no influence on them.

Despite our finding (see chapter 4) that most voters give the news a positive rating by the end of the election year, the news media are failing voters in many respects. Voters' specific evaluations of news content do not reflect positively on the institutional performance of the news media in their coverage of the 1996 presidential campaign. In short, much of the information that voters find in their news sources is not the kind of information they want. Voters want information that can help them cast an informed vote—issue positions, information on third party as well as major party candidates, and information about how the election might impact the voter. Instead, to a large extent what voters get is an overabundance of stories about the personalities involved and many updates on who is ahead in the race. From the journalists' perspective, these stories are crucial to developing and unfolding a dramatic story of an electoral contest. But they do not address voters' needs.

Voters wade through the many superfluous stories offered by the media to get the information they need. And, according to our study, they do receive enough of the right information to cast a vote, despite the belief of some that the news they are using is biased. So it appears that news organizations appear to be fulfilling the most basic requirements of their role in democratic politics. There is, however, much room for improvement.

# 7
—

# The Consequences of
# Poor Media Performance

In this chapter, we ask whether the specific problems that voters see in the news media affect their viewing behavior. Do dissatisfied voters use the news less, or do they continue to wade through the tide of information, much of which they consider to be substandard or tangential to their concerns? When fewer voters had criticisms of the news media, did more of them use the news? What the voters do—their behavior as opposed to their attitudes—matters. After all, it is news usage that provides incentives to media organizations. If voters who are dissatisfied watch less news, then ratings will suffer and the news organizations, with their need for ratings and advertising revenues, might respond. On the other hand, if voters continue to use the different news media even if they are dissatisfied, then they will have no impact on ratings and media organizations will have little financial incentive to change their programming.

We also ask whether voters who are dissatisfied with the media learn less. And we will analyze the extent to which specific negative evaluations have an impact on overall evaluations of the news media.

The organization of this chapter follows the different phases of the campaign: the conventions, the debates, and the final weeks of the general election campaign. After putting the 1996 election in context, we describe for each phase of the campaign whether voters who were more dissatisfied with the news media were less likely to follow these events (conventions and debates), and whether the critical voters were less likely to pay attention to the news as the election progressed.

We show that, although evaluation of the media sometimes had an impact on media use, that impact was generally small compared to the influence of individuals' established media habits. Those who had already established the habit of gathering information from television news, elite media, or print media generally maintained high levels of use of those media. In addition, those who had the habit of using the television for gathering information, either from network news or from elite media such as the *NewsHour,* were more likely to watch the conventions, debates, and associated coverage. Examination of turnover tables shows that most people maintained their level of use of any given type of media, from wave to wave across the panel. This implies that, although those with criticisms of the media were somewhat less likely to use it as frequently, any changes that led to this tendency occurred before the election season began. Dissatisfaction did not tend to change media use over the course of the election cycle.

We also look at whether people with different habits of media use thought they learned more from the major campaign events. For example, those in the habit of using the television to gather information thought that they learned more directly from the conventions and debates; those who get more information from newspapers or radio were more likely to learn from journalists' commentary. We show that dissatisfaction with media does not affect perceived learning, but it does make voters more likely to prefer direct exposure to events such as the conventions and debates.

Finally, we look at how specific complaints regarding the media affected overall evaluations of the media. We show that, whereas voters' dissatisfaction with specific aspects of the media does not affect their tendency to continue to use the news, it does affect their overall rating of the news media's performance. Voters are more likely to give the media positive ratings if they perceive it to be fair and if they think that news organizations are not overstepping their roles.

We suggested in earlier chapters that voters might give relatively high ratings to the news media if they were able to learn what they need from it, despite the negative aspects of news that they perceive. Reflecting this, the greatest positive impact on ratings comes from whether voters learned from coverage of conventions and debates.

## The Responsiveness of the Media to Voters' Opinions

In focusing on the continued viewing behavior of voters, we are drawing attention to the vital role of the media as a political institution in U.S.

politics. The organizations that comprise the news media have the responsibility for transmitting messages from candidates to mass audiences of voters. The news media provide other information to voters as well, helping them understand how the economy, international security, crime, the environment, and a host of other factors may affect their lives.

The news media also have taken on the responsibility for monitoring the accuracy and plausibility of candidates' statements, and for explaining to voters which techniques are being used to attempt to manipulate them (Patterson 1993). The media may encourage policy makers to take real positions on controversial issues of importance. When candidates try to emphasize consensus issues, the media can encourage them to take positions that may alienate part of the electorate. When candidates take positions to please part of their constituencies, the media can publicize their stances so that everyone has the possibility of sharing information and making a more informed choice.

The media organizations that play these roles are private corporations. They must balance their other goals with their responsibilities to stockholders. To an extent, corporations may own news organizations for the prestige this brings them. Increasingly, however, companies require that news organizations turn a profit.

What questions are raised by the private status of this important political institution? The question we address here is whether we can expect the news media to be responsive to the electorate. It is instructive to compare the incentives of media organizations with those of other political institutions, such as the executive branch and the legislature. Elections may provide a mechanism for encouraging the accountability of legislators and the executive.[1] Elected officials must consider what ramifications any action (or inaction) may have for the next election. They may choose to act against prevailing opinion, but it is at least possible that their tendency to do so will be limited to circumstances where vital national interests are at stake, or when they think that opinion in their constituency may change before the next election. In addition, during campaigns candidates may try to use tactics to manipulate voters; but they must also consider that their unprincipled behavior might result in backlash, with potential supporters voting against them or failing to vote.[2]

As with other institutional actors, the professional norms of journalists, editors, and producers have an impact on their actions. Moreover, the organizational structure of media organizations also constrains individual actors. Here we consider the ways in which voters can influence the media as an institution. This focus exposes a key difference between the news media and other political institutions: for the news media, the public's leverage comes not through the vote but through the market. Media organizations need high ratings—a large audience—to maintain their advertising revenues. Because of this, voter feedback comes through their viewing behavior. Viewers dissatisfied with the content of a news medium have the option of switching channels, changing the medium they use (e.g., television to newspapers), or simply throwing up their hands and reducing the amount of effort they put into gathering the news. Thus, it becomes important for us to know whether the negative evaluations of election coverage we identified in earlier chapters result in a specific behavior: less use of the news media. If dissatisfaction results in lower use, then media organizations may detect this and respond. On the other hand, if dissatisfaction has no impact on media use, then we might expect news organizations to remain unresponsive.

The media are not unique in their importance to electoral politics. Nor are questions about lack of responsiveness confined to the news media. Other institutional actors raise equally important questions—whether candidates tend to stake out issue positions only when there is consensus, whether incumbents enjoy too great an advantage over challengers, or whether campaign finance laws allow well-heeled interest groups to exert undue influence. But the media are unique because of the means by which they can be made accountable.

We now examine whether conditions exist that might lead media organizations to improve their political coverage relative to the public's standards and perceived needs. We explore whether those individuals who are dissatisfied tend to exercise their option to stop watching (or listening to or reading) particular news outlets, or whether voters continue to watch the news despite their dissatisfaction with aspects of the media's performance.

## Putting the 1996 Conventions and Debates in Context

Two main events mark the general election campaign, the Democratic and Republican national conventions and the debates between the candidates. Conventions, once a source of much excitement as party leaders engaged in backroom negotiations and led their followers among the delegates into successive ballots that chose their party's presidential candidate, have in recent decades become largely symbolic, as more delegates were committed by primary elections to support a particular candidate (Keeter and Zukin 1983). Recent conventions have been spectacularly staged, and 1996 was no exception. Nevertheless, because conventions now have predetermined conclusions, they have become little more than a source of free air time for the parties and an event to mark the beginning of the general election campaign. Tightly controlled by the winner of the primaries, conventions may provide information about the party to the uninitiated as well as an opportunity to see the candidates and party leaders present themselves, but they contain few surprises and little information for those who follow politics.

Audiences for the convention were down in 1996. Overall ratings were down compared to 1992, and they were substantially lower than the entertainment and news magazine programs that the conventions preempted. Ratings for what is, perhaps, the main event in the convention—the presidential candidates' acceptance speeches—were also down. Robert Dole's acceptance speech reached 17.9 million households, while four years before George Bush's acceptance speech had reached 23.7 million. At the Democratic national convention, Bill Clinton's 1996 acceptance speech drew an audience of 19.6 million households, compared with 24.3 million four years before (*Washington Post,* October 10, 1996).

Public opinion polls also showed a decline in the self-reported audience for the conventions. In 1984, a Gallup poll found that 53 percent of voters watched at least some of the Democratic convention (table 7.1). In 1992,

**TABLE 7.1** Self-Reported Audience for the Democratic and Republican National Conventions

|  | 1984 | 1992 | 1992 | 1996 | 1996 |
|---|---|---|---|---|---|
| Which convention: | Democratic | Democratic | Republican | Democratic | Republican |
| Watched ... |  |  |  |  |  |
| A great deal | 23 | 26 | 23 | 18 | 16% |
| Some of it | 30 | 32 | 35 | 29 | 29 |
| Very little | 27 | 26 | 28 | 28 | 31 |
| None of it | 20 | 17 | 14 | 24 | 24 |
| Don't know/Refused |  |  |  | 1 | 1 |
| Survey date | 7/20 | 7/17 | 8/23 | 8/29 | 8/15 |
| Sample size | 1006 | 955 | 939 | 738 | 874 |

Source: The Gallup Organization, telephone interviews. Respondents were asked if they registered to vote or do not need to register.

Question wording: How much, if any, of the [Republican or Democratic] convention did you watch on TV this week-none of it, very little, some of it, or a great deal?

when newcomer Bill Clinton made his acceptance speech, 58 percent of voters watched at least some of the Democratic national convention. In 1996, only 47 percent reported watching at least some of the Democratic national convention. Audiences watched less of the Republican convention as well: in 1992, 58 percent of voters watched at least some of the Republican convention, while in 1996 only 45 percent of voters tuned in.

In contrast to the conventions, debates between the presidential and vice-presidential candidates can be a source of greater excitement. Despite criticisms of the format of debates (e.g., Jamieson and Birdsell 1988), they can provide an opportunity for voters to learn about the character and stances of the candidates (Drew and Weaver 1991).

Viewership of the debates was also down in 1996 from previous years. Table 7.2 shows the Nielsen ratings of debates from 1960 to the present, which were in the 50s before 1980. Since that time, debates in which there were higher levels of conflict—the Mondale-Reagan debates in 1984, or the 1992 debates that included Ross Perot—drew ratings in the 40s (where each rating point represents 1 percent of television households), and other debates drew ratings in the 30s. The audience for the debates in 1996, however, drew very low ratings of 32 and 26. The average size of the audiences for the debates fell from sixty to seventy million individuals in 1992 to thirty-five to forty million in 1996.

This decline in viewership is reflected in the survey figures. Although ratings determine the average number of households tuning in to a debate at any minute, the survey asked whether each person saw the debate, without specifying how much of each they saw. For this reason, we can expect the percent of debate-watchers identified by the survey to be somewhat higher. Figure 7.1 shows that this tends to be the case. In this figure, diamonds and squares represent Nielsen ratings for the presidential debates conducted in various election years, while circles represent the percent of the public that reported viewing the debates. Both series fell in 1984, rose during the 1992 debates, and fell again during the 1996 debates.

## Following the Campaign During the Conventions

Overall, 55 percent of voters reported following the convention either very closely or somewhat closely. How closely individuals followed the conventions differed depending on their media viewing habits and also, to an extent, on their evaluation of the media.

**TABLE 7.2** Audience for the Presidential Debates

| | Nielsen Ratings | | | Self-Reported Viewership | | |
|---|---|---|---|---|---|---|
| | Debate | Rating | Audience (millions) | Watched debate | Survey Date | Sample |
| Nixon–Kennedy | September 26 | 59.5 | | | | |
| | October 7 | 59.1 | | | | |
| | October 13 | 61.0 | | | | |
| | October 21 | 57.8 | | | | |
| Ford–Carter | September 23 | 53.5 | 69.7 | | | |
| | October 6 | 52.4 | 63.9 | | | |
| | October 22 | 47.8 | 62.7 | | | |
| Carter–Reagan | October 28 | 58.9 | 80.6 | 83 | 10/28/80[1] | 1019 |
| Reagan–Mondale | October 7 | 45.3 | 65.1 | 66 | 10/7/84[2] | 476 |
| | October 21 | 46.0 | 67.3 | 57 | 10/21/84[2] | 494 |
| Bush–Dukakis | September 15 | 36.8 | 65.1 | | | |
| | October 13 | 35.9 | 67.3 | 58 | 10/13/88[2] | 729 |
| Bush–Clinton–Perot | October 11 | 38.3 | 62.4 | 70 | 10/11/92[1] | 489 |
| | October 15 | 46.3 | 69.9 | | | |
| | October 19 | 45.2 | 67.3 | 68 | 10/19/92[1] | 553 |
| Clinton–Dole | October 6 | 31.6 | 46.1 | 61 | 10/8/96[1] | 1294 |
| | | | | 63 | MSC Post-debate panel | 581 |
| | October 16 | 26.1 | 36.3 | 53 | 10/17/96[3] | 1479 |
| | | | | 61 | MSC Post-debate panel | 581 |

Source for ratings: Nielsen Media Research (1996), "Special Report: Presidential Debate Ratings." Rating is the average percent of all television households in the country that watched the debate (1 percent = 970,000 households).

Source of public opinion data: CBS News and CBS *News/New York Times* telephone poll.

Question wording: "Did you watch or listen to the debate between [candidate names] tonight?" Note that 1996 question wording referred to the day of the week.

1. Registered voters; 2. probable electorate; 3. national adult.

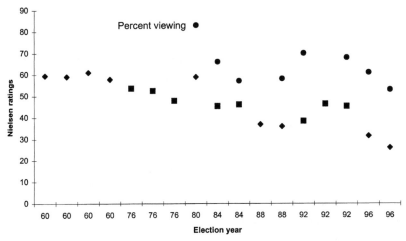

**FIGURE 7.1** Debate audiences from 1960 to 1996. Diamonds and squares represent Nielsen ratings; dots the percent of the public viewing the debates.

### Following the Convention

One possible variable related to media use during the conventions was personal taste, which led to different patterns of media viewing. In chapter 2, we segmented voters in our study into groups according to how much they used different types of media. Media use was measured at the beginning of the election season so that it would reflect, as closely as possible, individuals' habits of media use rather than media use that might be a response to the campaign. We defined six segmentation groups, which were constructed to reflect high levels of use of television news, elite media, print media, tabloid television shows, talk radio, and radio news. For each of these categories, individuals were put into a group reflecting a high, medium, or low level of use for that item (see chapter 2 for more details).

Table 7.3 shows that individuals were much more likely to watch the conventions if they were high users of television news: 63 percent of those who had high levels of TV news use reported following the convention at least somewhat closely, compared to only 46 percent of those with low levels of TV news use. In addition, those who reported watching elite media such as the *NewsHour* and Sunday morning political talk shows were far more likely to watch the conventions at least somewhat closely: 71 percent of those who have high levels of elite media use watched the convention at least somewhat closely, compared to only 47 percent of the individuals

**TABLE 7.3** Percent That Followed Conventions Very or Somewhat Closely

| | Television use | Elite media | Print media | Tabloid TV | Talk radio | Radio |
|---|---|---|---|---|---|---|
| High media use | 63 | 71 | 59 | 60 | 64 | 66 |
| Medium | 63 | 54 | 57 | | 56 | 48 |
| Low media use | 46 | 47 | 59 | 58 | 57 | 60 |

N = 494 registered voters.

with low levels of elite media use. The differences between those who watched a great deal of television news (a 17 percentage point difference) and followed closely the elite media (a 24 percentage point difference) were very high. In contrast, frequent users of other types of media were no more likely than their low-use counterparts to follow the conventions closely. Apparently, those individuals with the habit of reading newspapers regularly or listening to talk radio were not more likely to follow conventions than others who did not read newspapers or listen to talk radio regularly.

Although individuals with particular habits of news gathering appear to be more or less likely to use the media during the conventions, it is also plausible that individuals who are critical of the media are less likely to continue to follow the conventions and the news. To assess this hypothesis, we created scales for four different types of criticisms of the media, and we measured the criticisms in January before the campaign was fully underway. We asked individuals questions about whether they thought the media was fair and unbiased.[3] We also asked whether voters thought the news media paid too much attention to strategy, tactics, personality, and the horse race.[4] Voters signaled their perception of the usefulness of the news.[5] And finally, they were asked to agree or disagree with a series of questions about the media's role in the election (e.g., whether it had too much control in defining the issues of the campaign, whether it led candidates to perform for the cameras rather then focusing on issues, and whether it provided advantage to some candidates over than others).[6]

During the conventions we found that voters who were critical of the fairness of the news were less likely to be interested in the campaign and less likely to follow the convention closely. Those who perceived media to be fair and unbiased were more interested in the campaign in January: 82 percent reported being either "very" or "extremely" interested in the campaign, compared to 75 percent of those who did not have such criticisms. This gap in interest was maintained in September: 80 percent of those who thought media coverage was fair had high levels of interest in the campaign, whereas 74 percent of the more critical voters had high levels of interest. Those who saw coverage as unfair were also less likely to follow the convention closely. Although 63 percent of those who thought that the news media were fair followed the convention closely, only 53 percent of their critical counterparts did so (table 7.4).

Table 7.4 also shows that other types of criticism of the media had less of an effect. Those who thought the media were paying too much attention to candidate strategy were no more likely to follow conventions closely than those who thought the media's focus on strategy and the horse race was acceptable (59% vs. 57%). Those who thought that the media were less useful, and those who agreed with media analysts' criticisms of the role of the media in the political process, were no more likely than their less critical counterparts to be very interested in the campaign or to watch the conventions.

*Using the News*

Certain types of dissatisfaction and not others also had an effect on continued media use. Again, these effects tended to be small. Those who thought that media was fair and unbiased were more likely to watch television news

**TABLE 7.4** Effect of Satisfaction on Following Convention Closely and Interest in Campaign

| | January | September | |
| --- | --- | --- | --- |
| | Interest in campaign | Follow Convention closely | Interest in campaign |
| **Media fair and unbiased** | | | |
| Is fair and unbiased | 82 | 63 | 80 |
| Unfair and biased | 75 | 53 | 74 |
| **Attention to strategy** | | | |
| Not too much | 82 | 59 | 78 |
| Too much | 77 | 57 | 76 |
| **Usefulness of news** | | | |
| Useful | 78 | 57 | 74 |
| Not useful | 79 | 59 | 80 |
| **Role of media** | | | |
| Agree with fewer criticisms | 80 | 58 | 79 |
| Agree with more criticisms | 77 | 58 | 75 |

N = 494 registered voters.

frequently: 83 percent of those with positive evaluations of the fairness of media watched television news daily compared to 72 percent of those who thought more types of media were unfair and biased (table 7.5). Those who thought that media is fair and unbiased in January also tended to watch more television news in September: 82 percent of those with positive fairness evaluations watched TV news frequently, compared to 74 percent of their more critical counterparts. Table 7.5 also shows that other types of dissatisfaction with the media, such as problems with paying too much attention to strategy (81 vs. 76% in January, 77 vs. 79% in September), the usefulness of the news (76 vs. 79% in January, 78 vs. 79% in September), and the role of the media (76 vs. 78% in January, 81 vs. 79% in September), had limited or no effect on television use. In addition, these four criticisms had little or no effect on the use of radio news or newspapers.

The effect of dissatisfaction with media on talk radio use was different. Only one criticism, paying too much attention to strategy, led people to listen less to talk radio (28 vs. 18% in January, 31 vs. 23% in September). Other criticism of news—its fairness, its usefulness and the role of the media in elections—tended to lead *more* people to listen to talk radio. The reason for this may be found in table 7.6.

Scholars have suggested that talk radio functions as an alternative source of information for those who are dissatisfied with the mainstream media, which for most voters is television news. In our survey, we asked whether respondents saw television news as being fair and unbiased. Table 7.6 shows that those who think television news is less fair and more biased tend to use more alternatives such as talk radio (29 vs. 13% in January, 31 vs. 18% in September) and radio news (58 vs. 48% in September). In contrast, those who perceive television news as being fair continue to use it (80 vs. 74% in January, 80 vs. 76% in September) and newspapers (72 vs. 61% in January, 66 vs. 62% in September).

So far, we have shown that voters who are more critical of the news media may use it somewhat less. It should be noted, however, that this tendency may have already been in place before the election began. Because we collected panel data, we were able to look at change in media use over the course of the campaign. Table 7.7 shows that, for television news, 77 percent of voters maintained their same level of use between January and September. A great many of those who watched television news every evening in January continued this pattern of usage in September; and many of those who never watched television news continued not to do so in the second phase of the campaign. For television news, the 11 percent of

**TABLE 7.5** Effect of Satisfaction on Media Use (percent using news on every day, several times a week for talk radio)

| | January | | | | September | | | |
|---|---|---|---|---|---|---|---|---|
| | TV News | Newspaper | Talk radio | Radio news | TV News | Newspaper | Talk radio | Radio news |
| **Media fair and unbiased** | | | | | | | | |
| Is fair and unbiased | 83 | 70 | 17 | 57 | 82 | 66 | 21 | 52 |
| Unfair and biased | 72 | 64 | 26 | 57 | 74 | 63 | 30 | 55 |
| **Attention to strategy** | | | | | | | | |
| Not too much | 81 | 65 | 28 | 62 | 77 | 64 | 31 | 58 |
| Too much | 76 | 68 | 18 | 55 | 79 | 64 | 23 | 52 |
| **Usefulness of news** | | | | | | | | |
| Useful | 76 | 67 | 20 | 56 | 78 | 65 | 22 | 51 |
| Not useful | 79 | 67 | 24 | 59 | 79 | 64 | 29 | 58 |
| **Role of media** | | | | | | | | |
| Agree with fewer criticisms | 76 | 67 | 17 | 58 | 81 | 66 | 20 | 53 |
| Agree with more criticisms | 78 | 66 | 25 | 57 | 76 | 63 | 30 | 54 |

N = 494 registered voters.

**TABLE 7.6** Impact of Criticisms of Mainstream Media on Use of Alternative Sources of Media (percent that use one of four types of media frequently by perceptions of TV news' fairness)

|  | TV News | Newspaper | Talk radio | Radio news |
|---|---|---|---|---|
| **January** | | | | |
| Percent using these media frequently who ... | | | | |
| See TV news as fair and unbiased | 80 | 72 | 13 | 56 |
| See TV news unfair and biased | 74 | 61 | 29 | 58 |
| **September** | | | | |
| Percent using these media frequently who ... | | | | |
| See TV news as fair and unbiased | 80 | 66 | 18 | 48 |
| See TV news unfair and biased | 76 | 62 | 31 | 58 |

N = 494 registered voters.

**TABLE 7.7** Individual-level Change in Media Use

|  | January to September | | | |
|---|---|---|---|---|
|  | TV News | Newspaper | Talk radio | Radio news |
| **Change in media use** | | | | |
| Decrease in use | 11% | 17 | 20 | 23 |
| Same use | 77 | 71 | 51 | 57 |
| Increase in use | 12 | 11 | 30 | 20 |
| **Change in primary source of information** | | | | |
| From news media to conversations/ads | 10 | | | |
| Same | 73 | | | |
| From conversations/ads to news media | 17 | | | |
| **Change from TV to newspaper, radio, other as primary source of media information** | | | | |
| Change from TV to other | 15 | | | |
| Same | 69 | | | |
| Change from other to TV | 16 | | | |

N = 494 registered voters.

individuals who decreased their use were offset by the 12 percent who increased their use. Those with more criticisms of the news were no more likely to increase or decrease their television news consumption, so at the aggregate level we saw no change. At the individual level, as well, relatively few voters changed their patterns of media use. The same patterns were found for newspaper, talk radio, and radio news use.

Table 7.7 also examines whether individuals changed their primary source of information over the course of the campaign. It does not appear that individuals changed sources. Only 10 percent of voters changed from having some form of news media as their primary source of information to conversations, advertisements, or some other nonmass media source. Only 11 percent changed from relying primarily on conversations or advertisements to the news media. Fully 73 percent maintained their primary source of information.

The same patterns were found when we asked whether they changed their primary source of *news* information. Of those who relied on television news as their primary source of information (the most popular choice), 69 percent remained the same. Only 15 percent changed from some other source (e.g., newspaper, radio news) to television, and only 16 percent changed from some other source to television news. Again, these changes did not appear to be related to voters' negative evaluations of the media.

### Learning from Convention Coverage

Many voters reported learning from the conventions: 58 percent said that they learned something about the candidates and the parties from the conventions. Although many voters reported learning something from the conventions, however, the information did little to help them make a vote choice. A much smaller proportion of voters, 37 percent, reported that the national conventions helped them make a decision regarding whom to choose.

Table 7.8 also shows that most media-intensive voters did not think that they learned more from convention coverage than less frequent users of news. Voters who typically made an effort to gain information by using mainstream or alternative sources were no more likely to have learned something from the convention than those who paid less attention to the news. In fact, those who tended to use TV news and talk radio more frequently were slightly *less* likely to report learning from convention coverage. Similarly, those who use the news intensively were no more likely to have obtained the information needed to help them make a vote choice than others. These findings suggest that, although many voters (albeit fewer than in previous years) followed one or both of the conventions, paying more attention to commentators, news coverage, and analysis did not provide them with enough information to make a vote choice.

We suggested in earlier chapters that voters' desire to learn about the campaign overshadows possible criticisms of election coverage. We find some support for this hypothesis here. When asked whether they thought that they got most of their information about the conventions from watching them

**TABLE 7.8** Effect of Media Use Habits on Perceived Learning from Direct and Mediated Information About the Convention

| | Television use | Elite media | Print media | Tabloid TV | Talk radio | Radio |
|---|---|---|---|---|---|---|
| **Coverage:** | | | | | | |
| Learned a lot or some from coverage of conventions | | | | | | |
| High | 52 | 58 | 54 | 61 | 51 | 58 |
| Medium | 62 | 55 | 61 | | 62 | 50 |
| Low | 60 | 59 | 57 | 56 | 58 | 63 |
| Convention coverage helped make a voting decision | | | | | | |
| High | 34 | 34 | 32 | 39 | 36 | 34 |
| Medium | 38 | 31 | 34 | | 33 | 35 |
| Low | 32 | 42 | 45 | 34 | 36 | 37 |
| **Direct vs. Mediated Information** | | | | | | |
| Got most information about conventions from watching them directly | | | | | | |
| High | 72 | 69 | 62 | 81 | 71 | 61 |
| Medium | 65 | 66 | 70 | | 60 | 68 |
| Low | 64 | 68 | 77 | 64 | 70 | 75 |
| Prefer watching conventions without commentary | | | | | | |
| High | 58 | 54 | 50 | 48 | 68 | 54 |
| Medium | 48 | 46 | 58 | | 50 | 51 |
| Low | 56 | 63 | 56 | 56 | 51 | 58 |

N = 494 registered voters.

directly or from news stories or conversations, most voters reported that they got their information directly from the source: 64 percent of voters said that they got most of their information about the conventions from watching them live on television. In comparison, only 23 percent said that they got most of their information from news stories, and only 6 percent reported getting most of their information from conversations with others.

Not surprisingly, those who spent more time listening to radio or reading newspapers were less likely to have gotten most of their information about the conventions from watching them directly. After all, for many people the scheduling constraints of their daily lives led them to miss the television news and seek alternate sources of information. These same constraints could have led them to miss the televised conventions. Those who typically used the television a great deal—including frequent television news users and tabloid television viewers—were more likely (72 vs. 64%) to have gotten most of their information from watching the conventions directly. When we asked voters whether they preferred watching the conventions with or without commentary, about half preferred watching them without commentary. Frequent talk radio listeners were much more likely to prefer unmediated convention coverage (68 vs. 51%); those more likely to appreciate journalistic commentary included elite media users (63 vs. 54%) and those reading newspapers (56 vs. 50%) (see table 7.8).

Is voter dissatisfaction with news commentary one of the factors driving the preference for unmediated coverage? Table 7.9 examines the effect of voters' evaluations on learning and the preference for mediated versus unmediated coverage. We found that those who thought the news was more useful were actually more likely to have been helped in their vote decision by the convention coverage (39 vs. 30%). In most areas, however, those who were critical of the news media were no more or less likely to have learned from the conventions or to have been helped in making their voting decisions. We did find that those who were more critical of the news said that they were much more likely to prefer conventions without commentary. Fully 60 percent of those who thought the news media was unfair and biased said that they preferred conventions without analysis, whereas only 48 percent of those who saw the news as fair wanted unmediated coverage. Similarly, 58 percent of those who thought that the news paid too much

**TABLE 7.9** Effect of Satisfaction on Perceived Learning from Conventions and Media Coverage

| | Watching conventions | | Direct vs. mediated information | |
|---|---|---|---|---|
| | Learned a lot or some | Helped make voting decision | Got most information from watching directly | Prefer conventions without commentary |
| **Media fair and unbiased** | | | | |
| Is fair and unbiased | 59 | 38 | 68 | 48 |
| Unfair and biased | 55 | 33 | 68 | 60 |
| **Attention to strategy** | | | | |
| Not too much | 55 | 41 | 74 | 46 |
| Too much | 57 | 33 | 65 | 58 |
| **Usefulness of news** | | | | |
| Useful | 56 | 39 | 67 | 49 |
| Not useful | 57 | 30 | 69 | 61 |
| **Role of media** | | | | |
| Agree with fewer criticisms | 57 | 36 | 73 | 47 |
| Agree with more criticisms | 56 | 35 | 64 | 60 |

N = 494 registered voters

attention to strategy and tactics preferred unmediated coverage, compared to 46 percent of their less critical counterparts. Of those who thought news was not useful, 61 percent preferred unmediated coverage, but only 49 percent of those finding the news useful preferred unmediated coverage. And 60 percent of those who agreed with criticisms about the role of the media reported that they would prefer convention coverage without journalists' analysis, while only 47 percent of their less critical counterparts said that they preferred to watch the conventions without analysis.

Overall, our findings show that many viewers did pay attention to the conventions despite the fact that they came packaged with journalists' commentary, which many found to be less than satisfactory. In this part of the election season, voters were more likely to use the news if they had the habit of using these media already, and they were only a little more likely to use the different news outlets as a result of greater satisfaction. The perceived fairness of news had the greatest impact on continued use of mainstream media; those who saw mainstream news as focusing too much on strategy tended to use more talk radio.

If criticisms of the media's coverage had little impact on continued use of the news media, they did have an impact on whether voters reported preferring conventions with or without commentary. Perhaps not surprisingly, given voters' criticisms of the news media and the low overall ratings of the new media at this point in the election season, a majority of voters reported preferring unmediated information about the convention.[7]

*Rating Convention Coverage*

Overall, ratings of the convention coverage were relatively high: 64 percent of voters rated coverage of the Republican convention excellent or good, and 71 percent rated coverage of the Democratic convention excellent or good. Table 7.10 shows that individuals were much more likely to give the convention coverage high ratings if they generally saw the news as fair and unbiased (74 vs. 54%, and 80 vs. 67%), and useful (68 vs. 59%, and 80 vs. 67%). In addition, voters were more likely to give positive ratings to the news shows if they learned at least something from the coverage of the conventions: 70 percent of those who learned something from the Republican convention rated media coverage of it as excellent or good, and only 59 percent of those who learned little or nothing gave the news coverage an excellent or good rating.

It appears that, despite the conventions' symbolic role in bringing the primary season to a close and inaugurating the general election, voters

**TABLE 7.10** Effect of Satisfaction with Media Performance on Overall Rating of Media (percent rating media's job in covering conventions excellent or good)

| | Republican Convention | Democratic Convention |
|---|---|---|
| **Media fair and unbiased** | | |
| Is fair and unbiased | 74 | 80 |
| Unfair and biased | 54 | 67 |
| **Attention to strategy** | | |
| Not too much | 66 | 76 |
| Too much | 64 | 73 |
| **Usefulness of news** | | |
| Useful | 68 | 80 |
| Not useful | 59 | 67 |
| **Role of media** | | |
| Agree with fewer criticisms | 69 | 78 |
| Agree with more criticisms | 61 | 71 |
| **How much learned from coverage of conventions** | | |
| A lot/some | 70 | 79 |
| Little or nothing | 59 | 67 |

N = 494 registered voters.

expect to learn from their television viewing. When they do not, they give the media poorer grades. But they do not stop following the news.

## The Debates

Sixty-three percent of registered voters watched the first presidential debate, and 61 percent watched the second one. Surveys of the general population found that only 53 percent of the general public watched the second debate, so it would appear that those not registered to vote were much less likely to follow the second debate (see table 7.2).

This section parallels the first one, asking whether evaluation of the media and habits of use have an impact on whether people watched the debates, whether they learned from watching debates and the media coverage associated with it, and how they evaluated the media coverage of debates. In general, we found that media habits had much larger effects than media evaluation. Like the previous section, we will also show that it is the usefulness of media in providing information to voters that drives their evaluations, although it has a much smaller impact on their continued use of media.

### Media Use Habits

Because the debates are shorter in duration than conventions, we were better able to separate viewing the debates from watching commentary after the debates. Forty-four percent of voters watched commentary immediately after the debates, and 52 percent were exposed to commentary in the following days.

Table 7.11 shows the impact of media habits on whether voters watched the debates. As occurred during the conventions, many more of those who frequently watched television news and elite media (also mostly found on television) watched both debates. Compared to the 58 percent of frequent viewers of television news, only 41 percent of those who infrequently saw TV news watched both debates. And while 69 percent of those who frequently used elite media watched both debates, only 42 percent of those who infrequently used elite media were exposed directly to both debates. During the debates the frequent print media users also were more likely to view both debates. This did not occur during the conventions.

Frequent television and elite media viewers and frequent newspaper readers were more likely to view the commentary that occurred both

**TABLE 7.11** Effect of Media Use Habits on Viewing Debates
(percent who followed debates and debate coverage)

| | Television use | Elite media | Print media | Tabloid TV | Talk radio | Radio |
|---|---|---|---|---|---|---|
| **Percent who watched both debates** | | | | | | |
| High media use | 58 | 69 | 55 | 57 | 58 | 61 |
| Medium | 60 | 47 | 56 | | 51 | 48 |
| Low media use | 41 | 42 | 45 | 53 | 53 | 51 |
| **Percent watched commentary immediately after debates** | | | | | | |
| High | 47 | 58 | 50 | 48 | 35 | 41 |
| Medium | 49 | 33 | 42 | | 48 | 39 |
| Low | 31 | 35 | 32 | 42 | 44 | 49 |
| **Percent watched commentary in the days after debates** | | | | | | |
| High | 57 | 62 | 57 | 50 | 70 | 58 |
| Medium | 55 | 54 | 56 | | 50 | 54 |
| Low | 48 | 44 | 41 | 55 | 49 | 49 |

N = 494 registered voters.

immediately after the debates and in the following days. In contrast to these market segments, the voters who were frequent talk radio and radio news listeners were *less* likely to see the commentary that immediately followed the debates. They were, however, more likely to be exposed to commentary in the days following the debate: 70 percent of frequent talk radio listeners were exposed to commentary in the days after the debates, compared to only 49 percent of those who seldom listened to talk radio. This pattern of debate viewing for the talk radio market segment may reflect not interest but logistics. People who listen frequently to radio news and talk radio may do so because watching television news—or debates on television—does not fit into their schedules.

Unlike the dramatic effects of media habits, most media evaluations appear to have had a much smaller effect on whether or not individuals watched the debates (table 7.12). Those who were critical of the news media were no less likely to watch debates than their less critical counterparts. The only differences were found among those who watched journalists'

TABLE 7.12 Effect of Satisfaction on Watching the Debates and Journalistic Commentary (percent following debates very or somewhat closely; percent at least very interested in campaign)

| | September | October Watched journalistic commentary after debates | | | |
|---|---|---|---|---|---|
| | Interest in campaign | Watched both debates | immediately after | in days after debates | Interest in campaign |
| **Media fair and unbiased** | | | | | |
| Is fair and unbiased | 80 | 57 | 48 | 52 | 78 |
| Unfair and biased | 74 | 50 | 38 | 55 | 73 |
| **Attention to strategy** | | | | | |
| Not too much | 78 | 56 | 44 | 51 | 75 |
| Too much | 76 | 53 | 43 | 55 | 75 |
| **Usefulness of news** | | | | | |
| Useful | 74 | 52 | 46 | 55 | 72 |
| Not useful | 80 | 56 | 39 | 52 | 79 |
| **Role of media** | | | | | |
| Agree with fewer criticisms | 79 | 51 | 44 | 53 | 73 |
| Agree with more criticisms | 75 | 56 | 42 | 54 | 78 |

N = 494 registered voters.

commentary immediately after the debates. As occurred during the conventions phase, perceptions of fairness and lack of bias had an impact, with 48 percent of those who thought that the media was fair and unbiased watching coverage immediately after the debates, and only 38 percent of those who thought news is unfair and biased doing so. No other significant differences between the more and less critical groups were found.

### Using the News

We tracked individuals' use of the news—television, newspaper, radio news and talk radio—during the debates. During this phase of the election cycle, we again found that those who thought the media was fair and unbiased were more likely to follow the mainstream news. Fully 77 percent of those who thought the media was fair and unbiased were frequent users of television news, while only 61 percent of those who thought media was unfair were frequent television news viewers. Similarly, among those who thought the media was fair, a greater percentage were frequent readers of newspapers (66%), and among those who were less critical a smaller fraction (57%) were newspaper readers. Unlike the convention phase of the election, media evaluation had little other impact on continued media use. During the debates, we did not find that those dissatisfied with the fairness or role of the media were more likely to listen to talk radio; nor we did not find as large a tendency of those who thought there was too much strategy to listen less to talk radio (table 7.13).

As with the conventions phase, we again found that those who were critical of television news—a proxy for mainstream news—were more likely to use talk radio (28 vs. 17%) and radio (56 vs. 44%). In contrast, those who thought that television news was fair and unbiased were more likely to watch television news frequently, and somewhat more likely to read newspapers (table 7.14).

Once again, we have shown that those who are less satisfied with certain aspects of media coverage are less likely to use mainstream media, and may be more likely to use alternative sources of information such as talk radio. However, we again found no signs that a movement toward talk radio occurred during the election campaign. Table 7.15 shows that there was little change in media use between panel waves 2 (September) and 3 (October). For television news, 76 percent of voters maintained the same level of use between September and October. For newspaper readers, 74 percent maintained the same level. Somewhat fewer talk radio and radio news listeners maintained the same level of use (54 and 66%, respectively). Across

**TABLE 7.13** Effect of Satisfaction on Media Use (percent using news during debates on every day, several times a week for talk radio)

| | TV News | Newspaper | Talk radio | Radio news |
|---|---|---|---|---|
| **September (Conventions)** | | | | |
| Media fair and unbiased | | | | |
| Is fair and unbiased | 82 | 66 | 21 | 52 |
| Unfair and biased | 74 | 63 | 30 | 55 |
| Attention to strategy | | | | |
| Not too much | 77 | 64 | 31 | 58 |
| Too much | 79 | 64 | 23 | 52 |
| Usefulness of news | | | | |
| Useful | 78 | 65 | 22 | 51 |
| Not useful | 79 | 64 | 29 | 58 |
| Role of media | | | | |
| Agree with fewer criticisms | 81 | 66 | 20 | 53 |
| Agree with more criticisms | 76 | 63 | 30 | 54 |
| **October (Debates)** | | | | |
| Media fair and unbiased | | | | |
| Is fair and unbiased | 77 | 66 | 23 | 49 |
| Unfair and biased | 61 | 57 | 23 | 53 |
| Attention to strategy | | | | |
| Not too much | 70 | 58 | 28 | 54 |
| Too much | 68 | 63 | 21 | 49 |
| Usefulness of news | | | | |
| Useful | 70 | 61 | 21 | 49 |
| Not useful | 68 | 62 | 25 | 53 |
| Role of media | | | | |
| Agree with fewer criticisms | 71 | 61 | 19 | 51 |
| Agree with more criticisms | 67 | 61 | 26 | 51 |

N = 494 registered voters.

the different types of criticisms, we found little consistent evidence that those voters more critical of the media were likely to start listening to talk radio as well (or instead). The data show large amounts of stability in media use, and no apparent explanations for why changes in media use occurred.

Table 7.15 also examines whether individuals changed their primary source of information. Here, again, we found remarkable stability. Fully 76 percent maintained their primary source of information. Those who relied primarily on news media for information in September continued to do so in October; those who relied more on conversations or advertisements maintained the same pattern of information gathering.

**TABLE 7.14** Impact of Criticisms of Mainstream Media on Use of Alternative Sources of Media

|  | TV News | Newspaper | Talk radio | Radio news |
|---|---|---|---|---|
| **September (Conventions)** | | | | |
| Percent that use this media frequently who | | | | |
| See TV news as fair and unbiased | 80 | 66 | 18 | 48 |
| See TV news unfair and biased | 76 | 62 | 31 | 58 |
| **October (Debates)** | | | | |
| Percent that use this media frequently who | | | | |
| See TV news as fair and unbiased | 73 | 64 | 17 | 44 |
| See TV news unfair and biased64 | 64 | 57 | 28 | 56 |

N = 494 registered voters

**TABLE 7.15** Individual-Level Change in Media Use, September to October

|  | TV News | Newspaper | Talk radio | Radio news |
|---|---|---|---|---|
| **Change in media use** | | | | |
| Decrease in use | 16 | 14 | 23 | 19 |
| Same use | 76 | 74 | 54 | 66 |
| Increase in use | 8 | 12 | 23 | 16 |
| **Change in primary source of information** | | | | |
| From news media to conversations/ads | 12 | | | |
| Same | 76 | | | |
| From conversations/ads to news media | 12 | | | |

N = 494 registered voters.

### Learning from Debate Coverage

Among voters as a whole, 53 percent said that they learned a lot or some about the candidates from watching the debates live. Of those who paid attention to postdebate analysis, about the same fraction (58%) said they learned something about the candidates.

Among the different market segments, television news users and elite media users (the very people who were more likely to have seen the debates) were less likely to say they learned more than a little from watching the candidates debate (table 7.16). Similarly, frequent print media users were less likely to say that they learned something from watching the debates live (51% learned a lot or some) than those who read the newspapers less often (60% learned a lot or some). From watching commentary in the days after the debates, elite media viewers were less likely to say they learned much, and talk radio listeners—who did tend to pay attention to commentary in the days after the debate—were less likely to say they learned a lot (50%) than those who seldom listen to talk radio (62% learned a lot or some). We found a similar pattern in the conventions phase of the campaign; it appears that those voters who had high levels of media use were also motivated to watch debates (as they earlier paid attention to the conventions). Yet these same attentive voters apparently gained information from their news exposure, and so were less likely to learn from the campaign events. In 1996, it appears, debates and conventions had little information to offer the attentive voter.

When asked whether they got more information about the debates from watching them directly or from news media or other indirect sources, 54 percent said that they got most of their information about the debates from watching them live on television. The bottom rows of table 7.16 show that voters were more likely to get most of their information from watching debates directly if they were frequent television news and elite media viewers. In contrast, they were less likely to get most of their information from watching debates directly if they were talk radio or radio listeners.

**TABLE 7.16** Effect of Media Use Habits on Perceived Learning from Debates

| | Television use | Elite media | Print media | Tabloid TV | Talk radio | Radio |
|---|---|---|---|---|---|---|
| Learned from direct information | | | | | | |
| Learned a lot or some from watching candidates debate | | | | | | |
| High | 48 | 48 | 51 | 59 | 53 | 47 |
| Medium | 54 | 52 | 49 | | 47 | 56 |
| Low | 55 | 58 | 60 | 50 | 53 | 53 |
| Learned from coverage | | | | | | |
| Learned a lot or some from watching commentary in days after debate | | | | | | |
| High | 60 | 58 | 61 | 62 | 50 | 56 |
| Medium | 57 | 50 | 55 | | 63 | 52 |
| Low | 59 | 70 | 62 | 58 | 62 | 69 |
| Got most information about debates from watching directly (not news/conversations) | | | | | | |
| High | 58 | 60 | 52 | 57 | 49 | 49 |
| Medium | 57 | 55 | 57 | | 51 | 52 |
| Low | 49 | 49 | 58 | 55 | 59 | 57 |

N = 494 registered voters.

In the third wave of the panel study, we looked again to see whether those who were more critical of the media might be less likely to learn from it. Recall that we are separating out groups who are more critical in general (because we asked these media evaluation questions in January) rather than asking people in wave three for their evaluations of contemporaneous media coverage. We found results different from the second wave, where there was little evidence that criticisms affected learning (only perceptions of the usefulness of media had an impact). In the third wave we were able to separate out learning from direct information versus learning from mediated information. We found a stronger relationship for learning from viewing the debates directly. Perceptions of usefulness had a large impact: although 62 percent of those who perceived media as being useful learned a lot or some from watching the debates directly, only 41 percent who thought media coverage was not useful said that they learned a lot (table 7.17). Those who thought media was fair and unbiased and those who thought the media was not paying too much attention to strategy and the horse race were also more likely to have learned from watching the debates directly. There was no evidence that satisfaction with the media had any impact on learning from journalistic commentary after the debates. Nor were those who were more critical more likely to have obtained most of their information about the debates directly.

**TABLE 7.17** Effect of Satisfaction on Perceived Learning from Debates Directly, and from Media Coverage of Debates

| | Learned a lot or some from | | |
| --- | --- | --- | --- |
| | Watching debates directly | Commentary in days after debates | Got most information about debates from watching directly |
| **Media fair and unbiased** | | | |
| Is fair and unbiased | 58 | 51 | 56 |
| Unfair and biased | 46 | 55 | 55 |
| **Attention to strategy** | | | |
| Not too much | 59 | 51 | 58 |
| Too much | 50 | 54 | 55 |
| **Usefulness of news** | | | |
| Useful | 62 | 54 | 55 |
| Not useful | 41 | 52 | 56 |
| **Role of media** | | | |
| Agree with fewer criticisms | 52 | 52 | 55 |
| Agree with more criticisms | 52 | 54 | 56 |

N = 494 registered voters

Overall, we find in the third wave that many viewers did watch the debates, although fewer than in previous election years. Voters were more likely to watch the debates if they had the habit of televised media use; voters' evaluation of the news media, on the other hand, had little impact on their tendency to watch the debates or the commentary that followed. Only perceptions of fairness and unbiasedness had an impact. Voters watched the debates and the commentary afterwards despite their dissatisfaction with aspects of the media's coverage.

We found that, similar to the conventions phase, talk radio and elite news users were less likely to say that they learned from commentary about the debates. Unlike the convention phase, however, during the debates we found that perceptions of the quality of the news had an impact on whether voters thought they had learned from the debates and the coverage of the debates. During the debates, many more voters who thought that the news media was fair and unbiased, many more voters who thought the news media was useful, and many more voters who thought the media did not pay too much attention to the horse race, thought that they had learned from the debates.

### Rating Debate Coverage

Rating of the media's coverage of the debates was fairly positive: 65 percent rated the job the news media did in covering the debates either excellent or good—about the same as the ratings the media got for coverage of the Republican national convention, and slightly lower than the media's ratings for the Democratic convention.

As we found in wave 2 of the panel study, people who learned something from the debates were more likely to give the media a positive rating: 80 percent of those who learned something gave the media positive ratings, and only 56 percent of those who learned little gave a positive assessment (table 7.18). All of the four types of criticisms also had an impact on ratings of the media in wave 3: those who thought the media was fair, those who thought they were not paying too much attention to strategy, those who thought the news was useful, and those who thought the media was not overstepping its role, were all more likely to give the media positive overall ratings for their coverage of the conventions.

Once again, it appears that voters expect to gain information from the efforts they expend in using the news media. When they do not learn, they give the media poorer grades. But even when dissatisfied in some ways, they do not stop following the news.

**TABLE 7.18** Effect of Satisfaction on Overall Media Rating (percent rating media's job in covering debates excellent or good)

| Rating Category | Percentage |
| --- | --- |
| **Media fair and unbiased** | |
| Is fair and unbiased | 80 |
| Unfair and biased | 60 |
| **Attention to strategy** | |
| Not too much | 78 |
| Too much | 66 |
| **Usefulness of news** | |
| Useful | 75 |
| Not useful | 63 |
| **Role of media** | |
| Agree with fewer criticisms | 80 |
| Agree with more criticisms | 62 |
| **How much learned from coverage of conventions** | |
| A lot or some | 80 |
| Little or nothing | 56 |

## The Final Weeks of the General Election

In the final weeks of the election campaign, about 35 percent of voters followed the election very closely, with another 43 percent following the election somewhat closely. This level of interest was somewhat lower than what we found in January (34 percent and 52 percent respectively). Interest declined after the conventions and remained fairly low.

*Following the Election in the Final Weeks*

The final weeks of the election lack a specific series of broadcast events that would allow us to ask more specific questions. But we again found that those who sought information through television, elite media, and the print media were much more likely to have followed the election at least somewhat closely during the final weeks of the election campaign. More frequent television and elite news viewers followed the campaign's final weeks (91% and 89% respectively), whereas fewer low-use individuals did so (64% and 74%). Those who most frequently read newspapers and magazines were more likely to follow the election closely (85%), whereas fewer of those who infrequently opened the pages of periodicals did so (66%). Unlike earlier phases of the campaign, we also found high users of other media—radio, talk radio and tabloid television—to be somewhat more likely to follow the election than their low-use counterparts (table 7.19).

In the final weeks of the election, criticisms of the media had less of an impact than in earlier phases. Individuals who thought the media was biased, or saw it paying too much attention to strategy, were no less likely to follow the campaign in the final weeks (84 vs. 78% and 83 vs. 79%). Similarly, perceptions of the usefulness of the news and the role of the media had no impact (table 7.20). As with earlier phases of the election, we found that media habits had a greater impact than dissatisfaction on whether or

**TABLE 7.19** Effect of Media Use Habits on Following Election Closely in Final Weeks

| | Television use | Elite media | Print media | Tabloid TV | Talk radio | Radio |
|---|---|---|---|---|---|---|
| Percent who followed election very/somewhat closely in final weeks | | | | | | |
| High media use | 91 | 89 | 85 | 88 | 86 | 85 |
| Medium | 85 | 78 | 84 | | 78 | 83 |
| Low media use | 64 | 74 | 66 | 79 | 80 | 76 |

N = 494 registered voters.

**TABLE 7.20** Effect of Satisfaction on Percent Following Election Very or Somewhat Closely

| | October | November |
|---|---|---|
| | Interest in campaign | Follow very closely or somewhat closely in last few weeks |
| Media fair and unbiased | | |
| Is fair and unbiased | 78 | 84 |
| Unfair and biased | 73 | 78 |
| Attention to strategy | | |
| Not too much | 75 | 83 |
| Too much | 75 | 79 |
| Usefulness of news | | |
| Useful | 72 | 81 |
| Not useful | 79 | 80 |
| Role of media | | |
| Agree with fewer criticisms | 73 | 79 |
| Agree with more criticisms | 78 | 82 |

N = 94 registered voters.

not people followed the campaign. Apparently, it is the news–gathering habits of voters, more than their dissatisfaction with aspects of the news, that determine whether or not they will continue to follow the various events that comprise the election campaign.

*Using the News*
During the final weeks of the election, we again found that those who rated the fairness of television news higher are more likely to be frequent TV news viewers (table 7.21). We found that the second wave's finding of

**TABLE 7.21** Effect of Satisfaction on Media Use in Final Weeks of Election (percent using news on every day, several times a week for talk radio)

|  | TV News | Newspaper | Talk radio | Radio news |
|---|---|---|---|---|
| **October** |  |  |  |  |
| Media fair and unbiased |  |  |  |  |
| Is fair and unbiased | 77 | 66 | 23 | 49 |
| Unfair and biased | 61 | 57 | 23 | 53 |
| Attention to strategy |  |  |  |  |
| Not too much | 70 | 58 | 28 | 54 |
| Too much | 68 | 63 | 21 | 49 |
| Usefulness of news |  |  |  |  |
| Useful | 70 | 61 | 21 | 49 |
| Not useful | 68 | 62 | 25 | 53 |
| Role of media |  |  |  |  |
| Agree with fewer criticisms | 71 | 61 | 19 | 51 |
| Agree with more criticisms | 67 | 61 | 26 | 51 |
| **November** |  |  |  |  |
| Media fair and unbiased |  |  |  |  |
| Is fair and unbiased | 80 | 64 | 25 | 51 |
| Unfair and biased | 67 | 63 | 28 | 53 |
| Attention to strategy |  |  |  |  |
| Not too much | 73 | 64 | 30 | 56 |
| Too much | 73 | 63 | 24 | 50 |
| Usefulness of news |  |  |  |  |
| Useful | 74 | 63 | 23 | 51 |
| Not useful | 72 | 64 | 30 | 54 |
| Role of media |  |  |  |  |
| Agree with fewer criticisms | 73 | 65 | 22 | 52 |
| Agree with more criticisms | 73 | 62 | 29 | 52 |

N = 494 registered voters

the impact of dissatisfaction on talk radio listeners was unique. During the final weeks of the campaign, we did not find that those dissatisfied with the fairness or role of the media as a whole were much more likely to listen to talk radio; nor did we find as large a tendency of those who thought there was too much strategy to listen less to talk radio (table 7.21).

Although dissatisfaction with the media as a whole did not have an impact on talk radio use, dissatisfaction with television news specifically did have an impact. We had assumed earlier that television news could serve as a proxy for mainstream news, because it dominates other information sources as U.S. voters' primary source of information. Table 7.22 shows that those satisfied with the fairness of television news were more likely to continue to watch television news, and perhaps more likely to read newspapers, in the final weeks of the election campaign. In contrast, those *dissatisfied* with the fairness of television news were more likely to listen to talk radio or radio.

Once again, these findings should not be taken to imply a large shift in voters' information gathering patterns in the final weeks of the election. Table 7.23 shows remarkable stability in media use over the course of the election cycle. From 80 to 59 percent of media users that we tracked in our panel retained the same level of usage from wave 3 to wave 4. Much smaller percentages increased or decreased their media use between October and November, and there was little systematic correlation between those changes and evaluation of the media. Table 7.23 also shows remarkable stability in voters' primary source of information. Most voters (75%) retained the same overall source of information. If they had used the news media for their primary source in October, they kept using the

**TABLE 7.22** Impact of Criticisms of Mainstream Media on Use of Alternative Sources of Media

|  | TV News | Newspaper | Talk radio | Radio news |
|---|---|---|---|---|
| **October** | | | | |
| Percent that use this media frequently who | | | | |
| See TV news as fair and unbiased | 73 | 64 | 17 | 44 |
| See TV news unfair and biased | 64 | 57 | 28 | 56 |
| **November** | | | | |
| Percent that use this media frequently who | | | | |
| See TV news as fair and unbiased | 77 | 67 | 19 | 47 |
| See TV news unfair and biased | 69 | 60 | 33 | 57 |

N = 494 registered voters.

**TABLE 7.23** Individual-Level Change in Media Use from October to November

|  | TV News | Newspaper | Talk radio | Radio news |
|---|---|---|---|---|
| **Change in media use** |  |  |  |  |
| Decrease in use | 7 | 9 | 18 | 13 |
| Same use | 80 | 80 | 59 | 70 |
| Increase in use | 13 | 11 | 23 | 17 |
| **Change in primary source of information** |  |  |  |  |
| From news media to conversations/ads | 14 |  |  |  |
| Same | 75 |  |  |  |
| From conversations/ads to news media | 11 |  |  |  |
| **Change from TV to newspaper, radio, other as primary source of media information (Wave 2 to Wave 4)** |  |  |  |  |
| Change from TV to other | 14 |  |  |  |
| Same | 70 |  |  |  |
| Change from other to TV | 15 |  |  |  |

N = 494 registered voters.

news media; if they had used conversations or advertisements as their primary source of information then this remained the case in the final weeks of the election. Finally, we see that between wave 3 (September) and wave 4 (November) most voters retained their reliance on the same medium. When asked for their primary source of information in the news, 70 percent said that it remained the same. Those relying on television news kept using the same source; and those relying on newspapers or radio (a much smaller percentage) maintained their reliance on those sources. The final weeks of the election confirm once again our finding that individuals continued to follow the news, despite their dissatisfaction with certain aspects of coverage.

*Rating the Late Election Coverage*

As we discussed in chapter 4, late in the campaign most voters gave the news good ratings for the job they did in covering the presidential campaign: 57 percent gave the news a rating of excellent or good, and 54 percent gave the media a grade of A or B. Once again, we found a strong relationship between how much individuals think they learned and their rating of the news. Our last subjective assessment of knowledge comes from the third wave of the election, and we found that those who thought they learned a lot or some from coverage of the debates were much more likely to give the media an overall rating of excellent or good: 71 percent of those who thought they learned something from debates coverage gave the media a rating of excellent or good, while only 51 percent of those who thought they learned little or nothing from coverage of the debates did so. Similarly, 63 percent of those who thought that they had learned something from debates coverage gave the media a rating of A or B, while only 45 percent of those who learned little or nothing from debates coverage did the same (table 7.24).

Satisfaction with the news media also had an impact on the final evaluation that voters gave to the news media. Seventy-two percent of those who thought the media was fair and unbiased gave it a rating of excellent or good, but only 48 percent of those who perceived news to be unfair or biased did so, a gap of 24 percentage points. A similar gap (24 percentage points) was found between those who saw the media as fair and unfair when we asked voters to grade the media. Usefulness of the media also had an impact on voters' evaluations of the news media. Compared to those who

**TABLE 7.24** Effect of Specific Criticisms of the Media on Overall Rating of the Media

| | Rating | |
|---|---|---|
| | Excellent or good | Grade: A or B |
| Media fair and unbiased | | |
| Is fair and unbiased | 72 | 66 |
| Unfair and biased | 48 | 42 |
| Attention to strategy | | |
| Not too much | 64 | 57 |
| Too much | 58 | 53 |
| Usefulness of news | | |
| Useful | 67 | 62 |
| Not useful | 52 | 44 |
| Role of media | | |
| Agree with fewer criticisms | 63 | 63 |
| Agree with more criticisms | 57 | 46 |
| How much learned from coverage of conventions | | |
| A lot/some | 63 | 54 |
| Little or nothing | 59 | 56 |
| How much learned from coverage of debates | | |
| A lot/some | 71 | 63 |
| Little or nothing | 51 | 45 |

N = 494 registered voters.

perceived the news to lack usefulness, those who thought the news was useful were 15 percentage points more likely to give it an excellent or good rating, and 18 percentage points more likely to give it a rating of A or B. Dissatisfaction with election news made voters less likely to give the media a grade of A or B, and slightly less likely to give the media a rating of excellent or good.

## Conclusion

Chapters 2 and 3 led us to expect that the specific criticisms voters have of the news media might not have an impact on whether they continued to use the news over the course of the campaign. These expectations were confirmed. Overall, the habits of media use are what drive voters to continue to use the news. According to our survey findings, of all of the ways in which voters are dissatisfied with the news media, only perceptions of bias have an impact on continued use of the media, and this impact is small relative to the impact of habits on media use.

The evidence presented in this chapter supports the contentions that voters' motivations for media use come from reasons that have little to do with the quality of coverage. They might watch television for entertainment, listen to the radio to pass the time, or read the newspaper to confirm their prior beliefs. But the criticisms that they have of the media— its lack of success in focusing on the issues at the expense of strategy, its failure to project itself as an unbiased source of information, and its unwanted new role in electoral campaigns—usually do not translate into a tendency to change the channel, turn off the television and pick up a newspaper, or simply tune out altogether.

This is not to say that voters' criticisms have no effect. More voters who had specific criticisms of the news media reported preferring to watch the conventions directly, rather than watching the conventions accompanied by journalists' commentary. During the debates, more voters who thought the news media did not focus too much on strategy and the horse race, more voters who thought the news was generally fair and unbiased, and more voters who thought the news was useful reported learning more from their exposure to the news media. In addition, at all phases of the campaign, specific criticisms of the news media had a significant impact on overall ratings of the news media. Criticisms matter to voters, but they do not translate into behavior.

This suggests one reason why mass media continues to produce news that dissatisfies the voters: The market mechanism that would give news organizations an incentive to change does not work. Without lower ratings impacting these organizations' advertising revenues, media organizations may be left with a professional desire for more substantive content but they may also perceive themselves to be constrained by their bottom line to continue coverage the way it is.

# 8

Conclusion

The main findings of this book are twofold. First, although voters are generally satisfied with the news media, especially as the presidential campaign progresses, they have a long list of specific criticisms of the news media that reflect many aspects of coverage that have come under fire by scholars. Second, this dissatisfaction is not accompanied by infrequent media use. We do not find that criticism of the news comes only from those who do not use it. Nor, disturbingly, do we find that criticism of the news media has a major impact on changes in media use over the course of the campaign. Without the latter, there appears to be no mechanism that will lead the news media to better satisfy the preferences of the U.S. voter.

The most important finding of this book is that voters share many, though not all, of political communication scholars' criticisms of election news. In particular, we noted in chapter 4 that voters were skeptical of the conduct of the mass media, in particular the process by which the media gathers and reports news and the perceived tendency of the mass media to interfere with the election process. Many voters perceive a tendency of the press to give an advantage to frontrunners. In addition, voters think that the media have too much control in defining campaign issues, and lead candidates to avoid issues and perform for the news cameras.

We examined the extent to which the public thinks the media are fair and unbiased. Scholars, who have looked for patterns of ideological bias across many elections, have generally concluded that the content of the news does not display a partisan or ideological bias (Lichter and Noyes 1996:9–16). In some elections, the tendency of the media to focus on strategy as an explanation for performance in the horse race polls, has given advantage to Republicans in some cases and Democrats in others. Media consideration of candidates' viability leads the news media at some times to favor the runner-up (while criticizing the trailing candidate's campaign organization and strategic decisions at other times) also leads them to favor the Republican candidates at some times, and the Democrats at others. In contrast to the conclusions of evenhandedness by scholars, however, we find that in 1996 voters *were* likely to see bias in the media. Especially for Republicans and some independents, the news media were thought to have a liberal bias. Like dissatisfaction with the role of the media, this could have ramifications for voters' overall evaluation of the news media, their trust in the news media, and their continued use of it to gather information.

Finally, we showed that voters turn a skeptical eye to the usefulness of the news, the extent to which the news pays attention to strategy, and the extent to which the media is perceived to be overstepping its bounds in its role as a democratic institution. Scholars have shown that the news contains a great deal of coverage of strategy and the horse race; the public perceives this as well. An increasing proportion of the public thought this way as the 1996 campaign wore on. Most voters on our panel also were dissatisfied with the media's tendency to air a great many stories that focused on candidates' personalities. Finally, most voters thought that there was too much coverage of strategy and tactics in the campaigns.

In contrast, our voter panel found too little coverage of candidates' issue positions and third party candidates, and too little information regarding how the outcome of the election might affect them. Not all voters thought this, of course, and those who used different types of media intensively differed somewhat in their evaluations of the usefulness of the media.

These criticisms do not necessarily imply low overall evaluations of the news media for many voters. Although voters' overall evaluations of the media were lower at the beginning of the election season, their evaluations improved as the campaign season progressed. One possible cause for the improvement in voters' overall rating of the news media was that, by the end of the campaign, most voters reported that they had received the information they needed to vote. It may be that ratings improved once the news media had (finally) satisfied this most basic demand.

The second main finding of this study is that many U.S. voters use a great deal of information sources when they follow the presidential campaign. The implication of this finding is that the news media are, de facto, the institution that voters rely on for current information, education, and encouragement during an election. When the news media fail in their duties, democracy suffers.

We found that many voters rely on the news, but also that at least some individuals in the electorate cast their net wide indeed, using a diverse variety of media to gather information. Others rely on the mainstream media, and still others have the habit of heavily using specialty sources of information such as elite media (to the exclusion of many other sources of information), or talk radio. Personal tastes and habits, enforced by the schedules of peoples' daily lives (such as needing to spend a lot of time in the car with the radio on), appear to have the most important impact on which news media individuals use. In addition, we suggest (see chapter 3) that people who perceive the outcome of the election to be more important to them—those for whom the benefits of gathering information are greater—tend to use the news more. We found more frequent use of the news among those who have voted before and who have higher levels of political information at the beginning of the campaign. Presumably, for those individuals the costs of making sense of the news is less. Finally, we showed that partisanship has only an inconsistent role to play in whether or not people use the news.

If our survey results suggest that factors such as convenience, personal taste, and political experience drive voters' use of the news, then we implicitly leave little role for the impact of the perceived quality of the news on whether voters continue to use the news. Chapter 7 shows that most types of voter dissatisfaction have little impact on media use. Turnover tables suggest that, for most voters, dissatisfaction with the news does not lead them to use the news less as the campaign goes on. (This may be because, in 1996, there was nowhere else for voters to turn for information.) Instead, it is their already established patterns of news use, described in chapter 2, that have a greater impact on who will watch the political party conventions and the associated news coverage, who will watch the debates and the attendant commentary, and who will watch the news in the final weeks of the campaign.

This does not mean that dissatisfaction has no impact: voters who perceive the news to be ideologically biased are a little less likely to use the news. But this tendency was already present in February 1996, and we did not find that those who perceived the news to be biased reduced their frequency of viewing from one wave of the panel study to the next. Voters who perceive bias may have adjusted their viewing habits before the election began, and then maintained those patterns of media use throughout the course of the election campaign.

Specific criticisms of the news media have other consequences, as well: they reduce voters' perceptions of learning from the news media used, they appear to make voters more likely to prefer unmediated coverage of events like conventions and debates, and they lower voters' overall ratings of the news media. But in their basic viewing behavior, voters tend to remain stable, gathering the news as tenaciously as ever, wading trough coverage perceived to be flawed, and ultimately (for most of them) gaining the information they need to cast their vote. In sum, negative evaluations do not affect overall use of the news media in the short term, which is the time frame that audience researchers use for monitoring ratings. In fact, specific evaluations even have a relatively small impact on overall evaluations by the end of the election season, once voters have done the work needed to gather the information they need.

To summarize, we find that voters start the campaign with relatively low overall evaluations of the news, but by the end of the election season those evaluations have, for the most, part risen. Nevertheless, voters have several specific criticisms of the news media, many jibing with criticisms made in scholarly work. We find, however, that voters who are less satisfied with the media are not less likely to continue to use the news media, at least over the course of a single presidential campaign.

What are the implications of our findings? The news media, as a political institution, gets its feedback from voters through the market. As often as journalists, editors, publishers, and producers call attention to the First Amendment's protection of the independence of the news media, they point to the need of the news media to raise the revenues needed to cover their costs and satisfy their stockholders. Revenues come from advertising, and attracting advertisers depends on retaining a mass audience. If voters do not display their dissatisfaction with their feet (or their remote controls and radio dials), then news organizations do not have a powerful incentive to improve the content of the news or to improve the way they conduct themselves in elections.

For the most part, we found that attitudes of dissatisfaction do have an impact on overall ratings; but dissatisfaction does not have an effect on behavior in the short term. Voters who dislike certain aspects of coverage are less likely to give the media a positive rating; but they are not less likely to use the media over the course of a few weeks or months. In addition, when dissatisfaction (specifically, perceptions of bias) does have an impact on media use, this impact does not appear to occur incrementally.

It seems that those who perceived political bias in the media had already changed their viewing habits in the months or years before the 1996 election began. Indeed, aggregate trends in Nielsen ratings have shown a long-term decline in ratings for the networks, and a rise in ratings of many niche providers of the news. Many attribute this to an increase in programming options for viewers. Even if dissatisfaction did contribute to the decline, audience researchers focus on the short term, so any effect that dissatisfaction had on ratings over the long term would be missed in the focus on the multitude of smaller changes in the short term.

It would appear that even if dissatisfaction does influence viewers' habits in the long run, audience researchers working for news organizations will not detect the incremental changes in viewership that might be due to perceived bias in the news, or because voters are tired of coverage of strategy and the candidates' private lives.

It looks as if media organizations have learned the lessons of the short term. Sometimes they focus on coverage that will increase ratings such as scandals. But they may be missing opportunities, potential viewers who have changed their viewing behavior because of perceived political bias and been lost over the long run. A focus on substantive issues might bring these same voters back—but this is a long-term proposition.

The lessons learned from this study are important for democracy, but might also be relevant to policy makers. Proposals of free air time, for example, might be targeted toward more direct information and less information that is mediated through journalists. The lessons we have learned also should be pondered by journalists, editors, and producers. Although our findings do not suggest that the incremental workings of the market will solve the problems of voter dissatisfaction with the news media, they do suggest longer-term market opportunities for the news media. For example, our findings summarized in chapter 2 suggest that niche providers, including the elite media (the *NewsHour* with Jim Lehrer, the Sunday Morning talk shows, *Inside Politics*, National Public Radio, and C-SPAN), provide information to a significant proportion of the electorate. To these providers, we suggest that they market their offerings more aggressively. They might begin by expanding their distribution networks without changing their content to emulate the networks. To the sponsors of these shows, we suggest that they provide the revenues needed to support such an experiment.

To the mainstream news, we suggest that they focus not only on ratings but on customer satisfaction. Our findings summarized in chapter 4 suggest that voters do find the information they need to decide how to vote, and that this may be a reason why overall ratings of the news rise as the election season progresses. But we also found (see chapter 5) that voters get this information from a source they perceive to be ideologically biased. Mainstream news sources could experiment with different formats, perhaps separating analysis and interpretation from description of events, and separating analysis of strategy from the reporting of issue positions (Jamieson 1992).

We suggested in chapter 6 that, despite voters' perceptions that they get the information they need, they also think that they are given too much analysis of strategy and too little information about issues. Mainstream news organizations could experiment with changes in the content of the news, giving more coverage to issues and substance. Changes in format could be tried, as well. Rather than leading with stories about the horse race, for example, the news media could lead with stories about issues. News organizations could see whether changes such as these result in changes in the perception that they are ideologically biased and too focused on strategy. But owners should not expect an immediate, incremental impact. Viewers' expectations and viewing habits are difficult to change in the short term (Neuman 1991).

Whether such experiments would work, we cannot say. Conventional wisdom would suggest that the market might not respond to an increase in substance. Viewers might not take advantage of an increase in the number of outlets for elite media, which give political elites a greater chance to directly air their views. Viewers might tune out mainstream sources that de-emphasized strategy or separated analysis from coverage of the facts. Those voters who call for more substance might not watch, listen to, or read news that features more substance (Bower 1973). We suggest, however, that experiments such as these might find a receptive audience among part of the electorate in the long term. If not, a highly publicized attempt by the news media to respond to the voters' dissatisfaction might, by itself, have an impact on voters' current perceptions of the news.

If news organizations do not respond to the voters' criticisms, they may leave themselves vulnerable to competition, as they have in the past. Our surveys have shown that the perennial predictions by political scientists that the Internet will emerge as a significant factor in political information and discourse may be coming true. Our panel data figures on Internet use to gather political information are extremely low—5 percent of voters at the beginning of the campaign and 8 percent at the end of the campaign. But Internet use may have begun to rise during this campaign, and may prove to be a more significant factor in the next presidential election. Much of the low use of the Internet is due to limited access, that is, a limit to the number of connections, not to the percent of the public that uses computers. Changes in software to incorporate networking, improvements in electronic transfer rates, as well as generational replacement, may allow growth in Internet use for gathering political information. If voters remain dissatisfied, and if Internet content remedies some of the perceived problems of the news media, then an increasing number of voters may, over the long term, switch from a primary reliance on traditional sources of media. Perhaps even more likely, voters may use information on the World Wide Web as an additional source of information. It may then be the case that news organizations will feel the impact of voters' negative evaluations on their bottom lines.

# notes

## 1. Campaigns Are Unthinkable, Save in Terms of the News Media

1. These data are drawn from a Media Studies Center/University of Connecticut national voter survey (N=1,000) conducted in November 1996.

2. As we discuss in chapter 2, one reason this occurs is that the news media serve several purposes. Besides providing information, they view themselves as providing entertainment. To the extent that a news organization's audience tunes in for entertainment rather than for information, a news organization's ratings may remain high, yet it will not be contributing to the enlightenment of the electorate.

3. At interview times one through three, respondents who said they were planning on registering before the election were also included.

## 2. Media Use in the 1996 Campaign

1. See Rosengren, Wenner, and Palmgreen (1985) and Garramone (1985). For summaries of uses and gratifications theories, see Graber (1993:212–214) and Owen (1991:3–10).

2. This habit of getting information from news media is part of a larger tendency of Americans to devote a considerable amount of time to overall media use—television, radio, and newspapers (Neuman 1991).

3. See Neuman and Pool (1986) for data on overall television use.

4. This could reflect the differences in media use between voters and the general public.

5. For many people, media use is both habitual and casual. People often watch or listen to the news while driving, eating, washing, talking, or reading (see Neuman 1986, 1991; and Graber 1993:218).

## 3. Explaining Media Use

1. For a discussion of costs and benefits in political participation, see Rosenstone and Hansen 1993.

2. Others have found that those with greater interest in the campaign are more likely to participate in other aspects of the political process (Verba and Nie 1972).

3. Fiorina (1981:chapter 3) had similar expectations—he thought he would find retrospective voting more common among those with less political information. His expectations were not met.

4. Rosenstone and Hansen (1993), for example, consider the efforts of elites to recruit participation in politics. Media organizations, through their advertising and strategies of news coverage, do the same. Explanations such as these, however, are beyond the scope of our analysis.

5. The first question was asked on the baseline survey; the second question was asked in wave 2. Some of the differences between the two questions may be due to changes in opinion between January and July 1996, which makes the relationship between the two variables weaker than it would otherwise be.

6. Chi-square(3)=19.2.

7. Zaller focuses on reception—understanding the news—rather than use. He finds that those with moderate levels of political knowledge are more likely to receive the news (and so change their attitudes) than those with little knowledge. Those with higher levels of knowledge are also likely to receive the news, but they also may have a greater ability to resist the messages contained in the news.

8. Two contrasting views of partisanship are Campbell et al. (1960) and Fiorina (1981).

9. It is worth noting, however, that there were few strong partisans who cared little about the outcome of the election (N=30). Conclusions drawn about these individuals should be treated with caution.

### 4. Scratching the Surface: Overall Ratings of Election Coverage

1. The survey was commissioned by the Freedom Forum Newseum and conducted by the University of Connecticut. The telephone survey of 1,500 U.S. adults was conducted in February 1997.

2. Table 4.3 shows that Democrats offered substantially higher ratings of the news media than did Republicans, particularly late in the election campaign. Partisan differences in perceptions of political bias are likely to be important contributing factors to these differences. This issue is addressed in chapter 5.

3. Both the Pew Center study and the Media Studies Center study asking these items were conducted within one week of election day, November 5. Both studies included a sample of recontacted respondents who indicated, prior to election day, that they would vote on election day. Wording of the Pew Center item was: "Students are often given the grades A, B, C, D, or Fail to describe the quality of their work. Looking back over the campaign, what grade would you give to each of the following groups for the way they conducted themselves in the campaign ... the press." Wording for the Media Studies Center item was: "If you had to give the media a grade for their coverage of the campaign, would you give an A, B, C, D, or F?"

### 5. Tilting Left: Perceptions of Political Bias in Election Coverage

1. Other factors that need to be explored include the ways in which information is processed by journalists (Lichter, Rothman, and Lichter 1986), the influence of professional norms of journalists (Weaver and Wilhoit 1996), and the ideology of gatekeepers such as editors and producers (Graber 1980).

2. For example, when asked to name the *people* that most influence whether a journalist thinks a story is newsworthy, the journalists were most likely to name those who were responsible for their training (73%) or their supervisors (51%). These same authors noted journalists' perceptions that they have freedom—albeit declining somewhat—to select stories as evidence that journalists have freedom to choose stories and to emphasize what they want(Weaver and Wilhoit 1996).

3. The Media Studies Center-University of Connecticut survey of members of Congress was conducted by mail in November and December of 1995. One hundred fifty-five members completed and returned the questionnaire.

4. For example, a survey conducted by Louis Harris and Associates for the Center for Media and Public Affairs (November 1996) found 75 percent saying that it is very important for the news media to hold public officials accountable. This survey also found that 67 percent endorsed the media function of protecting the public from abuses of power.

5. From a November 1996 national voter survey conducted by Fox News and Opinion Dynamics.

6. An October 1996 Fox News and Opinion Dynamics survey showed that 69 percent of all voters thought that TV reporters tried to influence the election outcome. Sixty-one percent of Democrats, 67 percent of independents, and 78 percent of Republicans thought this way.

7. A Fox News Opinion Dynamics survey of voters in October 1996 asked voters whether news coverage tipped to the left or the right, politically. In this item, respondents were not offered the option of saying coverage did not tip in either direction. The survey found that 41 percent thought coverage tipped to the left, 20 percent said it tipped to the right, and 39 percent volunteered that coverage was neutral.

8. These data are from wave 4 (November) of the voter panel study.

9. This is the sample base upon which the mean scores and the percentages responding "6" and "7" are based.

### 6. Evaluations of News Content and News Sources

1. These data are from "Campaign News Coverage Down from '92," Annenberg Public Policy School press release, October 15, 1996.

2. Annenberg Public Policy Center press release "1996 Better or Worse," November 4, 1996; Center for Media and Public Affairs press release "Campaign '96 Final," November 1996.

3. This finding is from an item included on the February wave of the voter panel study.

4. Twenty-four percent of TV-dependent voters were very interested in the horse race and another 38 percent were somewhat interested. About the same

percentage of newspaper-dependent voters were very interested(22%) or somewhat interested(42%) in the horse race, and 19 percent of radio-dependent voters were very interested and 54 percent were somewhat interested.

5. Here, level of interest in news about candidate positions may be in part responsible for the perceptions of "too little" focus on issues. Seventy-seven percent of TV-dependent voters were very interested in issues, compared to 82 percent of newspaper-dependents, and 91 percent of those relying mostly on radio.

6. Center for Media and Public Affairs press release "Campaign '96 Final" November 1996.

### 7. The Consequences of Poor Media Performance

1. Of course, the effectiveness of elections can be limited by their lack of frequency and the strategic behavior of incumbents and challengers.

2. Ansolabehere et al. (1994) found that negative campaigning did reduce voter turnout. Ansolabehere and Iyengar (1995) extended this analysis and found that all partisan groups viewing negative advertisements were a little less likely to vote, and that independents were much less likely to turn out.

3. The additive index was constructed from fourteen questions about perceptions of fairness and bias in campaign coverage. Each question focused on a particular media outlet. Questions had the following wording: "I'm going to read the names of some sources of information. For each, please tell me how fair and unbiased you think presidential campaign coverage is from that source. Use a scale of 1 to 7, where 1 means that you think that source is not at all fair and unbiased and 7 means it is completely fair and unbiased." Questions were asked about network and local newscasts, the Lehrer *NewsHour,* Sunday morning political talk shows, *Larry King Live!,* Rush Limbaugh, local talk radio, commercial all-news radio, CNN news, programs on C-SPAN, local newspaper, the *New York Times,* weekly news magazines, and the Internet.

4. This additive index was created from three questions of the form: "In general, do you think the news media devote too much attention, too little attention, or about the right amount of attention to stories on . . ." (a) which candidates are ahead and which ones are behind, (b) the personal lives of candidates, (c) campaign strategies and tactics."

5. The usefulness of the news index was created by summing responses to these questions: "Please tell me whether you agree or disagree with each of the following statements. First [insert subject] do you agree or disagree with this? Probe: Do you agree or disagree strongly or mildly? . . ." (a) News media coverage of presidential candidates is often confusing and unclear. (b) Media coverage of the presidential campaign helps me to make up my mind about who to vote for."

6. The role of the media index was created by summing responses to these questions: "Please tell me whether you agree or disagree with each of the following statements. First [insert subject] do you agree or disagree with this? Probe: Do you agree or disagree strongly or mildly? . . ." (a) The news media have too much control in defining the issues of the campaign.(b) Because of media coverage,

presidential candidates do not focus on important issues but perform for journalists and news cameras instead.(c) The news media give an undue advantage to front-running candidates because they focus on those in the lead at the expense of those behind in the polls.(d) The way the media cover presidential candidates discourages good people from running for president.

7. It is interesting to note, however, that users of elite media and newspaper readers were more likely than others to prefer mediated to unmediated coverage.

# bibliography

Abel, Elie. 1981. "The First Word." In Elie Abel, ed., *What's News*, 1, 3–9. San Francisco: Institute for Contemporary Studies.

Abramowitz, A. I., D. J. Lanoue, and S. Ramesh. 1988. "Economic Conditions, Causal Attributions, and Political Evaluations in the 1984 Presidential Election." *Journal of Politics* 50:848–63.

Abramson, Jeffrey B., Christopher Arterton, and Gary Orren. 1988. *The Electronic Commonwealth: The Impact of New Media Technologies on Democratic Politics*. New York: Basic Books.

Adams, William C., and Paul H. Ferber. 1977. "Television Interview Shows: The Politics of Visibility." *Journal of Broadcasting* 21:141–52.

Adatto, Kiku. 1990. *Sound Bite Democracy: Network Evening News Presidential Campaign Coverage, 1968 and 1988*. Politics and Public Policy Research Paper R-2. Harvard University: Joan Shorenstein Barone Center on the Press, John F. Kennedy School of Government.

Agranoff, Robert. 1976. *The New Style in Election Campaigns*. Boston: Hollbrook Press.

Aldrich, J. 1980. *Before the Convention: Strategies and Choices in Presidential Nomination Campaigns*. Chicago: University of Chicago Press.

Anderson, Kristi, and Stuart Thorson. 1989. "Public Discourse or Strategic Game? Changes in Our Conception of Elections." *Studies in American Political Development* 3:264.

Ansolabehere, Stephen, and Shanto Iyengar. 1995. *Going Negative*. New York: Free Press.

Ansolabehere, Stephen, Shanto Iyengar, and Adam Simon. 1994. "Does Attack Advertising Demobilize the Electorate?" *American Political Science Review* 88:829–38.

Arterton, Christopher F. 1984. *Media Politics: The News Strategies of Presidential Campaigns*. Lexington, MA: D. C. Heath.

Asher, Herb, and Mike Barr. 1994. "Popular Support of Congress and its Members." In Thomas E. Mann and Norman J. Ornstein, eds., *Congress, the Press and the Public,* 15–43. Washington, DC: Brookings.

Bartels, Larry M. 1985. "Expectations and Preferences in Presidential Nominating Campaigns." *American Political Science Review* 79:804–15.

———. 1988. *Presidential Primaries and the Dynamics of Public Choice.* Princeton, NJ: Princeton University Press.

Behr, Roy L., and Shanto Iyengar. 1985. "Television News, Real-world Cues, and Changes in the Public Agenda." *Public Opinion Quarterly* 49:38–57.

Bennett, W. Lance. 1988. *News: The Politics of Illusion,* 2d ed. New York: Longman.

Berelson, Bernard F., Paul R. Lazarsfeld, and William N. McPhee. 1954. *Voting: A Study of Opinion Formation in a Presidential Campaign.* Chicago: University of Chicago Press.

Bibby, John F. 1992. *Politics, Parties and Elections in America.* Chicago: Nelson-Hall.

Blume, Keith. 1985. *The Presidential Election Show: Campaign '84 and Beyond on the Nightly News.* South Hadley, MA: Bergin & Garvey.

Bogart, Leo. 1984. "The Public's Use And Perception of Newspapers." *Public Opinion Quarterly* 48:709–19.

Bolce, Louis, Gerald De Maio and Douglas Muzzio. 1996. "Dial-in Democracy: Talk Radio and the 1994 Election." *Political Science Quarterly* 111(3):457–81.

Bower, Robert T. 1973. *Television and the Public.* New York: Holt, Rinehart and Winston.

Brady, Henry E., and Richard Johnston. 1987. "What's The Primary Message: Horse Race or Issue Journalism." In Gary R. Orren and Nelson W. Polsby, eds., *Media and Momentum.* Chatham, NJ: Chatham House.

Broh, C. Anthony. 1980. "Horse-race journalism: Reporting the Polls in the 1976 Election." *Public Opinion Quarterly* 44:514–29.

———. 1983. "Presidential Preference Polls and Network News." In William C. Adams, ed., *Television Coverage of the 1980 Presidential Campaign.* Norwood, NJ: Ablex.

———. 1987. "A Horse of a Different Color." Washington, DC: Joint Center for Political Studies.

Buchanan, Bruce. 1990. *Electing a President: The Markle Commission Report on Campaign '88.* Austin: University of Texas Press.

Campbell, Angus, Philip E. Converse, Warren E. Miller, and Donald E. Stokes. 1960. *The American Voter.* New York: Wiley.

Cannon, Lou. 1997. "The Socialization of Reporters," in Shanto Iyengar and Richard Reeves, eds., *Do the Media Govern? Politicians, Voters and Reporters in America.* Thousand Oaks, CA: Sage.

Carey, John. 1976. "How Media Shape Campaigns." *Journal of Communication* 26:50–57.

Ceaser, James W., and Andrew E. Busch. 1997. *Losing to Win: The 1996 Elections in American Politics.* New York: Rowman and Littlefield.

Chaffee, S. H., and J. Dennis. 1979. "Presidential Debates: an Empirical Assessment."

In A. Ranney ed., *The Past and Future of Presidential Debates.* Washington, DC: American Enterprise Institute.

Chester, Edward W. 1969. *Radio, Television and American Politics.* New York: Sheed and Ward.

Clancy, Maura, and Michael Robinson. 1985. "General Election Coverage, Part I." In Michael J. Robinson and Austin Ranney, eds., *The Mass Media in Campaign '84.* Washington DC: American Enterprise Institute.

Clarke, Peter, and Eric Fredin. 1978. "Newspapers, Television, and Political Reasoning." *Public Opinion Quarterly* 42:143–60.

Columbia Broadcasting System (CBS). 1988. "Television Coverage of the 1988 Democratic Nomination For President of the United States."

Converse, Philip E. 1964. "The Nature of Belief Systems in Mass Publics." In David Apter, ed., *Ideology and Discontent,* 206—61. New York: Free Press.

———. 1966. "Information flow and the stability of partisan attitudes." In Angus Campbell, Phillip Converse, Warren E. Miller, and Donald E. Stokes, eds., *Elections and the Political Order,* 136—57. New York: Wiley.

Cook, Timothy E. 1989. *Making Laws and Making News: Media Strategies in the U.S. House of Representatives.* Washington, DC: Brookings Institution.

Crespi, Irving. 1980. "Polls as Journalism." *Public Opinion Quarterly* 44:462–76.

———. 1988. *Pre-Election Polling: Sources of Accuracy and Error.* New York: Russell Sage.

———. 1989. *Public Opinion, Polls, and Democracy.* Boulder, CO: Westview.

Crotty, W., and J. S. Jackson, III. 1985. *Presidential Primaries and Nominations.* Washington, DC: Congressional Quarterly Press.

Cundy, Donald T. 1986. "Political Commercials and Candidate Image: The Effect Can Be Substantial." In Linda L. Kaid, Dan Nimmo, and Keith R. Sanders, eds., *New Perspectives on Political Advertising.* Carbondale: Southern Illinois University Press.

Dautrich, Kenneth, and Thomas Hartley. 1997. "The Role of Pre-election Polls in the 1996 United States Presidential Campaign." In Frederick Turner and Friedrich Welsch, eds., *Opinion publica y elecciones en America.* Caracas: Nueva Sociedad.

Dautrich, Kenneth. "The Electorate Assesses Media Performance." In Regina Dougherty, ed., *America at the Polls, 1996.* Storrs, CT: Roper Center.

Delli Carpini, Michael X., and Scott Keeter. 1996. *What Americans Know About Politics.* New Haven: Yale University Press.

Diamond, Edwin, and Stephen Bates. 1984. *The Spot: The Rise of Political Advertising on Television.* Cambridge, MA: MIT Press.

Downs, Anthony. 1954. *An Economic Theory of Democracy.* New York: Harper.

Drew, Dan, and David Weaver. 1991. "Voter Learning in the 1988 Presidential Election: Did the Debates and the Media Matter?" *Journalism Quarterly* 68: 27–37.

Dye, Thomas R., and L. Harmon Zeigler. 1983. *American Politics in the Media Age.* Monterey, CA: Brooks/Cole.

Efron, Edith. 1971. *The News Twisters.* Los Angeles: Nash.

Enelow, J., and M. J. Hinich. 1981. "A New Approach to Voter Uncertainty in The Downsian Spatial Model." *American Journal of Political Science* 25:483–93.

Epstein, Edward Jay. 1975. *Between Fact and Fiction: The Problem of Journalism.* New York: Vintage Books.

Feldman, Stanley, and Lee Sigelman. 1985. "The Political Impact of Prime Time Television." *Journal of Politics* 47:556–78.

Fiorina, Morris P. 1981. *Retrospective Voting in American National Elections.* New Haven : Yale University Press.

Gamson, William A. 1992. *Talking Politics.* New York: Cambridge University Press.

Gans, Herbert J. 1980. *Deciding What's News: A Study of CBS Evening News, NBC Nightly News, Newsweek and Time.* New York: Vintage Books.

Garramone, Gina M. 1985. "Motivation and Political Information Processing: Extending the Gratifications Approach." In Sidney Kraus and Richard Perloff, eds., *Mass Media and Political Thought.* Beverly Hills, CA: Sage.

Geer, J. G. 1988. "The Effects of Presidential Debates on the Electorate's Preference for Candidates." *American Politics Quarterly* 16:486–501.

Gelman, Andrew, and Gary King. 1993. "Why are American Presidential Election Campaign Polls so Variable When Votes Are so Predictable?" *British Journal of Political Science* 23:409–51.

Gollin, Albert E. 1987. "Polling and the News Media." *Public Opinion Quarterly* 51:S86–S94.

Graber, Doris A. 1976. "Press and TV as Opinion Resources in Presidential Campaigns." *Public Opinion Quarterly* 40:285–303.

——. 1980. *Mass Media and American Politics.* Washington DC: Congressional Quarterly Press.

——. 1988. *Processing the News: How People Tame the Information Tide.* Lanham, MD: University Presses of America.

——. 1993. *Mass Media and American Politics,* 4th edition. Washington DC: CQ Press.

Graziano, Cecile, and Kristin McGrath. 1986. "Measuring the Concept of Credibility." *Journalism Quarterly* 63:451–62.

Hallin, Daniel C. 1990. "Sound Bite News." In Gary R. Orren, ed., *Blurring the lines.* New York: Free Press.

Hertsgaard, Mark. 1988. *On Bended Knee: The Press and the Reagan Presidency.* New York: Farrar, Straus, Giroux.

Hess, Stephen. 1981. *Washington Reporters.* Washington, DC: Brookings.

——. 1986. *The Ultimate Insiders: U.S. Senators in the National Media.* Washington, DC: Brookings.

——. 1988. *The Presidential Campaign,* 3d ed. Washington, DC: Brookings.

——. 1991. *Live from Capitol Hill.* Washington, DC: Brookings.

Hibbing, John R., and Elizabeth Theiss-Morse. 1995. *Congress as Public Enemy: Public Attitudes Toward American Political Institutions.* New York: Cambridge University Press.

Hofstetter, C. Richard. 1976. *Bias in the News: Network Television Coverage of the 1972 Election Campaign.* Columbus: Ohio State University Press.

———. 1978. "News Bias in the 1972 Campaign." *Journalism Monographs* No. 58, November.

Hofstetter, C. Richard, and Terry F. Buss. 1978. "Bias in Television News Coverage of Political Events: A Methodological Analysis." *Journal of Broadcasting* 22: 517–30.

Hofstetter, C. Richard, Mark C. Donovan, Melville R. Klauber, Alexandra Cole, Carolyn J. Huie, and Toshiyuki Yuasa. 1994. "Political Talk Radio: A Stereotype Reconsidered." *Political Research Quarterly* 47:467–79.

Hollander, Barry A. 1996. "Talk Radio: Predictors of Use And Effects on Attitudes About Government." *Journalism and Mass Communication Quarterly* 73 (Spring):102–13.

Hwang, H. 1989. "Public Opinion Polls, Mass Media, and the 1988 Presidential Election: Trends, Accuracy, Credibility, and Voting Behavior." Unpublished paper, Iowa State University.

Iyengar, Shanto. 1991. *Is Anyone Responsible? How Television Frames Political Issues.* Chicago: University of Chicago Press.

Iyengar, Shanto, and Donald R. Kinder. 1987. *News that Matters: Television and American Opinion.* Chicago: University of Chicago Press.

Iyenger, Shanto, Mark D. Peters, and Donald R. Kinder. 1982. "Experimental Demonstrations of the 'Not-so-minimal' Consequences of Television News Programs." *American Political Science Review* 76:848–58.

Jamieson, Kathleen Hall. 1992. *Dirty Politics: Deception, Distraction, and Democracy.* New York: Oxford University Press.

Jamieson, Kathleen Hall, and David S. Birdsell. 1988. *Presidential Debates: The Challenge of Creating an Informed Electorate.* New York: Oxford University Press.

Jamieson, Kathleen Hall, and Karlyn Campbell. 1988. *The Interplay of Influence: Mass Media and Their Publics in News and Politics.* Belmont, CA: Wadsworth.

Jennings, M. Kent, and Richard C. Niemi. 1983. *Generations and Politics.* New Jersey: Princeton University Press.

Johnson, Thomas J. 1993. "Filling Out the Racing Form: How the Media Covered the Horse Race in the 1988 Primaries." *Journalism Quarterly* 70(2):300–310.

Johnstone, John W.C., E. J. Slawski, and W. W. Bowman. 1976. *The News People.* Urbana: University of Illinois Press.

Joslyn, Richard. 1984. *Mass Media and Elections.* Reading, MA: Addison-Wesley.

Just, Marion, Ann N. Crigler, Dean E. Alger, Timothy E. Cook, Montague Kern, and Darrell M. West. 1996. *Crosstalk: Citizens, Candidates, and the Media in a Presidential Campaign.* Chicago: University of Chicago Press.

Katz, Jeffrey L. 1991. "The Power of Talk." *Governing* 4(March).

Keeley, Joseph. 1971. *The Left-Leaning Antenna: Political Bias in Television.* New Rochelle, NY: Arlington House.

Keenan, Kevin. 1986. "Polls in Network Newscasts in 1984 Presidential Race." *Journalism Quarterly* 63:616–18.

Keeter, Scott. 1987. "The Illusion of Intimacy: Television and the Role of Candidate Personal Qualities in Voter Choice." *Public Opinion Quarterly* 51:344–58.

Keeter, Scott, and Cliff Zukin. 1983. *Uninformed Choice: The Failure of the New Presidential Nominating System.* New York: Praeger.

Kernell, Samuel, and Gary C. Jacobson. 1987. "Congress and the Presidency as News in The Nineteenth Century." *Journal of Politics* 49:1016–35.

Key, V. O. 1966. *The Responsible Electorate: Rationality in Presidential Voting, 1936–1960.* New York: Vintage.

Klein, Malcolm W., and Nathan Maccoby. 1974. "Newspaper Objectivity in the 1952 Campaign." *Journalism Quarterly* 31:285–295.

Kramer, G. H. 1971. "Short-term Fluctuations in U.S. Voting Behavior, 1896–1964." *American Political Science Review* 65:131–43.

Kraus, Sidney. 1988. *Televised Presidential Debates and Public Policy.* Hillsdale, NJ: Lawrence Erlbaum.

Kraus, S., and R. G. Smith. 1962. "Issues and Images." In S. Kraus, ed., *The Great Debates,* 287–312. Bloomington: Indiana University Press.

Krosnick, Jon A. 1988. "Attitude Importance and Attitude Change." *Journal of Experimental Social Psychology* 24(May):240–55.

Krosnick, Jon A., and Donald R. Kinder. 1990. "Altering the Foundations of Popular Support for the President Through Priming." *American Political Science Review* 84:497–512.

Kuklinski, James, and Lee Sigelman. 1992. "When Objectivity Is Not Objective: Network Television News Coverage of U.S. Senators and the 'Paradox of Objectivity.'" *Journal of Politics* 54:810–33.

Lang, G. E., and K. Lang. 1968. *Politics and Television.* Chicago: Quadrangle.

——.1979. "Immediate and Mediated Responses: First Debate." In S. Kraus, ed., *The Great Debates: Carter vs. Ford, 1976.* Bloomington: Indiana University Press.

Lanoue, D. J., and P. Schrott. 1989a. "The Effects of Primary Season Debates on Public Opinion." *Political Behavior* 11:289–306.

——. 1989b. "Voters' Reactions to Televised Presidential Debates: Measurement of the Source and Magnitude of Opinion Change." *Political Psychology* 10:275–85.

Lazarsfeld, Paul F., Bernard Berelson, and Hazel Gaudet. 1944. *The People's Choice: How the Voter Makes Up His Mind in a Presidential Campaign.* New York: Buell, Sloan, and Pearce.

Lichter, S. Robert, Daniel Amundson, and Richard Noyes. 1988. *The Video Campaign: Network Coverage of the 1988 Primaries.* Washington, DC: American Enterprise Institute.

Lichter, S. Robert, and Richard E. Noyes. 1996. *Good Intentions Make Bad News: Why Americans Hate Campaign Journalism,* 2d edition. New York: Rowman and Littlefield.

Lichter, S. Robert, Stanley Rothman, and Linda S. Lichter. 1986. *The Media Elite.* Bethesda, MD: Adler & Adler.

Lippman, Walter. 1922. *Public Opinion.* New York: Harcourt, Brace & World.

——. 1925. *The Phantom Public.* New York: Harcourt, Brace.

Lipset, S. M. 1980. "Different Polls, Different Results in 1980 Politics." *Public Opinion* (August/September):19–20, 60.

Loomis, Burdett. 1988. *The New American Politician.* New York: Basic Books.

Lupia, Arthur. 1994. "Shortcuts Versus Encyclopedias: Information and Voting Behavior on California Insurance Reform Elections." *American Political Science Review* 88:63–76.

MacKuen, Michael B. 1983. "Political Drama, Economic Conditions, And The Dynamics of Presidential Popularity." *American Journal of Political Science* 27:165–92.

MacKuen, Michael B., and Steven L. Coombs, eds. 1981. *More Than News: Media Power in Public Affairs.* Beverly Hills: Sage.

Mann, Thomas E., and Norman J. Ornstein, eds. 1994. *Congress, the Press, and the Public.* Washington, D.C.: Brookings.

Mashek, John. 1997. *Lethargy '96: How the Media Covered a Listless Campaign.* Arlington, VA: Freedom Forum.

Matthews, Donald R. 1978. "'Winnowing': The News Media and the 1976 Presidential Nominations." In James David Barber, ed., *Race for the presidency: The Media and the Nominating Process,* 55–78. Englewood Cliffs, NJ: Prentice-Hall.

Mayer, William G. 1987. "The New Hampshire primary: A historical overview." In Gary R. Orren and Nelson W. Polsby, eds., *Media and Momentum: The New Hampshire Primary and Nomination Politics,* 9–41. Chatham, NJ: Chatham House.

Mayhew, David. 1974. Congress the Electoral Connection. New Haven: Yale University Press.

McClenegan, J. Sean. 1978. "Effects of Endorsements on News Space in Texas Newspapers." *Journalism Quarterly.*

Meadow, Robert G. 1973. "Cross-media Comparison of Coverage of the 1972 Presidential Campaign." *Journalism Quarterly* 50:482–88.

Medsger, Betty. 1996. *Winds of Change.* Arlington, VA: The Freedom Forum.

Miller, Arthur H., Eden Goldenberg, and Lutz Erbring. 1979. "Type-set Politics: Impact of Newspapers on Public Confidence." *American Political Science Review* 73:67–84.

Miller, Arthur H., Martin Wattenberg, and Oksana Malanchuk. 1986. "Schematic Assessments of Presidential Candidates." *American Political Science Review* 80: 521–40.

Mondach, Jeffrey. 1995. "Newspapers and Political Awareness." *American Journal of Political Science* 39:513–27.

National Broadcasting Company (NBC). 1988. "Television Coverage of the 1988 Democratic Nomination For President of the United States."

Nelson, Michael, ed. 1997. *The Elections of 1996.* Washington DC: CQ Press.

Nesbit, Dorothy Davidson. 1988. *Videostyle in Senate Campaigns.* Knoxville: University of Tennessee Press.

Neuman, W. Russell. 1986. *The Paradox of Mass Politics: Knowledge and Opinion in the American Electorate.* Cambridge, MA: Harvard University Press.

——. 1991. *The Future of the Mass Audience.* New York: Cambridge University Press.

Neuman, W. Russell, Marion Just, and Ann Crigler. 1992. *Common Knowledge: News and the Construction of Political Meaning.* Chicago: University of Chicago Press.

Neuman, W. Russell, and Ithiel de Sola Pool. 1986. "The Flow of Communications into the Home." In Sandra J. Ball-Rokeach and Muriel Cantor, eds., *Media, Audience and Social Structure,* 71–86. Beverly Hills: Sage.

Orren, Gary R., and Nelson W. Polsby, eds. 1987. *Media and Momentum: The New Hampshire Primary and Nomination Politics.* Chatham, NJ: Chatham House.

Owen, Diana. 1991. *Media Messages in American Presidential Elections.* New York: Greenwood Press.

Page, Benjamin I. 1976. "The Theory of Political Ambiguity." *American Political Science Review* 70:742–52.

Page, Benjamin I., and Robert Y. Shapiro. 1987. "What Moves Public Opinion?" *American Political Science Review* 81:23–43.

——. 1992. *The Rational Public: Fifty Years of Trends in Americans' Policy Preferences.* Chicago: University of Chicago Press.

Paletz, David L., and Robert M. Entman. 1981. *Media Power Politics.* New York: Free Press.

Paletz, David L., Jonathan Y. Short, Helen Baker, Barbara Cookman Campbell, Richard J. Cooper, and Rochelle M. Oeslander. 1980. "Polls in the Media: Content, Credibility, and Consequences." *Public Opinion Quarterly* 44: 495–513.

Patterson, Samuel C., and David B. Magleby. 1992. "The Polls: Public support for Congress." *Public Opinion Quarterly* 56:539–51.

Patterson, Thomas C. 1980. *The Mass Media Election: How Americans Choose Their President.* New York: Praeger.

——. 1989. "The Press and Its Missed Assignment." In Michael Nelson, ed., *The Elections of 1988,* 93–110. Washington, DC: Congressional Quarterly Press.

——. 1993. *Out of Order.* New York: Knopf.

Patterson, Thomas E., and Richard Davis. 1985. "The Media Campaign: Struggle for the Agenda." In Michael Nelson ed., *The Elections of 1984,* 111–28. Washington, DC: Congressional Quarterly.

Patterson, Thomas E., and Robert D. McClure. 1976. *The Unseeing Eye: The Myth of Television Power in National Elections.* New York: G. P. Putnam.

——. 1973. "Political Advertising: Voter Reaction to Televised Political Commercials." Princeton, NJ: Citizens' Research Foundation.

Pearson, Charles M. 1986. "Explaining National News Coverage of Members of the U.S. Congress, 1977–1980." Paper presented at the annual meeting of the American Political Science Association, Washington, DC.

Pomper, Gerald M. 1989. "The Presidential Nominations." In Gerald M. Pomper, ed., *The Election of 1988: Reports and Interpretations.* Chatham, NJ: Chatham House.

Popkin, Samuel. 1991. *The Reasoning Voter: Communication and Persuasion in Presidential Campaigns.* Chicago: University of Chicago Press.

Povich, Elain S. 1996. *Partners and Adversaries*. Washington, D.C.: The Freedom Forum.

Price, D. 1984. *Bringing Back the Parties*. Washington, DC: Congressional Quarterly Press.

Quattrone, George A., and Amos Tversky. 1988. "Contrasting Rational and Psychological Analyses of Political Choice." *American Political Science Review* 82:719–36.

Ranney, Austin. 1983. *Channels of Power: The Impact of Television on American Politics*. New York: Basic Books.

Ratzen, Scott C. 1989. "The Real Agenda Setters: Pollsters in the 1988 Presidential Campaign." *American Behavioral Scientist* 32:451–63.

Reese, S., and Shoemaker, P. 1991. *Mediating the Message: Theories of Influence on Mass Media Content*. New York: Longman.

Reeves, Richard. 1997. "The Question of Media Bias." In Shanto Iyengar and Richard Reeves, eds., *Do the Media Govern? Politicians, Voters and Reporters in America*. Thousand Oaks, CA: Sage.

Rivers, William. 1962. "The Correspondents After 25 Years." *Columbia Journalism Review* 1(Spring):5.

Robinson, John P., and Mark R. Levy. 1986. *The Main Source: Learning from Television News*. Beverly Hills: Sage.

Robinson, Michael J. 1976. "Public Affairs Television and the Growth of Political Malaise: The Case of 'The Selling of the Pentagon.'" *American Political Science Review* 70:409–32.

———. 1985. "Where's the Beef? Media and Media Elites in 1984." In Austin Ranney, ed., *The American Election of 1984*. Washington, DC: American Enterprise Institute.

Robinson, Michael J., and Andrew Kohut. 1988. "Believability and the Press." *Public Opinion Quarterly* 52: 174–89.

Robinson, Michael J., and Margaret A. Sheehan. 1983. *Over the Wire and on TV: CBS and UPI in Campaign '80*. New York: Russell Sage.

Rogers, Everett M., and James W. Dearing. 1988. "Agenda-setting Research: Where Has It Been and Where Is It Going?" In James A. Anderson, ed., *Communication Yearbook*, Vol. 11. Newbury Park, CA: Sage.

Rosengren, Karl Erik, Lawrence A. Wenner and Philip Palmgreen, eds. 1985. *Media Gratifications Research: Current Perspectives*. Beverly Hills: Sage.

Rosenstiel, Tom. 1997 "The Road to Here." In Larry J. Sabato, ed., *Toward the Millennium*. Boston: Allyn and Bacon.

Rosenstone, Steven J., and John Mark Hansen. 1993. *Mobilization, Participation, and Democracy in America*. New York: Macmillan.

Rosenthal, Alan. 1996. *Drawing the Line: Legislative Ethics in the States*. Lincoln: University of Nebraska Press.

Roshco, Bernard. 1975. *Newsmaking*. Chicago: University of Chicago Press.

Rosten, Leo. 1937. *The Washington Correspondents*. New York: Harcourt, Brace.

Russonello, John M., and Frank Wolf. 1979. "Newspaper Coverage of the 1976 and 1968 Presidential Campaigns." *Journalism Quarterly* 56:360–64, 432.

Sabato, Larry. 1993. *Feeding Frenzy: How Attack Journalism Has Transformed American Politics*. New York: Free Press.

Salmore, Barbara, and Stephen Salmore. 1989. *Candidates, Parties and Campaigns,* 2d ed. Washington, DC: Congressional Quarterly Press.

Salwen, M. B. 1985a. "Does Poll Coverage Improve as Presidential Vote Nears?" *Journalism Quarterly* 62(4):887–91.

——. 1985b. "The Reporting of Public Opinion Polls During Presidential Years, 1968–1984." *Journalism Quarterly* 62(2):272–77.

Sandman, Peter, David M. Rubin, and David B. Sachsman. 1982. *Media*. Englewood Cliffs, NJ: Prentice-Hall.

Schattschneider, E. E. 1942. *Party Government*. New York: Rinehart and Company.

Schudson, Michael. 1978. *Discovering the News: A Social History of American Newspapers*. New York: Basic Books.

——. 1995. *The Power of the News*. Cambridge: Harvard University Press.

Semetko, H. A. 1988. "The Role of Mass Media in Elections: What Can We Learn from 1988?" *The Political Science Teacher* 1(3):17–19.

Shepsle, Kenneth A. 1972. "The Strategy of Ambiguity: Uncertainty and Electoral Competition." *American Political Science Review* 66: 555–568.

Sigelman, Lee, and David Bullock. 1991. "Candidates, Issues, Horse Races and Hoopla" *American Politics Quarterly* 19:5–32.

Smith, Tom W. 1990. "The First Straw? A Study of the Origins of Election Polls." *Public Opinion Quarterly* 54:21–36.

Smoller, Fredric T. 1990. *The Six O'Clock Presidency: A Theory of Presidential Press Relations in the Age of Television*. New York: Praeger.

Sorauf, Frank. 1988. *Money in American Elections*. Boston: Little, Brown.

Southwell, P. L. 1982. "Alienation and Nonvoting in the United States: A Refined Operationalization." *Western Political Quarterly* 38:663–74.

Squire, Peverill. 1988. "Who Gets National News Coverage in the U.S. Senate?" *American Politics Quarterly* 16:139–56.

Stempel, Guido H., III. 1965. "The Prestige Press in Two Presidential Elections." *Journalism Quarterly* 42(Winter):15–21.

—— 1969. "The Prestige Press Meets the Third Party Challenge." *Journalism Quarterly*.

Stempel, Guido H., III, and John Windhauser. 1991. *The Media and the 1984 and 1988 Elections*. New York: Greenwood Press.

Stevenson, Robert L., and Mark T. Greene. 1980. "A Reconsideration of Bias in the News." *Journalism Quarterly* 57:115–121.

Stovall, James G. 1988. "Coverage of the 1984 Presidential Campaign." *Journalism Quarterly* 65:443–49.

Stovall, James G., and Jacqueline H. Solomon. 1984. "The Poll as a News Event in the 1980 Presidential Campaign." *Public Opinion Quarterly* 48:615–23.

Taylor, Paul. 1990. *See How They Run: Electing a President in an Age of Mediaocracy*. New York: Alfred Knopf.

*Times Mirror*. 1993. "The Vocal Minority in American Politics." Times Mirror Center for the People and the Press.

Traugott, Michael W. 1985. "The Media and the Nominating Process." In George Grassmuck, ed., *Before Nomination: Our Primary Problems,* 101–15. Washington, DC: American Enterprise Institute.

Verba, S., and N. H. Nie 1972. *Participation in America.* New York: Harper & Row.

Wagner, Joseph. 1983. "Media Do Make a Difference: the Differential Impact of Mass Media in the 1976 Presidential Race." *American Journal of Political Science* 27:407–30.

*Washington Post,* October 10, 1996. "As Vote Nears, Americans Tuning Out Campaign '96."

Wattenberg, Martin P. 1996. *The Decline of American Political Parties 1952–1994.* Cambridge, MA: Harvard University Press.

Wayne, Stephen J. 1981. *The Road to the White House: The Politics of Presidential Elections.* New York: St. Martin's.

Weaver, David H. and G. Cleveland Wilhoit. 1986. *The American Journalist,* 2nd edition. Bloomington: Indiana University Press.

———. 1996. *The American Journalist in the 1990s.* Mahwah, NJ: Lawrence Erlbaum.

Weaver, Paul H.. 1972. "Is Television News Biased?" *Public Interest* (Winter) 26: 57–74.

Weisberg, H. F., and B. Grofman. 1981. "Candidate Evaluation and Turnout." *American Politics Quarterly* 9:197–220.

White, T. H. 1961. *The Making of the President, 1960.* New York: Atheneum.

Wolfinger, R. E., and S. J. Rosenstone. 1980. *Who Votes?* New Haven, CT: Yale University Press.

Yeric, J. L., and J. R. Todd. 1989. *Public Opinion: The Visible Politics,* 2d ed. Itasca, IL: Peacock.

Zaller, John. 1992. *The Nature and Origins of Mass Opinion.* New York: Cambridge University Press.

# index

partisans using, 63*t;* political knowledge and use of, 58, 59*t;* salience of election and, 54, 55*t;* tabloid television watchers using, 44*t,* 45; talk radio listeners using, 41*t; see also* Sunday morning political talk shows

MSNBC, use of, 33, 33*t*

National Election Studies (NES): decline in partisanship shown by, 7, 8*t;* split-ticket voting and, 9

National Opinion Research Center (NORC), confidence in institutions measured by, 13

National panel survey, of Freedom Forum Media Studies Center, 3–4, 15–18, 17*t*

National Public Radio, 30, 32, 35, 36; frequency of use of, 32, 32*t;* network news watchers using, 42*t;* political knowledge and use of, 57*t,* 58; salience of election and use of, 53, 54*t;* tabloid television watchers using, 43, 44*t; see also* Elite media

NBC, 42; *see also* Network news watchers

Network newscasts, frequency of use of, 20, 27, 27*t*

Network news watchers, 35, 36; media viewing habits of, 42*t,* 42–43, 43*t*

News content, evaluation of, 78, 113–33, 173; commentary and, 11, 130–31, 131*f;* excessive coverage and, 118, 119*t,* 169, 173; horse race and, 10–11, 15, 114–15, 116–17, 118, 119*t,* 120, 121, 132, 169; issue positions and, 114, 115, 116, 117, 118, 119*t,* 120, 121, 132, 169, 173; news sources and, 121–25, 123*t,* 124*t,* 125*t;* outcome effect and, 119*t,*

120, 121, 132, 169; personality of candidate and, 114, 115, 116–17, 118, 119*t,* 120–21, 132, 169; recommendations for changes in, 173; responsiveness of to voter needs, 120–21; scholars and, 4, 9, 10–12; skepticism and, 4, 10–11; strategy and tactics and, 4, 10–11, 15, 118, 119*t,* 121, 169, 173; third party and independent candidates and, 119*t,* 120, 121, 132, 169; too little coverage and, 118, 119*t,* 120, 169, 173; voter interest in kinds of election stories and, 120–21

News gathering process, evaluation of, 87–88, 88*f*

*NewsHour* with Jim Lehrer, 35, 36; bias perceived in, 110, 110*t;* conventions followed with, 141; frequency of use of, 30, 31*t,* 32; network news watchers using, 42, 42*t;* news junkies using, 20; political knowledge and use of, 57, 57*t;* salience of election and use of, 53, 54*t;* tabloid television watchers using, 43, 44*t; see also* Elite media

News junkies, 36; media viewing habits of, 20, 37, 37*t,* 38*t,* 39

Newsletters, use of, 33, 33*t*

News magazines: bias perceived in, 110*t;* discriminating elite viewers using, 37, 37*t;* frequency of use of, 27; network news watchers using, 42; news junkies using, 37, 37*t;* partisans using, 62*t;* political knowledge and use of, 58, 58*t;* as primary source of information, 24*t;* salience of election and use of, 54, 54*t;* tabloid television watchers using, 43, 44*t;* talk radio listeners using, 40, 40*t;* voters learning from, 129, 130*t*